SPECIAL ISSUES

NCTE

SPECIAL ISSUES VOLUME 1 *is a topical compilation of current scholarship published in journals of the National Council of Teachers of English.*

TITLES IN THE SERIES

CRITICAL MEDIA LITERACY

Vol. 1: Bringing Lives to Texts

RACIAL LITERACY

Vol. 1: Implications for Curriculum, Pedagogy, & Policy

TRAUMA-INFORMED TEACHING

Vol. 1: Cultivating Healing-Centered ELA Classrooms

SPECIAL ISSUES

VOLUME 1 TRAUMA-INFORMED TEACHING

CULTIVATING HEALING-CENTERED ELA CLASSROOMS

EDITED BY SAKEENA EVERETT

NCTE National Council of Teachers of English®

Editor: Sakeena Everett
Series editor: James Sitar
Cover and interior design: Ash Goodwin
Cover images: Marvin Young
Typesetter: Jim Gallagher

ISBN: 978-0-8141-4494-7
eISBN: 978-0-8141-4495-4

It is the policy of NCTE in its journals and other publications to provide a forum for the open discussion of ideas concerning the content and the teaching of English and the language arts. Publicity accorded to any particular point of view does not imply endorsement by the Executive Committee, the Board of Directors, or the membership at large, except in announcements of policy, where such endorsement is clearly specified.

NCTE provides equal employment opportunity to all staff members and applicants for employment without regard to race, color, religion, sex, national origin, age, physical, mental or perceived handicap/disability, sexual orientation including gender identity or expression, ancestry, genetic information, marital status, military status, unfavorable discharge from military service, pregnancy, citizenship status, personal appearance, matriculation or political affiliation, or any other protected status under applicable federal, state, and local laws.

Every effort has been made to provide current URLs and email addresses, but, because of the rapidly changing nature of the web, some sites and addresses may no longer be accessible.

Library of Congress Cataloging-in-Publication Data applied for.

NCTE
340 N. Neil Street, Suite 104 | Champaign, IL 61820
www.ncte.org

VOLUME 1 TRAUMA-INFORMED TEACHING

SPECIAL ISSUES

CULTIVATING HEALING-CENTERED ELA CLASSROOMS

NUANCING THE DIVERSE SPECTRUM OF TRAUMA

BUILDING HEALING-CENTERED ELA PEDAGOGIES

EDITOR'S INTRODUCTION

SAKEENA EVERETT

WE LIVE IN A TIME that requires attention to trauma. Educators and students are learning how to live in this precarious COVID-19 pandemic, which has amplified preexisting health, racial, economic, and educational inequalities as well as how we manage unprecedented natural disasters. The pandemic has shaped us and our students in ways we have yet to understand fully. But we know we must adapt. In an effort to respond to pressing teaching and learning needs, I was asked to curate this special issue on trauma-informed teaching. Specifically, I have been tasked with selecting previously published articles from NCTE journals to help educators implement trauma-informed teaching approaches in K–12 and college classrooms while offering tips for how these articles can be incorporated into our classrooms. In my research for this volume, I learned it is imperative to not only consider *trauma-informed*, but also *healing-centered* teaching practices. This collection is a useful starting point—not ending point—to spark conversation, evoke deep internal and external reflection, and engage strategic pathways forward.

Contextualizing Trauma, Trauma-Informed Care, and Trauma-Informed Teaching

Adverse childhood experiences (ACEs) are potentially traumatic events that occur in childhood. ACEs can include violence, abuse, and growing up in a family with mental health or substance abuse problems (CDC Vital Signs, 2019). The Centers for Disease Control and Prevention (CDC) also argues that ACEs are linked to chronic health problems, mental illness, and substance misuse in adulthood. With ACEs in mind, it is important to explain how I use the terms *trauma* and *trauma-informed* to explain my approach for curating this special issue. My understandings of *trauma* draw from applied clinical scholarship, which explains that

> trauma is the result of an event, series of events, or set of circumstances that is experienced by an individual as physically or emotionally harmful or life threatening and that has lasting adverse effects on the individual's functioning and mental, physical, social, emotional, or spiritual well-being. (Substance Abuse and Mental Health Services Administration, 2015)

The Substance Abuse and Mental Health Services Administration (SAMHSA) is the governmental agency within the US Department of Health and Human Services that leads public behavioral health efforts. SAMSHA's mission is to reduce the impact of substance abuse and mental illness on America's communities. Furthermore, *trauma-informed care* "views trauma through an ecological and cultural lens and recognizes that context plays a significant role in how individuals perceive and process traumatic events." Trauma-informed care involves vigilance in anticipating and avoiding institutional processes and individual practices that are likely to retraumatize individuals who already have histories of trauma (SAMHSA, 2015). Informed by clinical understandings of trauma, I define *trauma-informed teaching* as teaching that views trauma through ecological and cultural lenses and recognizes how context plays a significant role in how students and teachers perceive and process traumatic events in educational settings.

Neighborhoods and student populations in the United States are largely clustered by racial and ethnic groups. So are rates of exposure to trauma-inducing events and experiences. Yet, trauma may be one of the most underexplored racial equity issues in education (Alvarez, 2020). Trauma can be natural or human-caused. Natural events are typically unavoidable, whereas human-caused traumas are caused by human failure (e.g., technological catastrophes, accidents, malevolence) or by human design (SAMHSA, 2015). The effects of human-caused *historical trauma*—such as genocide, slavery, and internment in concentration camps—can be felt across generations. People's stories, coping behaviors, and stress reactions can be passed across generational lines far removed from the actual event(s) or firsthand accounts.

To effectively engage in trauma-informed teaching, educators must thoughtfully consider the ecological, cultural, and racialized realities that shape exposure to traumatic events. These articles are meant to provide educators with a set of tools to help anticipate and avoid institutional processes and individual practices that are likely to retraumatize students who already have individual, collective, and/or historical trauma histories.

A Brief Snapshot of Prepandemic Trauma in the US

Millions of young people in grade school and college are processing trauma. Approximately 22 percent of students ages 12–18 reported being bullied at school during the school year in 2019. About 16 percent of students in grades 9–12 reported being electronically bullied during the previous 12 months (National Center for Education Statistics, 2021). Younger people are at the highest risk of sexual violence. According to Smith et al. (2018), 81.3 percent (approximately 20.8 million victims) of women under age 25 and 70.8 percent (approximately 2 million) of men under age 25 reported being victims of rape. A decade before the pandemic began, US school shootings became commonplace. According to a CNN report, in the decade leading up to the pandemic, there were 180 school shootings and 365 students killed at school (Walker, 2019). People who experience a tragic event—such as a school shooting, hurricane displacement, or pandemic—endure a *collective trauma*. Even if our students did not directly experience some of the named traumas, they might be processing *vicarious trauma*. Our students might be the children, siblings, partners, and friends of people with individual, collective, and/or historical trauma histories.

Depression and anxiety are the most common mental health issues in the country. Approximately 21 million people in the US struggle with depression (CDC Vital Signs, 2019). I was deeply alarmed to learn that "suicide is the second leading cause of death among 10 to 24 year-olds in the U.S." (Heron, 2021, p. 10). Some of those young people who were lost due to (un)intentional self-harm—how the government defines suicide—were our students. You may know their names. It is also worth noting this recent report, published in 2021, only includes death rates up until 2019. It does not include death rates in 2020 or 2021, when the unexpected impact of compounded traumas prompted by COVID-19 deaths and related pandemic losses like food and housing security, jobs, and mental wellness settled in. We need trauma-informed and healing-centered teaching approaches because we do not know our students' trauma histories. We may never know them.

Cultivating Trauma-Informed and Healing-Centered Teaching Frameworks in the Pandemic

Trauma before the pandemic did not go away. Rather, it has only been compounded by the complex traumas of the pandemic. Governmental agencies are still trying to document the ways the pandemic has amplified mental health issues. As Keisha L. Green aptly notes in this volume, "We have never been more in need of frameworks for considering counternarratives and perspectives from the margins toward justice-centered futures." In addition to compiling trauma-informed teaching resources, my research led me to healing-centered care, which acknowledges but extends the work of trauma-informed care. Ginwright (2018) has argued that "while the term trauma-informed care is important, it is incomplete . . . it presumes that trauma is an individual experience, rather than a collective one." Therefore, *healing-centered care* has four explicit tenets: (1) to build an awareness of (in)justices and is explicitly political; (2) to view healing as a restoration of cultural identities; (3) to focus on wellbeing, recognizing that people are more than the traumas they experience; and (4) to support adults in their healing as they work with young people. By overlapping trauma-informed and healing-centered frameworks, this volume attempts to support students and educators who are hurting too.

I am not a distant educator or writer. I, too, am entangled in the complexities of understanding, living, and supporting trauma-informed and healing-centered teaching in myriad ways. During the pandemic, our profession has become more stressful. Our schools and institutions of higher education rarely equip educators with the necessary interdisciplinary knowledge and skills we need to meet the increasing demands of teaching or attending to students' social-emotional needs. Furthermore, educators need to be mentally and emotionally well themselves. How can educators provide the trauma-informed teaching and healing-centered ELA classrooms our students desperately need, if we are struggling?

What You Will Find in This Special Issue

Any serious approach toward trauma-informed or healing-centered teaching must include a combination of micro- and macro-level supports. Micro-level supports include skills or individual practices that can support trauma-exposed people. Macro-level support includes programmatic and large-scale initiatives. No one single approach will be sufficient to minimize harm. I have divided this special issue into four sections: (1) navigating pandemic-specific trauma, (2) nuancing the diverse spectrum of trauma, (3) building healing-centered ELA pedagogies, and (4) supporting hurting educators. In carefully curating this special issue, I have examined a combination of micro- and macro-level supports that educators need to engage in trauma-informed/healing-centered teaching and learning.

In the first section, "Navigating Pandemic-Specific Trauma," you will encounter Waffle's poem "A School Is Not Meant to Be Empty," which captures what many educators felt when we were forced to shift our instruction to completely remote. Then, Green prompts us to historicize this unique moment. Garrigues explains how historic moments like the pandemic shape a generation, so we must change our curriculum in the process. Kittle challenges the now common discourse of "learning loss" and urges educators to reevaluate what counts as learning. Silvas describes, "writing is one way to confront, resist, and heal" in the face of trauma. Pazur explains learning management systems (LMS) are vehicles, not substitutes, for compelling teaching and learning and provides a framework for school districts to (re)design the future of distance learning pedagogy. Baxley and Sealey-Ruiz unpack the historical and contemporary significance of the arts in the Black radical imagination, namely poetry, to push back against anti-Blackness. Garcia problematizes pedagogical complicity in ELA classrooms. Through the tenets of opportunity-centered teaching, Milner et al. invite educators, administrators, and policy makers to assess and disrupt opportunity gaps to build humanizing curriculum, assessment, and relational policies. Kim provides context for the spike in anti-Asian violence during the pandemic and describes how honoring diverse name genealogies and identities might serve as decolonial English education.

The second section, "Nuancing the Diverse Spectrum of Trauma," makes often hidden traumas visible so educators are able to engage trauma-informed teaching in more equitable ways. Jiménez Garcia illustrates how transnational colonial violence against communities of color inform the very concepts of childhood, literacy, and knowledge production that is imagined and rewarded in schools. Nxumalo, through a lens of "Black geographies," expands perceptions of Black children's early childhood literacy learning and offers "decolonial world-building" through "pedagogies of relational reciprocity." Sabzalian centers Indigenous international "sovereign pedagogies" to disrupt colonial erasure of Indigenous peoples, relations to lands and waters, and to expand childhood literacy education. Saeed describes how childhood bullying made school unsafe and hindered her ability to participate in school until a teacher intervened. Homrich-Knieling invites educators to build sustainable relationships with students to "foster empathetic, democratic, and supportive communities." Konrad describes how issues of access appear to be procedural matters, but in reality impact the mental, emotional, and physical labor and wellness of people who live with disabilities. Rogers and Shafer prompt educators to (re)consider the precarious nature of homelessness in the US and Canada and how we work with students. Hadley offers transformative moments for educators to become more effective LGBTQ+ allies for their students. An anonymous parent calls for trans* narratives to support teachers, students, and families in navigating schools. Also, Tayles uses a trauma-informed lens to redesign course syllabi, course documents, assignments, classroom routines, student feedback, and conferencing strategies.

The third section, "Building Healing-Centered ELA Pedagogies," explores the truth that we are more than our trauma histories. As Ginwright (2018) explains, healing-centered approaches are holistic, involving culture, spirituality, civic action, and collective healing. Flores designs writing workshops for Latinx mothers and daughters to share their collective wisdom through stories about their lives. Ramirez and Donovan activate a guided antibias/antiracist (ABAR) reading protocol to nurture the capacity to notice harm and healing within texts and communities. Hunter and Colón provide a multimodal unit on critical micropoetry to support students in asserting and reclaiming their dignity and humanity. Gallo and Herrmann contextualize adverse childhood events (ACEs) and support teachers in using texts on "heavy topics" in the classroom to help trauma-exposed youth feel seen and validated. Eisenbach and Greathouse destigmatize mental illness and promote mental health support through classroom texts. Clark et al. use picturebooks to teach *with* and *against* social and emotional learning. Additionally, Durkin redesigns reading workshop to include flexible strategies for sparking empathy during COVID-19.

The fourth and final section, "Supporting Hurting Educators," acknowledges that while teachers have capacity to support students, they hurt too. Building from a healing-centered framework, the articles in this section consider ways to support educators in their own healing. Czaia's poem "I Don't to Write a Poem for My Dead Students" captures the angst and sorrow teachers might feel when they lose students. Husbye et al. name difficulties teachers might have in teaching texts that involve death and grief, and they provide modeled support for teachers. Dunn makes the "emotional labor of teaching" among preservice, inservice, and teacher educators both visible and valuable. Finally, Everett and Dunn advance a new framework, "intersectional grief," and offer practical micro- and macro-level considerations for educators and administrators to support grieving colleagues.

Being a trauma-informed or healing-centered educator is a career-long pursuit. This volume is designed to help educators build the capacity to do the arduous but necessary work of trauma-informed and healing-centered teaching. As you move through this volume, I invite you to consider: Who is most harmed by a given trauma? What can be done to support them? How might a shared trauma impact different groups of students and educators differently? As we think through ways to support the most harmed people in our teaching and learning communities, we will move closer to a more equitable and just healing-centered profession. In the pages that follow, you will find valuable insights, diverse perspectives, innovative and exciting pedagogies, as well as thought-provoking research methodologies that engage micro- and macro-level supports you need to get started today.

REFERENCES

Alvarez, A. (2020). Seeing race in the research on youth trauma and education: A critical review. *Review of Educational Research*, 90(5), 583–626.

CDC Vital Signs. (2019). *Adverse Childhood Experiences (ACEs): Preventing early trauma to improve adult health*. Centers for Disease Control and Prevention. https://www.cdc.gov/violenceprevention/aces/index.html

Ginwright, S. (2018, May 18). The future of healing: Shifting from trauma-informed care to healing-centered engagement. *Medium*. https://ginwright.medium.com/the-future-of-healing-shifting-from-trauma-informed-care-to-healing-centered-engagement-634f557ce69c

Heron, M. (2021). *Deaths: Leading causes for 2019* (National Vital Statistics Reports (70)9; pp. 1–141). National Center for Health Statistics. https://www.cdc.gov/nchs/data/nvsr/nvsr70/nvsr70-09-508.pdf

National Center for Education Statistics. (2021). *Bullying at School and Electronic Bullying*. U.S. Department of Education. https://nces.ed.gov/programs/coe/indicator/a10

Smith, S. G., Zhang, X., Basile, K. C., Merrick, M. T., Wang, J., Kresnow, M., & Chen, J. (2018). *National Intimate Partner and Sexual Violence Survey: 2015 Data Brief*. National Center for Injury Prevention and Control Centers for Disease Control and Prevention. https://www.cdc.gov/violenceprevention/pdf/2015data-brief508.pdf

Substance Abuse and Mental Health Services Administration (SAMHSA). (2015). *Trauma-informed care in behavioral health services: Knowledge Application Program (KAP) keys for clinicians* (pp. 1–15). Substance Abuse and Mental Health Services Administration (SAMHSA). https://store.samhsa.gov/sites/default/files/d7/priv/sma15-4420.pdf

Walker, C. (2019). *10 years. 180 school shootings. 356 victims*. CNN. https://www.cnn.com/interactive/2019/07/us/ten-years-of-school-shootings-trnd/#storystar

This poem originally appeared in *English Journal 110.4*

A SCHOOL IS NOT MEANT TO BE EMPTY

Who knew that day in March would be the last time
I'd hear their laughter, call their names, hear them speak
without tinny-tone or lag in time?

Who knew this would be the last time we'd share air
without it being electric, imagined, covered?

Who knew it would be the last time I would
ask *How are you?* and we could
meander through distracted answers?

If I had known . . . I'd shake their hands,
look them in the eyes, proffer a hearty
Good morning or pat on the back in front of
a living, breathing class one more time.

But instead, I abandon bits
of chalkboard review, half erased:
allusion, anecdote, antithesis–

I pull books off shelves and press them
into boxes, cover the world map with frosted plastic,
creating a Pangea, a cateracted ocean,
as if we never happened.

–Julene Waffle

JULENE WAFFLE is an English teacher and coach. She is an advisor for several student clubs at Morris Central School in Morris, New York. Julene has been a periodic member of NCTE since the late 1990s. She is an entrepreneur, a writer, and the mother of three boys. Julene can be contacted at jwaffle@morriscsd.org.

This article originally appeared
in *English Journal* 111.1

COUNTERSTORYTELLING THIS HISTORICAL MOMENT

KEISHA L. GREEN

So let us leave behind a country better than the one we were left with.

—AMANDA GORMAN, *THE HILL WE CLIMB* (26)

DURING ONE OF THE MOST PIVOTAL TIMES in our nation's history, the youngest inaugural poet in US history, a Black woman, and the first national youth poet laureate, Amanda Gorman, declared—through spoken word poetry—that we could "raise this wounded world into a wondrous one." This radical and collective act of raising or (re)shaping and (re)building a nation scarred by anti-Black violence, racial injustice, a health pandemic, and political upheaval requires English language arts (ELA) teachers to know, center, and sustain the diverse literary histories and polyvocal stories of the varied lifeways of our students. Ours and their lived experiences converge and diverge around triumph and tribulation, jubilee and judgment, as well as dignity and dispossession. Our counterstories and perspectives map the contours and complexities of our nation's historical development and contemporary conditions.

Literature that mirrors the vastness of our lives, struggles, viewpoints, and multiple literacies is the substance of counternarratives that provide teachers and students with alternate perspectives about the world often absent from our curriculum. As we make headway into a new school year marked by a heightened sense of urgency for racial justice and equity in education, more inclusive literary histories must be integral to our curriculum. It is, after all, through critical reading, thinking, and writing about stories such as *Giovanni's Room* by James Baldwin, *The Bluest Eye* by Toni Morrison, *Brown Girl Dreaming* by Jacqueline Woodson, or *Look Both Ways: A Tale Told in Ten Blocks* by Jason Reynolds that we are able to explore experiences and perspectives that differ from dominant or mainstream narratives. By doing so, we begin to widen our own views, making good on Gorman's invitation to "leave behind a country better than the one we were left with" (26).

In a similar way, James Baldwin's 1963 speech "A Talk to Teachers" continues to be instructive today, as he implores us to envision education as a site of possibility purposed "to create in a person the ability to look at the world for [themself], to make [their] own decisions." ELA classrooms have the potential to be generative spaces for counternarratives, critical perspectives, and justice-centered curricula, wherein teachers and students examine society and shift toward equity and social justice. Language and literacy scholars April Baker-Bell, Lamar Johnson, and Tamara Butler elaborate on this kind of conscious and responsive ELA classroom experience in their call for a Critical Race English Education, an approach to teaching and learning that centers race and seeks to (re)address racism, power, and injustice while affirming the plurality of students' identities and lived experiences through culturally sustaining, healing, and racially just pedagogies (123).

Storying This Historical Moment

We have never been more in need of frameworks for considering counternarratives and perspectives from the margins toward justice-centered futures. The global health crisis, as well as racial and political unrest, require an overhaul of the way we teach and learn. For example, in March 2020, we were mandated to shelter in place as the spread of COVID-19 surged. By May 2020, streets around the world were filled with justice-seekers demanding accountability for the police-state sanctioned murders of George Floyd, Breonna Taylor, and so many other unarmed Black men and women. On January 6, 2021, the world watched as insurrectionists stormed the US Capitol. The violent scene unfolded on live television and social media platforms viewed by millions, including our school-aged children and adolescents. Almost immediately, social media threads posted by educators asked: *What will we tell the children?* Just how will we write about this moment in time?

Teachers scrambled to make sense of the moment as curriculum in real time; we did so, in some cases, despite experiencing pushback from administrators, students, and parents. Media organizations, including *The New York Times*, PBS, NPR, and others, offered guidance on how to talk to young people about the insurrection and protests. Curriculum guides were created by organizations including Learning for Justice (formerly Teaching Tolerance) and Facing History and Ourselves. During critical global sociocultural, political, and historical moments, it behooves us to consider what might be learned and taught.

As these moments constitute our curriculum (see Ohito et al.), I recommend three guiding questions for ELA teachers to consider:

1. If we define curriculum as anything from which knowledge can be learned and generated, how might we (re)conceptualize these current events and moments as curricula?
2. If curriculum can be defined as everything occurring everywhere, how might we rethink teaching and learning in all modes in a racialized and politicized COVID-19 era?
3. How might we recognize and name our individual and collective wounds to heal ourselves and form a better country?

By attending to these questions, ELA teachers gesture toward developing classrooms that, according to Keith Gilyard, "further the development of authentic democracy . . . by helping to create informed, critical, powerful, independent, and culturally sensitive student voices" (74). Our language arts classrooms should be spaces for nurturing conscious civic actors.

As Nicole Mirra and Antero Garcia emphasize, "Civic education is not the exclusive domain or responsibility of social studies teachers. Teachers of all subjects can and must connect their subject areas to real-world issues if schools hope to sustain democracy." Counternarratives and perspectives are an effective pathway to enact a critical and culturally sustaining pedagogy as well as design a justice-seeking curriculum (Paris). Teachers who engage in critical pedagogy invite students to question the status quo, name and disrupt injustice, and encourage students to think about the relationship between power and oppression in our world.

Counterstorytelling for Reclamation and Reparation

An engagement with counternarratives and diverse literary histories helps us address the pandemics of racial violence, political insurrection, health disparities, and inequitable education. We do so to reclaim students' voices, identities, lifeways, and experiences. As Valerie Kinloch et al. espouse, "[W]e believe all educators must reimagine schooling practices in ways that both affirm students' knowledges, perspectives, community realities, and life goals, and critique systems of racism and inequity" (51). We do so to repair the harm schooling has inflicted on Black and Indigenous students' minds, bodies, and spirits. In the NCTE Statement Affirming #BlackLivesMatter, we are guided to "[U]se classrooms to help as opposed to harm, to transform our world and raise awareness of the crisis of racial injustice."

In the end, we do so to tell the children that this *is* America. Our classrooms should be spaces where young people develop and cultivate agency, love, joy, community, and justice. Talking to teachers, Baldwin explains, "[I]f America is going to become a nation, she must find a way—and this child [or adolescent] must help her to find a way to use the tremendous potential and tremendous energy which this child represents" (332). To our children and adolescents, what stories will you tell regarding this moment? What counternarratives and perspectives will we develop, as ELA teachers, to be studied by future generations? In the words of Amanda Gorman, I hope our stories reveal

> We've learned that quiet isn't always peace,
> And the norms and notions
> of what "just is"
> isn't always just-ice. (12)

And I hope our students believe

> we will raise this wounded world into a
> wondrous one
> We will rebuild, reconcile and recover (28)

And, finally, I hope our literature continues to teach

> the new dawn blooms as we free it.
> For there is always light,
> if only we're brave enough to see it.
> If only we're brave enough to be it. (29)

TEACHING TIPS

Green explains, "The global health crisis, as well as racial and political unrest, require an overhaul of the way we teach and learn." Rightly so, Green prompts readers to "map the contours and complexities of our nation's historical development and contemporary conditions." ELA educators are uniquely equipped with multimodal literacy skills and artistic insights to document and analyze these unprecedented, trauma-producing times. How have you been documenting and analyzing these historic moments? How, if at all, have you been supporting your students in documenting what's going on? How might you (re)conceptualize current events and moments as ELA curricula? Invite students to gather multimodal primary source documents about the global health crisis, as well as racial and political unrest. Ask students to craft counterstories that cultivate agency, love, joy, community, and justice. Invite students to share their counterstories inside and beyond the classroom walls. Alongside students, brainstorm ways to recognize and name individual and collective wounds to heal and form a better country.

WORKS CITED

Baker-Bell, April, et al. "Editorial: The Pain and the Wounds: A Call for Critical Race English Education in the Wake of Racial Violence." *English Education*, vol. 49, no. 2, Jan. 2017, pp. 116–29.

Baldwin, James. *Giovanni's Room*. Vintage Books, 2013.

——. "A Talk to Teachers." *The Price of the Ticket: Collected Nonfiction, 1948–1985*. 1985. Beacon Press, 2021, pp. 325–32.

Gilyard, Keith. *Let's Flip the Script: An African American Discourse on Language, Literature, and Learning*. Wayne State UP, 1996.

Gorman, Amanda. *The Hill We Climb: An Inaugural Poem for the Country*. Viking Books for Young Readers, 2021.

Kinloch, Valerie, et al. "When School Is Not Enough: Understanding the Lives and Literacies of Black Youth." *Research in the Teaching of English*, vol. 52, no. 1, 2017, pp. 34–54.

Mirra, Nicole, and Antero Garcia. "Same Old Civics Ed. Won't Save Us: We Must Fight White Supremacy in the Classroom, Not Dodge It." *Education Week*, Jan. 2021, www.edweek.org/teaching-learning/opinion-same-old-civics-ed-wont-save-us/2021/01.

Morrison, Toni. *The Bluest Eye*. 1970. Vintage Books, 2007.

NCTE/CCCC Black Caucus. NCTE *Statement Affirming #BlackLivesMatter*. https://ncte.org/wp-content/uploads/2020/04/Statement_Affirming_BlackLivesMatter.pdf

Ohito, Esther O., et al. "This Moment Is the Curriculum: Equity, Inclusion, and Collectivist Critical Curriculum Mapping for Study Abroad Programs in the COVID-19 Era." *Journal of Experiential Education*, vol. 44, no. 1, Mar. 2021, pp. 10–30.

Paris, Django. "Culturally Sustaining Pedagogy: A Needed Change in Stance, Terminology, and Practice." *Educational Researcher*, vol. 41, no. 3, 2012, pp. 93–97.

Reynolds, Jason. *Look Both Ways: A Tale Told in Ten Blocks*. Atheneum Books, 2020.

Woodson, Jacqueline. *Brown Girl Dreaming*. Puffin Books, 2016.

KEISHA L. GREEN is an associate professor of secondary English education at the University of Massachusetts, Amherst. She is a cofounding director of the Center of Racial Justice and Youth Engaged Research and a coeditor of *Equity and Excellence in Education*. Keisha is a longtime NCTE member and formerly served on the Standing Committee on Research. Also, she was an NCTE Cultivating New Voices among Scholars of Color fellow from 2008 to 2010. Keisha can be contacted at klgreen@umass.edu.

This article originally appeared in *English Journal* 111.1

PANDEMIC PAGES

As an educator and a survivor of COVID-19, the author explores the restorative power of writing with students in an online class.

LISA MATISON GARRIGUES

I STARTED MY FIRST SEMESTER of student teaching at an independent school in New York City, on a Thursday morning in September of 2001. The following Tuesday, seven subway stops from my classroom, terrorists attacked the World Trade Center, killing 2,977 people.

The 13/14s, as Bank Street School for Children calls its eighth graders, had begun a semester-long study of ancient Greece and the classics. But I felt compelled, with support from faculty, to develop a series of lessons that spoke to the immediate crisis. The unit, Finding Poetry in Tragedy, introduced students to historic examples of art created from the ashes of anguish—Homer's *Iliad*, Picasso's *Guernica*, Maya Lin's Memorial Wall—and then instructed them to assemble found poems from present-day newspaper clippings (see Figure 1). Students were required to submit, along with their final poems, process paragraphs explaining their poetic choices (meter, rhyme, form, and so forth) as well as reflections on their experience of the project, both intellectual and emotional. The unit spanned two weeks and culminated in a salon-style poetry reading. It proved illuminating and generative and, for some students, cathartic.

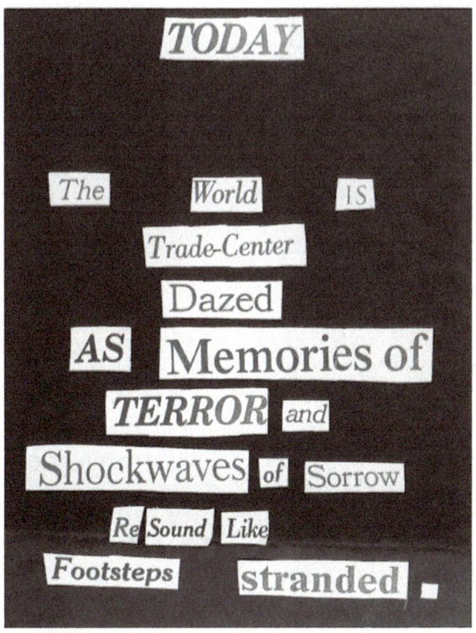

FIGURE 1
Grade 8 students assembled found poems from newspaper clippings in the wake of 9/11.

Back home in New Jersey, my own children, then twelve and ten, had spent the day on 9/11 nervously awaiting news of their father, who worked at the World Trade Center. Mark had just entered the second tower, at 8:46 that morning, when the first plane hit. He, thankfully, survived, but our children would go on to dream about the attack, they would talk about it in therapy, they would write about it in their college essays. Their friends, some of whom had lost a parent or relative in the attack, voiced similar experiences. Like other national catastrophes—the Depression, World War II, the Vietnam War—9/11 would come to define a generation.

The same will be true of the pandemic.

Face masks, quarantine, lockdown, social distancing, daily death tolls that far exceed the fatality count at Ground Zero—the pandemic is shaping our students and our children in ways we have yet to understand. But the message to educators is clear. While teachers and students have risen to the challenges of remote learning, gaining dexterity on Zoom, Google Classroom, and other virtual platforms, our courses of study remain much the same. I believe the content of what we teach, not just the container for how we teach it, must adapt to the terror and tumult of the times.

I have been teaching memoir writing in adult education for twenty years. Last spring, I was contracted to teach my signature course, Writing Womanhood, at a community college in northern California where I now live. Eighteen women signed up. Two weeks before the start of class, however, I tested positive for COVID-19. Mine was one of the first cases reported in my county, the first among my personal and professional circles. With advice from the chancellor of the college, we canceled my course without explanation.

Stephen King famously said that writing, once a way of life, became his way *back* to life the summer he was hit and nearly killed by an errant car on a country road (249). Writing saved me, too. Feverish and afraid, I opened my notebook and started writing. I wrote about the day, in early March, when my husband and I flew from San Francisco to New York City for my nephew's wedding, how we were up in the air, midway across the country, when the World Health Organization declared COVID-19 a pandemic. I wrote about the afternoon, soon after we returned home, when Mark began to cough and I followed him around with a spray bottle (two teaspoons of bleach diluted in sixteen ounces of water), wiping every surface he touched. I wrote about the morning my eggs tasted like sodium and my coffee smelled like sulfur. I wrote about the different ways our children rallied to our aid, our son putting into place an emergency protocol, our daughter depositing on our doorstep food and supplements known to support respiration and boost immunity. I wrote about our daily telephone calls with Nurse D from the local health services agency, the gratitude I felt knowing someone was out there, watching over us. From the day my sense of taste and smell went missing until now when it has yet fully to recover, writing has been a lifeline; my notebook has kept me afloat.

In July, recalling the unit I had developed in the wake of 9/11, I began teaching a virtual "writing together apart" workshop called Pandemic Pages (see Table 1). Part writing class, part restorative retreat, the five-week course invites students to document in a "pandemic notebook" the ordinary details of these extraordinary days. The twentieth-century poet Gwendolyn Brooks, the first African American author to win the Pulitzer Prize, insisted that writers collect words. "The more words you know," she said, "the better you will be able to express yourself, your thoughts" (qtd. in Heard 48). And so our first task is to create a "pandemic dictionary" (see Figure 2), complete with etymologies and definitions, both real and made up, of all the words that have been invented, reclaimed, and reimagined to describe this indescribable moment: *mask up, unmute, shelter in place, flatten the curve, anosmia, super spreader, essential worker, herd immunity, Zoom fog, long hauler* (Goldberg). With heartbreak and humor, we immerse ourselves in the language of the pandemic.

Pandemic Pages begins by inviting students to reflect back on their lives before the pandemic started, generating a list of "remember whens," and the course ends by asking students to look ahead to the day the coronavirus recedes, filling in the first week of their post-pandemic calendar (Gondelman). In between, we situate ourselves exactly where we are now—which, for most of us, is home. We prime our pens with a series of quick-writes called "postcards from home," an

TABLE 1

Pandemic Pages at a Glance

	Activity	Inquiry
Week 1	The Language of the Pandemic—Getting Acquainted, Getting Started	Facing Our Fears
Week 2	Before the Pandemic—Remember Whens	Embracing Loneliness and Longing
Week 3	Writing from Home—I Am Here	Finding Refuge
Week 4	After the Pandemic—My Post-pandemic Calendar	Walking in the New World
Week 5	Voices from the Pandemic—All-Class Reading	Writing Together Apart

pan· dem· ic

noun

1 : an outbreak of a disease that occurs over a wide geographic area and affects an exceptionally high proportion of the population

2 : from the Greek word "pan" (all) + "demos" (village or people)

3 : a mythological creature that visits our village every 100 years to teach us a vital lesson

FIGURE 2

A sample entry from the instructor's pandemic dictionary shows both real and made-up definitions.

TEACHING TIPS

Invite students to document in a "pandemic notebook" the ordinary details of the extraordinary days. Create "pandemic dictionaries" and study the definitions of "words that have been invented, reclaimed, and reimagined to describe this indescribable moment" like* "mask up; unmute; shelter in place; flatten the curve; anosmia; super spreader; essential worker; herd immunity; Zoom fog; and long hauler," *as Garrigues describes. Ask students to write about what they ate, what they wore, how they worked, studied, exercised, and socialized, as well as how they felt during all these activities to capture the creativity and complexity of the moment. Encourage students to reflect on their lives before and after the pandemic (a time in the future) in an effort to individually and collectively make sense of the moment and imagine what healing from these difficult moments might require. How has your school, district, or institution attended to the complexities of the pandemic? What can be done to improve the efforts?

activity inspired by the work of artist and graphic novelist Aidan Koch. We go on to write about what we eat and what we wear (our pandemic pantries and COVID closets). We write about how we work and study, exercise and socialize—all the creative and compromised ways we've been passing the time (Smith 23). We write about loneliness and fear (note that the word *pandemic* derives from the same Greek root as the words *panic* and *pandemonium*). Along the way, we examine newly published essays, poems, art, photographs, and podcasts as inspiration for writing, and we share our writing in small breakouts.

Wallace Stegner once described writing as a social act. "It is also," he said, "at its best, an affirmation—a way of joining the human race" (66). In that spirit, we gather on our final day for an all-class reading of our writing, Voices from the Pandemic. Sally reads a story titled "Home in Three Acts." Behnaz describes the view from her window. Victoria recounts an encounter with an anti-masker. Kayla recites a rhyming poem, "Pandemic Blues," in which languor dissolves into laughter. Xenia reads a lyrical narrative about longing. Together and apart, we share our collective stories, and in so doing we begin to heal ourselves, one another, and the earth.

The great neurologist and author Oliver Sacks, a few months before he died, looked up from his notepad one evening and said to his partner Bill Hayes, "The most we can do is to write—intelligently, creatively, critically, evocatively—about what it is like living in the world at this time" (qtd. in Hayes 13).

The year was 2015. Those words could not be more relevant today.

My parents, both Jews, came of age during World War II, and so I grew up hearing about the horrors of the Holocaust. My children, now thirty-two and thirty, will soon have children of their own. I wonder what these yet-to-be-born beings will know of the pandemic. What words will last? Which behaviors will persist? What fears—and hopes—will linger? What stories will we tell them? For now, all we can do is what every generation has done before us, and what every generation will do after us: lift ourselves out of the ashes of anguish and spin tragedy into poetry.

WORKS CITED

Brooks, Gwendolyn. *The Place My Words Are Looking For: What Poets Say about and through Their Work*, edited by B. Janeczko, Simon & Schuster, 1990.

Goldberg, Emma. "The New Words for Our New Misery." *The New York Times*, 24 Dec. 2020, www.nytimes.com/2020/12/24/opinion/coronavirus-language-words.html.

Gondelman, Josh. "When It's Safe: The First Week of My Post-pandemic Social Calendar." *The New York Times*, 14 Aug. 2020, www.newyorker.com/humor/daily-shouts/when-its-safe-the-first-week-of-my-post-pandemic-social-calendar.

Hayes, Bill. *How We Live Now: Scenes from the Pandemic*. Bloomsbury, 2020.

Heard, Georgia. *Writing toward Home: Tales and Lessons to Find Your Way*. Heinemann, 1995.

King, Stephen. *On Writing: A Memoir of the Craft*. Pocket Books, 2000.

Koch, Aidan. "Why You Should Write Postcards, Even from Home." *The New York Times*, 7 Aug. 2020, www.nytimes.com/2020/08/07/arts/aidan-koch-postcards.html.

Smith, Zadie. *Intimations*. Penguin, 2020.

Stegner, Wallace. *On Teaching and Writing Fiction*. Penguin, 2002.

LISA MATISON GARRIGUES is the author of *Writing Motherhood* (Scribner) and a freelance writer based in Santa Cruz, California. She has taught writing for twenty years, in secondary and adult education, and currently teaches at Cabrillo College. She is a fellow of the MacDowell, Hedgebrook, and Blue Mountain Center. She holds a master's degree in English education from Teachers College, Columbia University. Find out more at www.writingwomanhood.com.

This article originally appeared in *Voices from the Middle 28.4*

CULTURE, LOSS, AND SILENCE: It's on Us

PENNY KITTLE

ONE OF THE LAST TRIPS I took in 2020 was to visit Chad Everett, assistant principal at Horn Lake Middle School in Horn Lake, Mississippi. My colleague, Elaine Millen, and I are studying educational leaders. We followed Chad for two days: conferring with students and teachers, racing—seriously, as fast as we possibly could—to assist a student in distress, and orchestrating the flow of students in the cafeteria during lunch while talking about all things education. Just two weeks later, schools closed and we began this unwelcome shift to online learning.

Chad and I talked about reading soon after. He said, "If the culture of reading was not in place before we sent them home, there is no chance now." (C. Everett, personal communication, March 2020.)

Ah, the culture of reading.

In Chad's school, teachers have rich classroom libraries built on student interests and a determined and inspiring librarian. Chad's office is filled with books he can hand to a student sent to him for discipline. He expects teachers to lead all students to rewarding reading lives, so during the pandemic, Chad and his teachers made getting books in students' hands job one. As Gholdy Muhammad said in *Cultivating Genius*, historically responsive literacies call for such "urgent pedagogies" (2020). We can dismantle deficit thinking with a determined shift toward children.

You see, we used to lament summer reading loss. And now, after a year of unprecedented disruption, many students have experienced all-year reading loss.

But stop.

First, a clarification.

The idea of "loss" is a muddled mess. As Inigo Montoya said in *The Princess Bride*, "You keep using that word. I do not think it means what you think it means." You can't call it "learning loss" until we agree on what counts as learning and how we determine with integrity that it has or has not occurred. We have no agreement on this in American schools. I'm certain we all want sustained engagement across hundreds of pages for every student, one book after another. We want students to deepen their thinking about this life in all of its complexity year after year—no matter whose class they're in. That's a culture of reading. And I would agree that it has been lost for some time in many schools. We can't say that reciting a few things *about a book* but *not reading it* counts. Reading relevance and joy can disappear simply because teachers make all the choices about what counts as reading.

However, there is a solution. As Katherine Bomer says, "We need an air of expectancy with every child—which means we see what is brilliant and genius inside them." Amen. It means *we see them*. We give them books to read about issues and ideas that matter to them so that engaged reading increases both inside and outside of school. Many students are unlikely to seek books without us, and too many children simply won't *have* books without us.

So here we are.

Authentic reading is essential, yet I wonder if schools have lost it like we "lost" a tight-fitting skirt in the back of the closet once those pandemic survival cookies began to collect around our waistlines. We push aside what we don't want to face—and this idea that individual reading identities are our responsibility seems complicated. The National Literacy Trust reported in 2017 that kids who *enjoy* reading outperform their peers by a widening margin: from 1.3 years at age 10 to 3.3 years by age 14 (Clark, 2019). Those who enjoy reading read more. It just makes sense. What we fold into our identity brings us satisfaction, or why would we claim it?

We can ignore this and just pull out copies of a favorite whole-class novel, but that also gets tricky, doesn't it? You've heard that certain novels are essential for our culture. But whose culture?

We have to stop eating up so much class time with pretend reading. Swap the tired United States history textbook (that no one reads) for *Caste: The Origins of Our Discontents* by Isabel Wilkerson, the Pulitzer-prize-winning look at what our history of slavery tells us about our culture today. Students will wake up, trust me. Not just to engage, but to question and explore and seek to understand. Trade the slow weeks spent on *The Lord of the Flies* for book clubs centered on social justice. All students will read more.

Simply put: More reading matters.

It matters now.

It mattered before.

It matters whether we're in a room with students or online.

Everything has been harder with remote learning. It has revealed how much schools rely on compliance—and how far that is from engagement. The kid who turns off his camera might be the same kid in class with eyes open but his mind elsewhere.

When forced online, I started my 2020 school year with book clubs because my first goal was to bring students back into a community of readers. Online, yes, but not alone. To get my students talking, I selected a range of titles that would invite conversations about race and white privilege and the systems that suppress brilliance, that stereotype and intimidate people, and that prevent us all from living in community. We had two rounds of book clubs of four weeks each. The students chose two books from a list of nine, six of which explicitly deal with race. Every one of my students read one of these: *The Nickel Boys*; *Sing, Unburied, Sing*; *We Are Not from Here*; *Dear Martin*; *Long Way Down*; and *We Are Here*. Student-initiated conversations crossed into big territories: immigration, xenophobia, mass incarceration, police brutality, poverty, why #BlackLivesMatter, and mental health. We talked about the coronavirus and its outsized impact on communities of color. The *books* and the community of curious young people drove deep thinking.

Kieran, a first-year university student, was unsure what to make of #BlackLivesMatter from his northern New Hampshire town. He went to an almost all-white high school, and the media he consumes will not steer him out of that lane. Yet he said during a meeting this fall, "*Dear Martin* is helping me understand what is happening in our country right now . . . and I *want* to know. I mean, why couldn't we read books like this in high school?"

The book choices led to thorny conversations, for sure. And I wished I had Julia Torres or Cicely Lewis or Andria Nacina Cole in my classroom to lead me. I still have so much to learn—so much of my own antiracism work to do. But all my students had was me. All your students have is you. Remember the mantra of the Freedom Riders? "If not you, who? If not now, when?"

I asked students to listen and to question, to rephrase, and to challenge assumptions. We learned together. Sure, it was wobbly work at times, but it was better than pretending reading isn't urgent and relevant now. In a multiracial democracy there is no defense for an English curriculum of all white authors. There never was, you know that. But the fight for change can look like a maze of cactuses. We'd rather put our heads down, perhaps, and avoid considering the impact of that choice. We can remain silent about curriculum since the decision about which books to teach is often made far from classrooms. (It is too often true: Those in power rarely give teachers the agency to make important decisions.) But we still have choices, and they begin with what we commit to.

EVERYTHING HAS BEEN HARDER WITH REMOTE LEARNING. IT HAS REVEALED HOW MUCH SCHOOLS RELY ON COMPLIANCE—AND HOW FAR THAT IS FROM ENGAGEMENT.

For me, I will not ignore a culture of pretend reading.

I have braided two big ideas into this essay so far: culture and loss. There is an ancient power in the number three, so I have one last subject for you: silence.

We've seen social media elevate conversations about race and school curricula. But how many white teachers who are bold in tweets are as bold in their own English departments? This is big work and it is small work: Significant change begins in *your* classroom and *your* school.

I won't forget the stand-off one afternoon at a high school department meeting when a colleague said with a great deal of fire, "I won't let anyone leave my classroom without understanding the importance of the green light at the end of the dock in *Gatsby*."

And I replied, "I am determined that no one leaves my classroom without reading—really reading—a book." The uncomfortable silence that followed is something we all seek to avoid. Cornelius Minor reminds us, "There are far too many people in agreement with injustice. Expect people to disagree with you. One aspect of white supremacy culture is conflict avoidance. In our roles as builders, destroyers, healers, and organizers, we will upset others" (2021). More than a few of my colleagues were upset that day. But we simply must recognize that all teachers have clear, specific, and measurable commitments that drive all kinds of decisions we make each year. You have to ask: What do I make time for? What do students gain and lose when I make that choice?

The urgency of now requires us to move. When children return to you this fall, many will have not read a book for a year—and many more for many years. If that matters to you (and please tell me it does), what will you do to change that?

When I first made the transition from high school to college teaching, I expected to meet students ready and willing to read. Three girls arrived early to slurp iced coffee and show me TikTok videos. They were soon deep in thought, writing and fiddling with words in notebooks in response to the power of spoken word poetry. They slumped back against their chairs, however, when I handed them books. They came to college having learned not to expect much in those pages. We taught them that.

YOU HAVE TO ASK: WHAT DO I MAKE TIME FOR? WHAT DO STUDENTS GAIN AND LOSE WHEN I MAKE THAT CHOICE?

When I saw them unwilling to stop reading a week later, I smiled. It wasn't me, of course; it was the books that kept them reading. Elizabeth Acevedo and Tiffany D. Jackson did the hard work of engaging them. I just gave them choices and time to read.

TEACHING TIPS

Kittle argues, "You can't call it 'learning loss' until we agree on what counts as learning and how we determine with integrity that it has or has not occurred." What is your definition of learning? How, if at all, has the pandemic influenced how you define and assess your students' learning? How do you determine your students' reading and writing needs, especially during the pandemic? Compose your definition of learning in a notebook or online. Share your definition of learning with your students. Ask your students how they define learning and how they determine for themselves if they have learned something well. Compare and contrast you and your students' definitions of learning. Kittle explains, "everything has been harder with remote learning. It has revealed how much schools rely on compliance—and how far that is from engagement." Rather than assume, ask your students what makes remote learning difficult? Ask students for suggestions to improve remote learning. Find ways to include your students' compelling suggestions into your classroom. Invite your students to share their compelling suggestions with administrators.

In the high school English department I was in for 21 years, teachers worked to connect a classic novel to current events. Those efforts rarely increased reading. What do we lose when we stop reading? If standardized tests are the measure, our most well-resourced schools will say not much. High test scores can be used to justify a curriculum where almost no one reads. But those of you reading this—you know. We lose an opportunity to be the change we seek in our classrooms, our schools, and in our nation.

I recorded interviews with students to show how choice and personalization had transformed so many young people (my colleagues' former students) from disinterested readers to empowered ones. I shared it and endured the uncomfortable silence that followed. You know I wasn't welcome at their lunch table, but I refused to pass on the curriculum my mother (who is 86) remembered from high school. She found *East of Eden* fascinating and 1984 haunting—terrifying, even. But now? Most teens meet these texts with a ho-hum shrug and fake read for weeks. Too many teachers shrug back, "We've got to get through this. It's in the curriculum." *Please.* We only hand out novels written long before our students' grandparents were born and call that the best we can do?

We *can* find a balance. We must.

What if we saw contemporary books as a portal: an opportunity to bring the past forward, to make history relevant now? It isn't that modern books ignore history—it percolates in the events characters live through. And it isn't that the book alone works on us; we personalize reading as we bounce the ideas there against our understanding of what is happening in our streets. What is literature if not an opportunity to look both in and outside of yourself and your experiences? This is the conversation in book clubs when we ask, what does the book say to you?

During this pandemic I have tuned into television I have rarely watched in the past. Episodes of "Love It or List It" have stolen hours. When people are looking for a new house, the word that bothers me the most is *need*. Everyone seems to *need* a larger closet. We use that word carelessly, incompletely. Our needs trample others'. How do we determine what students need from the reading and writing lives we hold captive in middle and high school? Who do we serve: curriculum or students?

Jason Reynolds revealed in a keynote address last fall that he never read in high school (2020). He said he wants to tell his former English teachers, "You traded *my* engagement for books *you* cared about." You might start the conversation in your school with that simple truth. Your school will never develop a culture of wide reading if we don't face the silence we find so comfortable. And that's learning loss we can't deny.

Have the courage to create a culture where young people wrap themselves around the haunting importance of *King and the Dragonflies* and *Dig* and *This Is My America* and *Furia*.

Books are brave and true. Are we?

REFERENCES

Bomer, K. (2021, Feb. 27). "Come back to radical joy" [Workshop]. Teaching Literacy in Times of Change and Uncertainty Conference, Literacy Consultants Coalition.

Callender, K. (2020). *King and the dragonflies.*

Clark, C. (2019). Children and young people's reading in 2017/18: Findings from our Annual Literacy Survey. National Literacy Trust.

Fitzgerald, F. S. (1925). *The great Gatsby.*

Golding, W. (1954). *The lord of the flies.*

Goldman, W. (Director). (1987). *The princess bride* [Film].

Johnson, K. (2020). *This is my America.*

King, A. S. (2019). *Dig.*

Méndez, Y. S. (2020). *Furia.*

Minor, C. (2021, Feb. 27). Keynote address. Teaching Literacy in Times of Change and Uncertainty Conference, Literacy Consultants Coalition.

Muhammad, G. (2020). *Cultivating genius: An equity framework for historically and culturally responsive literacy*. Scholastic.

Orwell, G. (1949). 1984.

Reynolds, J. (2017). *Long way down.*

Reynolds, J. (2020, Oct. 26). Keynote address. Literacy for All Conference, October 26.

Reynolds, J., & Kiely, B. (2015). *All American boys.*

Sanchez, J. T. (2020). *We are not from here.*

Steinbeck, J. (1952). *East of Eden.*

Stone, N. (2017). *Dear Martin.*

Tauheed, I. (2021, Feb. 27). "Poetry as a practice of freedom" [Workshop]. Teaching Literacy in Times of Change and Uncertainty Conference, Literacy Consultants Coalition.

Twain, M. (1885). *Huckleberry Finn.*

Ward, J. (2017). *Sing, unburied, sing.*

Whitehead, C. (2019). *The nickel boys.*

Wilkerson, I. (2020). *Caste: The origin of our discontents.*

PENNY KITTLE teaches writing at Plymouth State University in New Hampshire. She taught in public schools for 34 years and learned two essential things: all students will build independent reading lives of joy, curiosity, and hunger when given agency; and teachers who write *with* their students generate community and creative power. Kittle is the founder of the Book Love Foundation. She has written eight books on teaching and travels the world to learn beside teachers and students.

This article originally appeared in *English Leadership Quarterly* 43.2

FROM CRISIS TO CONTINUITY: The Role of the LMS in the Future of Learning

SARAH PAZUR

The Case for Continuity

I was a senior in high school in the late '90s when I gave birth to my son. Adults in my Catholic high school questioned whether or not I could continue my education from a distance, and, quite frankly, whether they felt I deserved the opportunity. Those questions still haunt me today. In the end, my teachers prepared work packets for me and every day for three weeks between Halloween and Thanksgiving, as I acclimated to young motherhood, I labored over math problems in an antiquated textbook and typed essays on my Brother word processor. I kept pace with the daily curriculum during and after my absence and graduated high school with my peers.

As I look back on these experiences, it is clear to me it did not have to be that way. If my school had only been humanized in a manner that permitted me access to flexible, asynchronous learning, I would have been spared a significant amount of shame and anxiety from not being there in person. Those like me—young moms; students with chronic illness; youth who have experienced trauma; incarcerated, displaced, and homeless teens—understand that learning continuity is not a new challenge in education; but widespread school closures have suddenly made it an urgent one for the mainstream population.

The education landscape has evolved since the '90s, and blended and virtual classrooms are certainly more common than when I attended high school, but the COVID-19 pandemic catapulted brick and mortar classrooms into the cloud faster than anything we had experienced before. To manage this rapid shift, state education departments required districts to submit Continuity of Learning Plans that outlined how they would transition their students from in-person to remote instruction with minimal disruption to learning. These plans mandated that district leaders address equity and access issues exacerbated by the pandemic. In response, administrators rethought everything from meal distribution to internet access in a matter of a couple weeks. Nevertheless, inequities abound.

At the same time school administrators scrambled to implement an emergency online learning program, they battled virtual learning's stigmatized legacy. Traditionally, educators and stakeholders have not wholeheartedly embraced virtual learning, pointing to low course completion rates and lack of compelling student performance data as indicators of its ineffectiveness. Furthermore, online learning

INEQUITY IN EDUCATION HIGHLIGHTED BY SCHOOL CLOSURES

The coronavirus crisis shines light on educational inequalities, *Washington Post*

The Disparate Impact of School Closures: Measuring the Unequal Educational Costs of the Coronavirus Pandemic, *Forbes* has been stigmatized in the eyes of those who see it as a last resort for "nonconforming" or "alternative" students. It is true that virtual high schools disproportionately provide credit recovery solutions for students at risk of not graduating on time; it is also true they offer second chances for students no longer welcome at their home districts.

To add to this skepticism of online learning, the mass closures prompted a heavy dose of nostalgia. Parents, students, and educators now refer to school using evaluative binaries—pre- versus post- pandemic school, online versus in-person learning—but the reality is that technology in education is an ever-evolving ecology, and we are on a change continuum. Neil Postman (1992) in his anti-technology manifesto, *Technopoly*, described this continuum best:

> Technological change is neither additive [n]or subtractive. It is ecological. I mean ecological in the same sense as the word is used by environmental scientists. One significant change generates total change. If you remove the caterpillars from a given habitat, you are not left with the same environment minus caterpillars: you have a new environment, and you have reconstituted the conditions of survival; the same is true if you add caterpillars to an environment that has had none. (p. 18)

Despite his polemical opposition to educational technology, Postman's caterpillar metaphor ironically serves an important point about the nature of virtual learning: When we introduce distance learning—at scale—to mainstream education, we reconstitute the conditions for student achievement. Of course, the necessity for a coordinated distance learning pedagogy that is available to all students predated and will postdate this crisis. But now, as leaders plan for students to return to school this fall, they must honor what virtual learning environments can do to reach all students. They must embrace the many ways that virtual school environments reflect and affirm our students' realities outside of the physical school building. An important and overdue step in that process: implementing a district-wide learning management system (LMS).

WHEN WE INTRODUCE DISTANCE LEARNING—AT SCALE—TO MAINSTREAM EDUCATION, WE RECONSTITUTE THE CONDITIONS FOR STUDENT ACHIEVEMENT.

The LMS as a Third Teacher

Loris Maluguzzi, founder of the Reggio Emilia approach to education referred to a child's environment as the "third teacher." Reggio Emilia ambassadors believe the environment shapes and is shaped by the learning process, creating a "constant dialogue between architecture and pedagogy" (Reggio Emilia Approach, 2020). In our present learning ecosystem, the architecture of school has changed. Classroom walls are permeable, school is amorphous. In this version of school, the LMS functions like a classroom environment, a third teacher.

IN OUR PRESENT LEARNING ECOSYSTEM, THE ARCHITECTURE OF SCHOOL HAS CHANGED. CLASSROOM WALLS ARE PERMEABLE, SCHOOL IS AMORPHOUS. IN THIS VERSION OF SCHOOL, THE LMS FUNCTIONS LIKE A CLASSROOM ENVIRONMENT, A THIRD TEACHER.

LMSs are software applications used to deliver educational programming, but like a good teacher, an effective LMS is inclusive, supportive, responsive, rich with resources, and able to foster connections within and across communities. Unfortunately, the abrupt shift to remote teaching outpaced many districts' readiness and capacity to implement a coordinated web-based or remote infrastructure; for districts who were not already using an LMS, the transition to online learning was especially disjointed and difficult.

Lessons Learned from the Pandemic

Michigan Virtual, a nonprofit organization that provides online courses and professional development for educators, in partnership with design firm Sundberg-Ferar, conducted a qualitative study on the effects of the pandemic on educational leaders, teachers, parents, and students. They found across the board that districts with an LMS in place were relieved they had one, and those who did not have one were frustrated (Byron, 2020). One English teacher said this:

> I can't imagine how I'd tackle online learning without our LMS. I use it and the tools within it to give students information, videos, docs, models, etc. We use Zoom and Meet for online meetings. It is effective because my students know how to do it. I didn't need to train them much. I also put up plenty of mentor texts and videos of my lessons and my own modeling, so that helps them.

The schools that lacked an LMS specifically discussed their districts' inability to communicate effectively. An administrator shared her frustration:

> The biggest challenge has been to have a central place to go for all communication. Not e-mail, not a Classroom stream. Messages get lost in those formats. We need to have a bulletin board/dashboard that all people expect to go to. This is true for parents, for students, for staff to get questions answered. (Different boards for different audiences.) We need to have an infrastructure for learning so that everyone knows where to find the resources they will use most. Students need to have a place to keep work that is in progress, and students and parents and teachers all need to be clear on what the priorities are and what work needs to be turned in.

In other words, remote instruction during the pandemic taught schools the importance of a universal, coordinated platform with common social and communication norms to facilitate the flow of information between all stakeholders. The lack of a district-wide LMS caused a hyper-decentralization of school: multiple sign-ins for students and parents, slews of applications to navigate, confusion on where to go for information, too few or too many places to store and share documents, the list goes on. An LMS can mitigate a significant number of those frustrations.

Selecting the Right LMS

Having an LMS in place is not a substitute for a compelling vision for teaching and learning; it is the vehicle to help districts achieve that vision. Like any effective initiative, implementing an LMS into your school district will require careful and long-term planning as well as dedicated resources and thoughtful and ongoing professional development for all users. Michigan educational leaders developed a guide to assist districts in choosing the best-fit LMS that aligns to their school's mission ("Guide to selecting," 2020). The guide outlines a comprehensive selection process; to summarize the essence of the selection process, consider these four questions on the role that your LMS will play on the future of learning:

- Does the LMS facilitate student-driven learning?
- Does the LMS integrate with other tools and applications so students can work, learn, and collaborate seamlessly?
- Can the LMS be altered in scope and functionality so that it grows over time with our district?
- Does the district have the commitment, time, and resources it will take to effectively implement the system across all user groups—students, teachers, administrators, and parents?

Answering these questions can assist with choosing an LMS that fosters learning continuity; continuity

HOW AN LMS CAN SUPPORT LEARNING

How to Align Your LMS with the Science of Learning, *Edutopia*

Teaching SEL skills in online education, *NEO Blog*

TEACHING TIPS

Pazur explains, "When we introduce distance learning—at scale—to mainstream education, we reconstitute the conditions for student achievement" and "Having an LMS in place is not a substitute for a compelling vision for teaching and learning; it is a vehicle to help districts achieve that vision." What is your vision for teaching and learning? Compose your vision in a notebook or online. How has your vision for teaching and learning shifted during the pandemic, if at all? What lessons have you learned about your vision for teaching and learning during the pandemic? Ask your students about their vision for teaching and learning. Does your school district have a central LMS? If so, then how have you implemented your vision for teaching and learning through your LMS? If your district does not have a central LMS, then how are you managing learning opportunities? Rather than assume, ask your students about the experiences with navigating your classroom (or district) LMS. Ask students how the classroom or institutional LMS challenged and contributed to their learning. How are you carrying these lessons forward?

that empowers students to work synchronously and asynchronously, to collaborate, to communicate, and to feel connected to the school community and culture.

The LMS as Social Connector

In addition to leveraging the LMS as a common learning platform, it will be important to leverage it as a way to keep students socially connected as they move from face-to-face to online classrooms. The new reality of school will include in-person, hybrid, and 100% virtual experiences—and students will flow between these models. David Jakes, educational design thinker, wrote about the concept of using the LMS to create a "virtual third place," a place for students to socialize with other students that is not exclusively an academic space, or exclusively a social space, but something in between (Jakes, 2020). This concept is another illustration of the way that technology is neither additive, nor subtractive, but transformative. Previously, students relied on school as a place to stay connected with their peers. But now that face time with their peers at school will be reduced and fragmented with longer periods of virtual time in between, they will need a school-sponsored social application to satisfy these gaps. The LMS is one way to address the need for a virtual school-social space.

The LMS and the Future of Learning

The history of distance learning is storied and complex. Its legacy is wrought with bias against disenfranchised learners. It has been misappropriated in a way that alienates students from their learning communities. Distance learning, however, can also be extremely redemptive. Students who otherwise would not have been able to complete school have earned their diplomas and degrees. Students against difficult odds—COVID-19 being one of them—have persisted and succeeded. The LMS plays a critical role in supporting learning continuity for all students. The right-fit LMS promotes networked learning and social connectedness. A district-wide LMS is no longer a perk; it's an integral part of distance learning pedagogy. As Nicholas Negroponte (1998) said in his prescient article, "Beyond Digital": "Like air and drinking water, being digital will be noticed only by its absence, not its presence." COVID-19 demanded that school systems provide learning continuity at scale and the LMS will prove to be a ubiquitous presence in the future of learning.

REFERENCES

Byron, D. (2020, June). Future of remote learning (Google Slides). Presented at Keep Michigan Learning workgroup meeting, Michigan Virtual.

Champion, A. (2015). Self-efficacy and online learning for expelled students. *The Exchange*, 4(1). ssrn.com/abstract=2676862

Guide to selecting an LMS in K–12. (2020, June 25). kmlearning.wpengine.com/guide-to-selecting-an-lms-for-k-12/

Heinrich, C., Darling-Aduana, J., Good, A., & Huiping, C. (2019, May 14). A look inside online learning settings in high schools. Brookings. Retrieved from www.brookings.edu/blog/brown-center-chalkboard/2019/05/14/a-look-inside-online-learning-settings-in-high-schools/

Jakes, D. (2020, June 21). Designing a virtual third place for schools. David Jakes Designs. davidjakesdesigns.com/ideas/2020/6/20/designing-a-virtual-third-place-for-schools

Loeb, S. (2020, Mar. 20). How effective is online learning? What the research does and doesn't tell us. *EdWeek*. www.edweek.org/ew/articles/2020/03/23/how-effective-is- online-learning-what-the.html

Negroponte, N. (1998, Jan. 12). Beyond digital. *Wired*. web.media.mit.edu/~nicholas/Wired/WIRED6-12.html

Reggio Emilia Approach. (2020, June 25). www.reggiochildren.it/en/reggio-emilia-approach/

SARAH PAZUR is the director of school leadership for a network of public school academies across Michigan and is the co-founder of FlexTech Education. She earned a PhD in educational leadership from Oakland University. She writes scholarly articles, creative non-fiction, short stories, and poetry; her work has been published in places like *Pithead Chapel, JMWW, EdWeek, Phi Delta Kappan, Ed Surge, Principal Leadership Magazine and Hybrid Pedagogy*. You can follow her education publications here: https://authory.com/SarahPazur or find her on Twitter @saypa.

This article originally appeared in *Language Arts 98.2*

WRITING FOR LIBERATION

Tiana Silvas, 2019 recipient of the Donald H. Graves Award for Excellence in the Teaching of Writing, explains how writing is a tool for liberation.

TIANA SILVAS

Tiana Silvas, 2019 recipient of the Donald H. Graves Award for Excellence in the Teaching of Writing

MY JOURNEY as a writing teacher started long before I took my first breath on this earth. As a Mexican American educator, my teaching practices around writing are deeply rooted in the history of my family. For this piece, I call on the name of my father, Manuel Silvas. He and many elders have and continue to walk through this world with strength and resilience.

My heart as a writing teacher comes from the power and courage of my father's stories, such as the one about my grandfather being convicted of murder in 1962 and sentenced to death. His execution changed my father's life forever. That death penalty stole the innocence of my father's childhood, which he spent his life reclaiming through writing and action.

My father once shared a memory of the first moment he took a step forward in reclaiming his life. "I had no one else to fall on," he said. "You see, I was alone and struggling. I tried to write about it in school. I wrote, but I was silenced. I was told by a teacher that school wasn't a place to share my story." My father faced barriers but continued to push through with writing. Throughout my father's life he continues to show my brother and me that writing is one way to confront life, resist, and heal. Paper and pen are the companions that have never left his side.

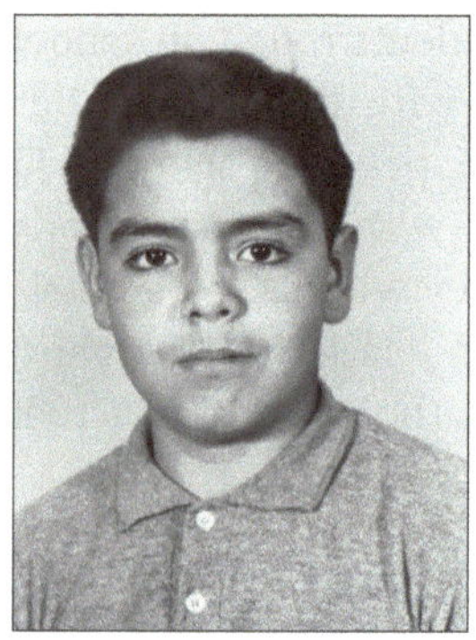

Tiana's father, Manuel Silvas, age 9. This school picture was taken the year his father was charged.

My father's stories allow me to reflect on my practice working with young writers. How can I bridge the gap between our current teaching practices and pathways for students to use writing as a tool for liberation?

Reflection on My Practice

Along with my elders, my students have been another guiding light. I've always felt uncertain when things seem to be going smoothly. Some time ago, that feeling came as I watched my students write. Where was the energy? Where was the magic? It appeared the students were just going through the motions of writing. I wondered how they really felt about writing. I wondered if they could see there was a larger purpose for writing beyond school. One day, as we were finishing up the writing workshop, I decided to ask a group of students, "Why do you write?" So many students answered that, since this was school, they wrote because they were told to. These responses were both telling and devastating. Little did I know that questioning my practice was the step in the direction Donald H. Graves encouraged: learning to listen.

Learning to Listen with Our Hearts

I knew that there could be a plethora of causes affecting my ability to listen to learn, such as the structure of units, mandates, and high-stakes tests. What was it about writing that led students to think it was only relevant for school? I needed to think about what was in our sphere of influence. When I did, I realized the answer: We needed to reframe the purpose of writing to move beyond "the assignment" and shift towards an experience that embodies creating pathways to process the world and reclaim our stories.

Listening with our hearts is at the foundation of our writing community. As a community of learners, we established a culture embodying the words of Donald Graves (1990):

> Listening is at the heart of learning for both children and teacher. Unless we listen we have no window on the world. We can see, touch, and feel, but the world of words is lost to us. But if we are to live the life of words in our teaching and in our writing, we need to hear the words of children and adults, both when they speak and when they write. (p.83)

Listening is an act of mindful inquiry about ourselves, others, and the world around us. It is a pathway for writing to discover, name, and confront the world in which we live. We did this as a community by spending time learning about each other in both our school and home lives. In our fifth-grade class, Zabrina offered insights as she critically examined the world. Early on, I noticed how she would use the power of her words to share her perspective and express herself. Zabrina's writing opened another lens of learning for our community. Here is a snippet of her writing:

THE ROAD TO MY INDEPENDENCE

> In your life you have your own rules. Everyone handles everything differently. Some just lock their emotions in and some just send a message by using other sources to help themselves. You're gonna be stuck in quicksand and want to get out but you keep sinking. You sink, and sink, and sink until you save yourself. You save yourself with what you can depend on. You just look at it and you smile. It's like something is pulling you out of the conflict or issue that is happening. It's like a hand pulling you out. In the quicksand you may have expectations from people, expectations like you can't get out, as if you're doomed. And you're probably wondering what was the hand pulling me out of the quicksand. Mine was music.

Our learning extended far beyond a set of questions; listening to write was about listening to learn what matters in students' lives. As Bettina Love (2019) says, "Mattering is civics because it is the quest for humanity" (p. 7). Our students matter. Their stories matter. It matters when there is a wall of injustice built and students' lives are dehumanized; it matters that listening and writing can be a place to humanize the world.

Discovering the Power of Words

Building a community was one of the essential steps in creating a space for students to write with courage. Throughout this journey, writers started to feel comfortable as they tried out new writing movements, played around with styles, and shared the stories they were ready to share. Most importantly, students began to redefine the workshop by taking agency through choice. With the support of the community, students felt brave as they told their stories. Another student in our classroom, Marz, shared that she just needed to write her memoir to set the

TEACHING TIPS

Silvas explains, "listening is an act of mindful inquiry about ourselves, others, and the world around us . . . and writing can be a place to humanize the world." Invite your ELA students to compose multimodal texts that confront, resist, and make suggestions for healing from the issues of this historical moment. Listen carefully to your students' issues. What promotes and prevents your ability to listen to your students concerns? Facilitate opportunities for your students to share their concerns with your school, district, or institution.

story straight because people have made too many assumptions about her quietness. Here is an example of Marz using the power of words to inform and reclaim her world:

> When most people think about the word fierce, they probably think of a superhero flying into a destroyed building to save a child. Or a random person risking their life for someone they don't even know. I think fierce means to stand up for yourself and to face challenges life holds. Facing those challenges is being fierce. Owning your power is being fierce. Not letting those nasty words get to you is being fierce! Most people will underestimate a person by the way they look, but sometimes what people see on the outside doesn't determine what is on the inside. If people really got to know me, they'd know that I am fierce.

Like Marz, so many students continued to construct a writing experience that embraces their abilities and honors their identities, to nurture their voices as writers and write with purpose and power. As a teacher, it was essential for me to take a learning stance, listen, and trust the process as the students created their writing community. To quote Graves (1990), "Writing is learning to listen to yourself and your own voice, to watch for the sense of self that emerges, and to trust what you see coming" (p. 26). Writing is about the "sense of self" that can emerge from us. When this happens, the pen and paper become our companions to confront life, resist injustice, and heal.

REFERENCES

Graves, D. H. (1990). *Discover your own literacy*. Heinemann.

Love, B. L. (2019). *We want to do more than survive: Abolitionist teaching and the pursuit of educational freedom*. Beacon Press.

TIANA SILVAS is a fifth-grade teacher at PS 59 in New York City. She served as a Heinemann Fellow from 2016 to 2018 and can be reached at tiana.silvasbrunetti@gmail.com.

This article originally appeared in
Research in the Teaching of English 55.3

IN THE BLACK RADICAL TRADITION: Poetry as a Praxis for Healing and Resistance in Education

This In Dialogue essay stands on the shoulders of ancestry and centers on the nexus of the Black Radical Tradition and healing – specifically through poetry. Poetry has historically been leveraged as a tool of protest, helping to capture current realities and imagine new ones into existence (Lorde, 2007; Neal, 1969). Baxley and Sealey-Ruiz share their poetry as a form of resistance; a way to bare their souls and restore themselves against the anti-Blackness that is rampant in our society. By showcasing how this art form has been healing and affirming for them individually and collectively, they also advocate to practitioners and educational leaders that poetry be central to the curriculum for Black children in schools.

GWENDOLYN BAXLEY &
YOLANDA SEALEY-RUIZ

Introduction: Say *These* Names

> Jonathan Mattingly. Brett Hankison. Aaron Dean. Anthony Holzhauer. Myles Cosgrove. Timothy Loehmann. Gregory McMichael. Travis McMichael. William Bryan Jr. Percy Dupra. George Zimmerman. Bryan Myers. David Ried. Terrence Mercadal. Jared Robinet. Amber Guyger. Joseph Weekley. Derek Chauvin. J. Alexander Kueng. Thomas Lane. Tou Thao. Edward McMellon. Sean Carroll. Kenneth Boss. Richard Murphy. Jeronimo Yanez. Blane Salamoni. Darren Wilson. Peter Liang. Daniel Pantaleo. Scott Aldridge. Jason Van Dyke . . .

These are the names of just a few police officers and vigilantes who have brutally killed Black adults and children.[1] We must say *these* names, too, as they stand to remind us of the work that must be done to hold murderers accountable while we strive to dismantle the criminalization and disposability of Black people.[2] Law enforcement and schools are two of several institutions complicit in robbing Black bodies of innocence and social protections (Dumas, 2014; Dumas & Nelson, 2016; Goff et al., 2014; Morris, 2016; Shange, 2019). Think for a moment about Tamir Rice: shot and killed at the age of 12 by Timothy Loehmann. Tamir's tragic murder is the distinct reason our children are cautious of police and almost instinctively hide in fear of being harmed when cops pass by in their neighborhoods—for example, 10-year-old Elijah hid from police while playing solo basketball in his family's driveway in Connecticut (Brito, 2020). Or think of 15-year-old Grace, who (just a few weeks before Elijah hid), was arrested and incarcerated for not completing her schoolwork during the COVID pandemic and the transition to remote learning (Jurado, 2020). This pandemic has further unleashed violence on Black communities nationwide, showcasing the violent systems and structures that disproportionately impact affect the lives, health, and well-being of Black people. It has also highlighted the Black-led movement and uprisings against these various forms of violence (Fowkles & Walters, 2020; Camera, 2020) and the lack of social safety nets for so many in our nation.

At such times, the arts offer a mirror to Black resistance and a window through which we can see our collective struggle. Audre Lorde (2007) reminded us specifically of the importance of poetry to serve as a mirror and window (Sims-Bishop, 1990) for those marginalized by society's ills of racism, sexism, and homophobia. In her essay, she noted "poetry is not a luxury." It is a vital necessity of our existence. It forms the quality of the light within which we predicate our hopes and dreams toward survival and change, first made into language, then into idea, then into more tangible action" (Lorde, 2007, p. 37).

It is from this assertion that our work emerges. At a time when anti-Blackness is further unmasked, and our collective resistance continues, healing seems both elusive and urgent. This In Dialogue essay seeks to offer rays of hope and resistance: a tribute to our continued collective protest, and a reprieve from the wounding and suffering experienced by so many Black people in our country. In the historic tradition of using art to affirm Black Dignity against dehumanization, we turn to the Black Radical Tradition as a concept; we share our poetry as a way to bare our souls, release our pain and sadness, and restore ourselves. We view the writing and sharing of our poetry as a form of healing—for ourselves and, we hope, for *RTE* In Dialogue readers—in the wake of persistent state-sanctioned violence against Black people and supporters of the current Black Lives Matter movement for justice. By showcasing how this art form has been healing and affirming for us individually and collectively, we also advocate to practitioners and educational leaders that poetry be central to the curriculum for Black children in schools.

Literature Review

BLACK RADICAL TRADITION: POETRY AS A FORM OF RESISTANCE, DIGNITY, AND HEALING

From Phiyllis Wheaitley and Langston Hughes to Amiri Baraka and Mahogany L. Browne, poetry has historically been a part of a broader Black Radical Tradition—the collection of customs, beliefs, and values through which Black people call out and disrupt systems of oppression that deny them humanity and (re/pro)claim their worth and dignity (Robinson, 2000; Thomas, 2019). The Black Radical Tradition, which is what we leverage for the duration of this article, is the focus on historical Black resistance, struggle, and dignity (Robinson, 2000, foreword by Kelley, p. xiii; Stern & Hussain, 2015). Cedric Robinson characterized the Black Radical Tradition as the continued collection of ways—from uprisings to the arts—that Black people not only call out and disrupt systems of oppression that deny them personhood, but also imagine something different. Robinson stated, "The Black Radical Tradition was an accretion, over generations, of collective intelligence gathered from struggle. . . . As a culture of liberation, the tradition crossed the familiar bounds of social and historical narrative." The Black Radical Tradition is both "resistance against structures" and the maintenance of an ontology through Black cultural traditions, values, and beliefs (Thomas, 2019, para. 2). "From ship revolts to maroon communities, from abolition to civil rights, from Black Power to Black Lives Matter, the major goal [of the Black Radical Tradition] has to be strategic action to maintain the dignity and humanity of Black people," according to Thomas (2019). Poetry has a particular way of sustaining and healing our souls by serving as a tool of resistance, helping to capture our current realities and imagine new realities and identities into existence (Lorde, 2007; Neal, 1969). Healing, the process of restoring health and well-being to individuals and communities, is essential for continued individual and collective resistance and the fight for justice, such as through poetry (Ginwright, 2011). As Lucille Clifton reminded us, "Poetry can heal. Because it comes from a heart, it can speak to another heart. . . . [Poetry] feeds us. And if one is not fed, one starves. If you don't get any food, you starve physically and if you don't get any food for the inside, your soul starves" (Lamon, 2012, para. 4). Through our poetry, we strive to continue the tradition of our elders to heal, resist, and proclaim our worth and dignity.

POETRY AS EMPOWERMENT AMONG YOUTH

Given the power and history of poetry in the Black Radical Tradition, we advocate, along with other literacy scholars, that poetry be central to the curriculum for Black children in schools. School leaders, such as deans and supervisors of curriculum and instruction, set the ethos in schools for children and their families, and can be advocates for the implementation of poetry in the curriculum. Poetry is part of Black youth and families' ancestral tradition, and there are clear benefits—articulated by poets, educational leaders, and scholars—associated with the positive impact of poetry and spoken word on academics. Spoken word has especially been overlooked as a valuable writing and performance genre. While poetry (and especially spoken word) has proven to be a "balm in Gilead" for Black and Brown students, its utilization as an outlet for exploring trauma and developing one's sense of self has been underexamined, despite the work that documents its transformative impact on youth of color (Camangian, 2008; Fisher, 2005). Prominent literacy scholars have offered compelling arguments about the ability of poetry to empower students and create a space for worthy and responsive witnessing (Camangian, 2008; Fisher, 2005; Jocson, 2005; Kinloch, 2005; Wissman & Wiseman, 2011). Specifically, for urban youth, McCormick (2000) explained how the genre welcomes the opportunity for students to "play out conflict and imagine multiple possibilities for identity" (p. 194). In her article "'There's a Better Word': Urban Youth Rewriting Their Social Worlds through Poetry," Jocson (2005) advocated for youth poetry and described how a poetry program helped students gain writing skills, increase their motivation to learn and confidence in their learning style, and build self-awareness and social consciousness. In the historic tradition of using art to affirm Black Dignity and resistance against dehumanization, and specifically the art of poetry (McClure, 2017; Neal, 1969), we offer our poems as social commentary, resistance, and a form of healing. Black people's lives *are* poetry. As Toni Morrison (2015) wrote, "We speak, we write, we do language. That is how civilizations heal" (para. 12).

POETRY IN THE PANDEMIC: A PORTAL OF POSSIBILITY FOR HEALING

In his article in *The Atlantic Monthly*, Ibram X. Kendi (2020) offered an indicting analysis of America and its disdain for people of color, including Black people, as manifested in fatalities from COVID-19. After experiencing personal loss, bearing witness to continued police brutality during the time of COVID-19, and reading and discussing Kendi's article, we were inspired to write poetry[3] to get our feelings out on paper and invite others to do the same. Each of us coordinated and participated in the other's public poetry event. Baxley's "Get Free" event (sponsored by the New Jersey Public Library) and Sealey-Ruiz's "Word Up/Wine Down" event invited poets to share their work in an online Zoom space to heal. Both events were live-streamed with the hope of maximum viewership and community. Understanding the value of poetry in our own lives to get us through challenges and hardships (Baxley, 2019; Sealey-Ruiz, 2020), we each decided to create virtual communities of expression for others to share their feelings and struggles during these difficult times. In the following section, we share poems that we recently wrote as an attempt to express, "go public" with, and release the pain of what we were/are witnessing at this historic moment. We offer an analysis of each other's poems as an additional step of affirmation of the other and collective healing. We also hope that our poetic analysis can be an example of a pedagogical tool school leaders and practitioners can employ in their local context to cultivate youth voice, critical consciousness, and social-emotional learning via art in ways that move beyond notions of kindness and character development (Watson, 2020).

Miss Rona
by Gwendolyn Baxley

Dear Miss Rona,

YOU GOT ME FUCKED UP

Thought you just gonna kill me
Have me bleeding
On the floor
Like a dog

Have my lungs
Heavy as Sandbags
Filled with your petty and poison

Take the wind from my skin?

You got me all the way fucked up,
Thought I was just gonna lie down here
and die

don't you know I've died so many times before
I've lost count?
Don't know you are merely De Ja Vu
I've been choked
Been whipped
Been shot
Been got swine from your crooked cousin
    named cop
We've been here before, boo

And I've always been Birthed back anew
Because that's what Black do

Don't you know
I am lit
I am live
I am life
Even when you strip me of my last breath

I am spirit
I am sky
I am the fly cat with more than nine lives
I am the pulse of my people
I am the fist and the fight
I am the protest before protest before the
protest
I am still here
standing

How dare you
Try me.

"Miss Rona": Poetic Analysis by Yolanda Sealey-Ruiz. In this stirring poem, Baxley uses her pen to express righteous anger, frustration, and the pain that comes from witnessing continued injustice against Black people in moments of crisis. Baxley shares the heaviness of what Kendi (2020) and other scholars exposed about how COVID-19 has hit Black communities the hardest. There is a parallel between the lack of mercy when racist police officers murder innocent Black people and the mercilessness of the "Rona" that came to kill, "take the wind from [the] skin," and snatch the lives of its victims. There is one distinction: the Rona took lives without judgment, while the officers mentioned at the beginning of this article made the judgment that being Black was a crime punishable by death. In this heartfelt conversation with "Miss Rona," Baxley reminds the virus of the resistance of those who look like her—Black people across time who have lost their lives to enslavement, Jim Crow, mass incarceration, inequity, unjust policies, miseducation, and state-sanctioned violence against Black bodies. Baxley's soliloquy evokes the temperament of Angelou's (1978) "Still I Rise" in her reminder that "I've always been Birthed back anew / Because that's what Black do." In "Miss Rona," Baxley simultaneously offers both an ode to Blackness in all of its beauty and resistance, and an indictment of white racism and the damage it has exacted—and continues to exact—on Black communities. In her poem of praise and indictment, there is an echoing of Giovanni's (1973) "Ego-Tripping" as Baxley reminds "Miss Rona" of her and Black people's fierceness: "I am sky / I am the fly cat with more than nine lives / I am the pulse of my people / I am the fist and the fight / I am the protest before protest before the protest / I am still here / standing / How dare you / Try me."

Like the Black Radical Tradition poets before her, Baxley uses her art to comment on the history, struggle, and collective liberation of Black people, reminding all—deadly viruses and police officers—that in spite of all that is hurled against us, Black people will rise. Baxley, like other poets who write in the Black Radical Tradition, understands the importance of using the art of language to document our struggles, share our hopes, and enunciate the triumphant beauty of Black survival. Baxley uses poetry in a poignant and powerful way to articulate the strength, focus, determination, and fierce will of Black people—a will that has allowed us not only to survive, but to thrive during four centuries in a country that is not our home.

American Dreams
by Yolanda Sealey-Ruiz

As America talks about humanity,
Theirs, but not quite ours—
Let's remember Breonna & Ahmaud
Trayvon & Sandra
Kayla & Tamir
Mother Eleanor & Brother Amadou—
All shot down
like rabid dogs.
Angelic and Black,
mistaken
for red and blue demons
  in White dreams.

I will lift my pen & my voice to
resist & persist in resistance,
& remember their innocence.
Going about their daily lives—
sitting, jogging, walking, driving,
resting, working, and playing while Black
& blue & White reigned in terror
snatching breaths and quiet lives
when no one & everyone
looked on in silent amazement.

"American Dreams": Poetic Analysis by Gwendolyn Baxley. In "American Dreams," Sealey-Ruiz describes the ways in which this country denies Black people personhood. When she writes, "America talks about humanity," she highlights the rhetoric rather than the reality of life in the United States for Black people. For me, the beginning of this poem unearths the mix of feelings I have around the mythical story of America. This "American Dream" and rhetoric about humanity include stories about the United States as a "melting pot" where people of every race and creed belong, and about how, through hard work and sacrifice (a concept better known by its other name, *meritocracy*), anyone can thrive holistically (Parrish, 2006). I remember this idea of meritocracy from when my elementary school classmates and I regularly recited our school motto, that "all students will achieve—no exceptions, no excuses"; I was also told throughout my childhood that credentials through schooling were the means of prosperity. But Sealey-Ruiz calls on us to "remember" and resist the falsehood in this narrative. She points to the lives of Breonna, Ahmaud, Trayvon, Sandra, Kayla, Tamir, Eleanor, and Amadou, who were

Baxley and Sealey-Ruiz discuss how this pandemic has further unleashed violence on Black communities nationwide, showcasing the violent systems and structures that disproportionately affect the lives, health, and well-being of Black people. They also explain school and institutional leaders set the ethos for students and families. Has your school, district, or institution acknowledged the violent systems and structures unleashed during the pandemic? How so? Are you satisfied with their response? In this moment, you can learn from the Black radical (arts) tradition, which affirms Black dignity against dehumanization. For Black people, as Audre Lorde once said, "poetry is not a luxury." Extend your poetry teaching and learning to include deep analytic study of Black poets, across the generations. Provide opportunities for students to process pandemic trauma through poetry as a "portal of possibility for healing." Where are the pandemic poetry spaces in your classroom, school, or institution? If they do not exist, then what will you do to change this?

wrongly and viciously murdered; the bullet(s) piercing their skin becomes both a metaphor and a reminder of the fierce anti-Blackness sentiment that reigns in this country—here, where they did not see that Amadou was the oldest of four siblings or that Eleanor was a grandmother. Here: where we are not only murdered like animals, but then described as demons after death (as Mike Brown was) to justify the murder (Thomas, 2014). Here: where there are no social protections while we navigate various structural forms of "nobodyness": lacking quality education, housing, affordable healthcare, and living wages (Hill, 2016). Here: where my own family and community in Jersey City, New Jersey, have been harmed by the multiple systems of oppression, including police brutality, even as we strive to thrive (Love, 2019). Here: where the "American Dream" is an "American Nightmare" for Black people who are killed for living: "sitting, jogging, walking, driving, / resting, working, and playing while Black." Reading this poem was a form of catharsis for me because it concisely captures my feelings around the dark paradox of America, the "talk" versus the anti-Black reality—where my niece's generation, my generation, my mother's and grandmother's generations, and countless others continue to navigate, call out, and fight against brutality and marginalization.

"American Dreams" also brings to mind Langston Hughes's poem "I, Too," in which Hughes (2004) wrestles with the tension surrounding this anti-Black reality. "I, too, sing America. / I am the darker brother. / They send me to eat in the kitchen / When company comes," he writes, describing his "Americanness" and yet denial of the basic customs and respect of communal eating with guests at the dinner table. While both Hughes and Sealey-Ruiz recognize the denial of basic human decency when Black people engage in everyday activities, what most strikes me is the implicit and explicit ways Black dreaming is captured, in contrast to white dreams. Sealey-Ruiz draws our attention to whiteness in the last line of the first stanza, the first line in the poem to mention whiteness explicitly. By noting a "White dream," she suggests that the white fantasy that is the United States is different, antithetical to Black dreaming, where Black people strive to celebrate and honor our personhood as well as "remember [our] innocence." Hughes, too, brings this point home, with somewhat of a celebration and acknowledgment of Black personhood and dignity. "But I laugh, / And eat well, / And grow strong," he asserts after being denied a seat at the table. "Tomorrow, / I'll be at the table / When company comes. / Nobody'll dare / Say to me, / 'Eat in the kitchen,' / Then," he triumphantly continues. It is through this positioning of resistance—whether sitting at the table or etching Black dreams in between the lines and stanzas—where our humanity, our Black Lives Matter. This is where the essence of the Black Radical Tradition stands strong, even though these poems were written at least 90 years apart: through the recollection and calling out of our pain, while we still sustain the continued struggle for a different reality. They each offer a framework for healing.

Conclusion

In line with the Black Radical Tradition, we maintain Black Dignity despite continued attempts to minimize, erase, commodify, and brutalize our existence. We resist and refute these efforts. We will not be contained by them. We use our poetry to get free from these efforts. We use our poetry to call out these systems that oppress us. We also use words to heal. Writing has been a way of shedding the burdens of this world into words for us. As much as this process has been healing and refueling for us, we hope this article is a respite for you as well. We also hope that educational leaders and practitioners will provide space for young people to utilize poetry as a tool for healing, affirmation, and liberation.

NOTES

1. These are the murderers involved in the killings of Breonna Taylor, George Floyd, Ahmaud Arbery, Trayvon Martin, Laquan McDonald, Janisha Fonville, Tanisha Anderson, Akai Gurley, Eric Garner, Atatiana Jefferson, Aiyana Stanley-Jones, Michelle Cusseaux, Alton Sterling, Aura Rosser, Stephon Clark, Botham Jean, Philando Castile, Michael Brown, Amadou Diallo, and Tamir Rice.

2. #SayTheirNames is a hashtag movement inspired by the Black Lives Matter movement and made popular in association with Kimberlé Crenshaw's #SayHerName, which draws attention to Black women who have been slain by the police.

3. "American Dreams" by Yolanda Sealey-Ruiz and "Miss Rona" by Gwendolyn Baxley were first published in *The Brooklyn Rail* (September 2020).

REFERENCES

Angelou, M. (1978). *And still I rise*. Random House.

Baxley, G. (2019). Black magic. *International Journal of Qualitative Studies in Education*, 32(8), 1064–1066.

Brito, C. (2020, June 16). *A 10-year-old boy was shooting hoops in his driveway when a cop car drove by. Video captured him hiding until it passed*. CBSNews. www.cbsnews.com/news/boy-hides-from-police-car-george-floyd-lebron-james-connecticut/

Camangian, P. R. (2008). Untempered tongues: Teaching performance poetry for social justice. *English Teaching: Practice & Critique*, 7(2), 35–55.

Camera, L. (2020). *The End of Police in Schools*. US News. www.usnews.com/news/the-report/articles/2020-06-12/schools-districts-end-contracts-with-police-amid-ongoing-protests

Dumas, M. J. (2014). 'Losing an arm': Schooling as a site of Black suffering. *Race Ethnicity and Education*, 17(1), 1–29.

Dumas, M. J., & Nelson, J. D. (2016). (Re)Imagining Black boyhood: Toward a critical framework for educational research. *Harvard Educational Review*, 86(1), 27–47.

Fisher, M. (2005). From the coffee house to the school house: The promise and potential of spoken word poetry in school contexts. *English Education*, 37(2), 115–131. www.jstor.org/stable/40173176?seq=1

Fowlkes, T., & Walters, A. (2020). *Freedom Inc. protest calls for immediate end to police in Madison schools*. Wisconsin State Journal. madison.com/wsj/news/local/education/local_schools/freedom-inc-protest-calls-for-immediate-end-to-police-in-madison-schools/article_b41932b1-6767-5abd-a3a9-854955030536.html

Ginwright, S. (2011). Hope, healing, and care. *Liberal Education*, 97(2), 34–39.

Giovanni, N. (1973). *Ego-tripping and other poems for young people* (G. Ford, Illus.). Lawrence Hill.

Goff, P. A., Jackson, M. C., Di Leone, B. A. L., Culotta, C. M., & DiTomasso, N. A. (2014). The essence of innocence: Consequences of dehumanizing Black children. *Journal of Personality and Social Psychology*, 106(4), 526–545.

Hill, M. L. (2016). *Nobody: Casualties of America's war on the vulnerable, from Ferguson to Flint and beyond*. Simon and Schuster.

Hughes, L. (2004). I, too. Poetry Foundation. www.poetryfoundation.org/poems/47558/i-too

Jocson, K. (2005). "Taking it to the mic": Pedagogy of June Jordan's *Poetry for the people* and partnership with an urban high school. *English Education*, 37(2), 132–148. www.jstor.org/stable/40173177?seq=1

Jurado, J. (2020, July 21). *Judge denies release for 15-year-old detained for not doing homework*. The Root. www.theroot.com/judge-denies-release-for-15-year-old-detained-for-not-d-1844460017

Kendi, I. X. (2020, April 6). What the racial data show: The pandemic seems to be hitting people of color the hardest. *The Atlantic*. www.theatlantic.com/ideas/archive/2020/04/coronavirus-exposing-our-racial-divides/609526/

Kinloch, V. (2005). Poetry, literacy, and creativity: Fostering effective learning strategies in an urban classroom. *English Education*, 37(2), 96–114. www.jstor.org/stable/40173175?seq=1

Lamon, J. J. (2012, August 28). Lucille Clifton: Interview. *Mosaic*. mosaicmagazine.org/lucille-clifton-interview/#.Xy9S8017k0o

Lorde, A. (2007). *Sister outsider: Essays and speeches*. Crossing Press.

Love, B. L. (2019). *We want to do more than survive: Abolitionist teaching and the pursuit of educational freedom*. Beacon Press.

McClure, D. (2017). "Who will survive in America?": Gil Scott-Heron, the Black radical tradition, and the critique of neoliberalism. In M. Mitchell & D. Covin (Eds.), *Broadening the contours in the study of Black politics* (pp. 11–34). Routledge.

Morris, M. (2016). *Pushout: The criminalization of Black girls in schools*. The New Press.

Morrison, T. (2015, March 23). No place for self-pity, no room for fear. *The Nation*. www.thenation.com/article/archive/no-place-self-pity-no-room-fear/

Neal, L. (1969). Any day now: Black art and Black liberation. *Ebony*, 24(10), 54–58, 62.

Parrish, R. (2006). The meritocracy myth: A *Dollars & sense* interview with Lani Guinier. *Dollars & Sense*, 263. Retrieved from www.dollarsandsense.org/archives/2006/0106guinierB.html

Robinson, C. J. (with Kelley, R. D. G.). (2000). *Black Marxism: The making of the Black radical tradition*. University of North Carolina Press.

Sealey-Ruiz, Y. (2020). *Love from the vortex and other poems*. Kaleidoscope Vibrations.

Shange, S. (2019). *Progressive dystopia: Abolition, antiblackness, and schooling in San Francisco*. Duke University Press.

Sims-Bishop, R. (1990). Mirrors, windows, and sliding glass doors. *Perspectives: Choosing and Using Books for the Classroom*, 6(3), ix–xi.

Stern, M., & Hussain, K. (2015). On the charter question: Black Marxism and Black nationalism. *Race Ethnicity and Education*, 18(1), 61–88.

Thomas, D. (2014). *Michael Brown was not a boy, he was a "demon."* Al Jazeera. www.aljazeera.com/indepth/opinion/2014/11/michael-brown-demon-ferguson- 2014112672358760344.html

Thomas, D. (2019). The Black radical tradition of resistance. Medium. medium.com/national-center-for-institutional-diversity/the-black-radical-tradition-of-resistance-7277f09ef396

Watson, T. N. (2020, June 6). Where was the kindness – for George Floyd? *Classroom Q&A with Larry Ferlazzo*. blogs.edweek.org/teachers/classroom_qa_with_larry_ferlazzo/2020/06/the_problem_with_kindness_sel_the_death_of_george_floyd.html

Wissman, K. K., & Wiseman, A. M. (2011). "That's my worst nightmare": Poetry and trauma in the middle school classroom. *Pedagogies*, 6(3), 234–249.

GWENDOLYN BAXLEY is an assistant professor in the Department of Educational Leadership and Policy at the State University of New York at Buffalo. She investigates how school and community leaders cultivate nurturing and affirming spaces for Black youth. Baxley also examines the structures, practices, and ideologies that facilitate or hinder the development of such spaces, including the role of anti-Blackness.

YOLANDA SEALEY-RUIZ is an award-winning associate professor at Teachers College, Columbia University. Her research focuses on racial literacy in teacher education, Black girl literacies, and the schooling experiences of Black and Latinx male high school students. Sealey-Ruiz appeared in Spike Lee's *2 Fists Up: We Gon' Be Alright*, a documentary about the Black Lives Matter movement and the campus protests at the University of Missouri. Her first full-length poetry collection is *Love from the Vortex and Other Poems* (Kaleidoscope Vibrations, 2020). She can be reached at sealeyruiz@tc.edu.

This article originally appeared in *English Journal* 111.1

PEDAGOGIES OF COMPLICITY: Perspective Taking and Healing

A teacher educator and researcher questions complicity in the classroom and recommends a new approach.

ANTERO GARCIA

We thrive on negative criticism, which is fun to write and to read.
—PETER O'TOOLE AS ANTON EGO, *RATATOUILLE* (FILM)

I WRITE THIS in the still-waking dawn of early 2021, overwrought by the state of the world. On January 6, two weeks ago (and months ago for you as readers), an insurrection was attempted. Hundreds of thousands of people in the United States died as a result of a grossly mismanaged response to a global pandemic. Our country continues to punt any kind of meaningful response to the legacies of anti-Blackness that continue to harm our families, friends, and communities. I *feel* these phenomena deeply, and they weigh on my perspective of what must be done by teachers and students in English language arts (ELA) classrooms.

From where I am looking right now, conditions in schools are not good. While I can imagine and sympathize with teachers eager to find a sense of banal normality after the seemingly bottomless freefall that was 2020 and the early parts of 2021, we cannot go back. Even more so, we must reject the calls for such a return to "normal" from our colleagues and administrators. Let us make no mistake: some of the ways we engaged in ELA instruction when times were "normal" caused harm and unintentionally contributed to the devastation we are still processing today. A few ways ELA teachers contributed to the state of the world include the following:

1. providing space for debating and arguing over topics that are fundamental human rights, such as gender identity and the treatment of individuals based on legal status in the United States;
2. reteaching literature that may reinforce Whiteness and settler-colonial values as reflected in a self-perpetuating and limited literary canon; and
3. remaining silent when our colleagues contributed to acts of harm, ranging from verbal microaggressions in schools to vocal support of, or participation in, acts of insurrection during Trump's US presidency.

As ELA teachers, we can be complicit in the harm that rocks our country. Our ability to sustain multiple perspectives may have been, in fact, a central way that ideas like insurrection, questioning the validity of our country's election, or casting doubt on the safety of vaccination maintained steam. Questioning the veracity of claims and eliciting new perspectives: these skills we teach (and often teach well) bring us to crisis. If we want to move forward collectively, we must recognize and own the fact that teachers—ELA teachers included—bear some responsibility for the here and now.

I write this essay from a place of fury and hope.

Even in light of the substantial weight of teaching in this moment, I remain hopeful about the fact that English teachers are more than capable to meet this moment. Looking inward, evaluating the complex world around us, and communicating new civic ideas based on the multiple needs that are converging in our lives: these are skills that flourish in ELA classrooms. Our classrooms can be—must be—sites of joy and solidarity as we provide a necessary space for students to reflect and process the present.

Approaching Freedom

In the months and years to come, we must guide young people to try to understand the seemingly nonsensical. We must work collectively for young people to see (1) their full humanity reflected in the world around them; (2) the failure of some political leaders to recognize and respond to generations of climate devastation; and (3) the illogical nature of a pandemic and the lives lost by it. These are complicated issues that will require that we not shy away from conversations that have been deemed political and, as a result, have left us flatfooted for the urgency of healing and action needed today.

Our students and colleagues may be hurting. We may be, too. Let us build from this place of vulnerability and use it as the whetstone on which we sharpen the dulled pedagogy that has, for too long, failed to cut meaningfully into new directions of possibility and liberation. Put simply, if you are not intentionally naming for yourself and for your students the ways your minute-to-minute lessons are working toward freedom, then your lessons need reevaluation.

Just as we saw schools rapidly (and necessarily) transform their structures to meet the logistical demands of the global pandemic in 2020, our pedagogies are overdue for such radical metamorphosis and hope for our students and their future. Where structures shifted so that students might try to learn in hybrid and distance-based learning environments, the content and teaching approaches these students encountered typically stayed the same.

And while some of our past pedagogical strategies need to be discarded, I want to offer three directions that our teaching practice might shift toward as we consider the perspectives and questions with which the communicative and empathetic power of our ELA discipline can grapple.

Dialogue over Debate

One challenge with invoking increased attention to perspectives and counternarratives in classrooms is the assumption that *every* topic merits multiple perspectives. The notion that "both sides" of a belief need equal air is one way that the practices of ELA classrooms provided air to the echo chambers of partisanship in the United States, allowed for disinformation to cloud the most recent presidential election, and permitted aspects fundamental to individuals' personhood to be questioned and scrutinized. ELA classrooms afford necessary space for students to explore hard and sometimes controversial topics.

HOW ARE YOU ENSURING THAT THE DEVELOPMENT OF RHETORICAL WRITING PRACTICES REINFORCES STUDENTS' ABILITIES TO ACT IN SOLIDARITY WITH CLASSMATES AND MOVEMENTS FOR JUSTICE?

Students, too, need a place to raise topics they may not know about beyond a limited stream of information funneled through online algorithms or local familial contexts. However, rather than emphasizing argumentation as the baseline approach for exploring topics such as immigration, guns, police funding, or gender identity—topics that received prominent attention during the past election—perhaps we can shift classrooms as sources for *dialogue*. In recent research with Nicole Mirra, for example (295), Mirra and I found powerful moments of interpreting and *hearing* new perspectives when young people were offered space to engage in online conversation with peers dispersed across the United States.

Similar to these debate-focused recommendations, the kinds of writing practices we focus on do not have to be framed as the winner-take-all form of argumentation that is embedded in how we evaluate student essays. Rather than focusing on persuasion in our classes, for example, what might it mean to have students draft reasoned statements of solidarity? How might we reframe writing practices—that still evaluate student growth—as sources for affirming the ideas students have rather than as reasons for casting vitriolic skepticism on an uncertain *other*?

As you approach the standards in your classroom that focus on argumentation and persuasion, consider this: How are you ensuring that the development of rhetorical writing practices reinforces students' abilities to act in solidarity with classmates and movements for justice?

Youth Expertise over Historical Fact-Finding

Perhaps one of the most exciting aspects of this issue's emphasis on perspectives and counternarratives is the opportunity for teachers to (re)commit to the voices and experiences of the students in our classrooms. From my experience working with young people through models of youth participatory action research (Mirra et al. 49), student knowledge not only offers innovative pathways forward but also bolsters the credibility and nuance of the ideas that students contribute.

Further, while we may have a litany of texts and facts we might offer students that can help them reflect on deep issues of inequity in the current moment, there is no text that fully captures what it meant to your individual students to experience the ongoing effects of a global pandemic here in 2021. This is tacit and complex knowledge. Encouraging students to communicate these narratives validates the polyphonic nature of civic engagement today. The many perspectives, feelings, and questions that students bring into our classrooms speak to civic learning that extends beyond linear and singular forms of knowledge.

To be clear, this emphasis on student experiences does not mean eschewing your responsibility of curating meaningful texts for students, or disregarding the opportunities in your classroom to hold up literary windows, mirrors, and sliding glass doors that support students to gain further nuance about the world around them (Bishop ix). Rather, by allowing youth experience to guide the questions and hopes that students have about the world, we can reorient literature and nonfiction texts to better serve justice.

Overall, literature can help propel student innovation in the present moment, but it must do so as part of how young people actively dialogue with ideas from the past as we help them innovate for the future.

People over Tools

During the months of social distancing, far too many of us had to get very familiar with the use of digital tools such as Zoom and Google Classroom to ensure we were providing as powerful a learning experience as the hardships of teaching in a pandemic would allow. I urge teachers to recognize that our teaching practices can move forward by acknowledging the fact that was seemingly overlooked during all of the preparations for school reopening last year: schools are only as productive and transformative as the imaginations of the people they house. Students and teachers *must* be the focus of what we invest in. For teachers, this means we must not assume that there is (or ever will be) a tool or digital app that can fix any of the inequities that young people are facing. In the face of recent politics, it is clear that digital tools, software for surveillance, and algorithmic resources may make our abilities to communicate and understand one another quantifiably worse and even disenfranchise the young people we seek to engage in learning and understanding.

Rather than worrying about what students in today's digital age might need, we must center the fact that we live and interact in an analog world and attend to the feelings and fears that young people and teachers alike are experiencing and attempting to understand.

ELA Perspectives for Justice

In the climactic showdown in the film *Ratatouille*, food critic Anton Ego states what he's craving: "A little

TEACHING TIPS

Garcia argues, "Our classrooms can be—must be—sites of joy and solidarity as we provide a necessary space for students to reflect and process the present." In your ELA classroom, facilitate the three pedagogical suggestions offered by Garcia—organize a dialogue, support youth in historical fact-finding, and leverage the power of people over digital apps and tools. Start by inviting your students to compose reasoned statements of solidarity and justice. How might your classroom dialogue emphasize solidarity, justice, and joy with pandemic-specific issues? Layer classroom texts for your students to communicate narratives that "validates the polyphonic nature of civic engagement" as students living through the pandemic. Invite your students to compose and rhetorically reframe writing practices that reinforce students' abilities to act in solidarity with classmates and movements for justice. What, if any, rhetorical writing has your school, district, or institution engaged that promotes solidarity, justice, and joy? How can you and your students work toward supporting institutional-level acts of solidarity, justice, and joy?

perspective. That's it: I'd like some fresh, clear, well-seasoned perspective." As the meal that follows makes clear, both the content that is explored *and* the sources that produce it can surprise and transform one's beliefs about the world.

For Ego, the perspective that is served (a titular, traditional ratatouille) shakes him so profoundly that his notion of what is possible is expanded over the course of a meal.

While we educators may not have the luxury of sous-chefs and cabinets of sundry seasonings at our disposal, our ability to transform through the perspectives we uphold or excise matters. The perspectives we offer in our classrooms are finite, and we harbor a responsibility for ensuring that we do not simply cast skepticism on the ethical and moral dimensions of humanity.

At the same time, perspective—as Ego reminds us—is multi-sensical. *Seeing* is one way of interpreting the world, and the multimodality of where, how, and with whom we discuss issues of justice remains a core aspect of what we, as ELA teachers, offer and what students experience in our classrooms. As we ensure our classrooms emphasize the myriad questions and concerns that shape students' perspectives, our pedagogies must always reach toward freedom across the stories that challenge and counter what is unjust.

WORKS CITED

Bishop, Rudine Sims. "Mirrors, Windows, and Sliding Glass Doors." *Perspectives*, vol. 6, no. 3, 1991, pp. ix–xi.

Mirra, Nicole, and Antero Garcia. "'I Hesitate but I Do Have Hope': Youth Speculative Civic Literacies for Troubled Times." *Harvard Educational Review*, vol. 90, no. 2, 2020, pp. 295–321.

Mirra, Nicole, et al. "Revolutionizing Inquiry in Urban English Classrooms: Pursuing Voice and Justice through Youth Participatory Action Research." *English Journal*, vol. 105, no. 2, 2015, pp. 49–57.

Ratatouille. Directed by Brad Bird and Jan Pinkava. Pixar, 2007.

ANTERO GARCIA is an associate professor in the Graduate School of Education at Stanford University. His recent books include *Everyday Advocacy: Teachers Who Change the Literacy Narrative*; *Compose Our World: Project-Based Learning in Secondary English Language Arts*; and *Good Reception: Teens, Teachers, and Mobile Media in a Los Angeles High School*. He has been a member of NCTE since 2010 and can be reached at antero.garcia@stanford.edu.

This article originally appeared in *Language Arts* 99.1

OPPORTUNITY CENTERED TEACHING FOR RACIAL JUSTICE IN ELEMENTARY ENGLISH LANGUAGE ARTS CLASSROOMS

This column advances tenets of opportunity centered teaching to help educators in the work of racial justice disrupt opportunity gaps in elementary ELA classrooms.

H. RICHARD MILNER IV, JALEEL HOWARD, TEQUILA CORNELIOUS, BRYANT O. BEST & LAURA FITTZ

EVEN AS THE COVID-19 pandemic spread across the world, the Black Lives Matter movement was able to amplify its message dramatically as millions of people in the United States took to the streets protesting police violence toward Black bodies and other forms of racial discrimination and oppression. Teachers have an incredible opportunity to leverage this momentum and reimagine their curriculum, instructional, assessment, and relational practice with students in support of racial justice. Why not, for example, acknowledge and center current events as a way to facilitate powerful conversations in classrooms?

In this column, we draw from our own experiences in education over the years to shed light and expand on what opportunity centered teaching (OCT) practices might look like for elementary English language arts (ELA) teachers as they build practices with students in pursuit of racial justice.

When we use the term *racial justice* in elementary ELA classrooms, we refer to the stance teachers take to understand and build classroom policies and practices that directly and explicitly resist racism and injustice for students of color generally but especially for Black students. This resistance happens when teachers actively pursue racial justice in their work. Racial justice practice is not automatic; it does not just magically happen because teachers consider themselves "good" people. Racial justice work is not a checklist practice or a process that can be completed and done with. Instead, it must be sought after, pressed toward, and consistently centered in all facets of teachers' work. When centering the pursuit of racial justice, elementary ELA teachers must constantly question their own practices and the practices of others, as they recognize and disrupt the ways in which schools contribute to racial inequity, anti-Blackness, and discrimination.

RACIAL JUSTICE WORK IS NOT A CHECKLIST PRACTICE OR A PROCESS THAT CAN BE COMPLETED AND DONE WITH. INSTEAD, IT MUST BE SOUGHT AFTER, PRESSED TOWARD, AND CONSISTENTLY CENTERED IN ALL FACETS OF TEACHERS' WORK.

Opportunity gaps which result in lack of access to high-quality ELA instruction persists among too many students of color. The National Assessment of Educational Progress (NAEP) evaluates a representative sample of fourth, eighth, and twelfth grade students at the national and state levels for reading comprehension of literary and informational texts. In 2019, the group found that Black students showed a smaller increase in average reading scores than students in any other racial category except Native Americans (NAEP, 2019).

Opportunity gaps exist and persist in early childhood education, too. Students from low income backgrounds (Milner, 2013, 2015) especially benefit from access to high-quality education according to a 2016 research policy brief from the National Council of Teachers of English (NCTE). So the process of disrupting inequitable schooling practices should begin in early childhood. The NCTE policy brief posits three essential dimensions of high-quality early childhood education: (1) culturally competent teachers who engage students on issues of social justice and equity; (2) consistent and equitable communication between students, teachers, and families; and (3) inclusive classroom environments that encourage collaboration among students and allow them to make decisions about their own learning.

Prioritizing what Ladson-Billings (2006) refers to as "education debt," we intentionally refer to *opportunity gaps* instead of *achievement gaps* to center educational mechanisms that systemically marginalize and oppress Black and other minoritized students (Milner, 2020b). We rely on an established body of theory and research focused on racially just experiences, policies, structures, and practices that honor diverse students and that see and center them fully in the ELA context (Au, 2011; Edwards et al., 2009; Gay, 2018; Ladson-Billings, 2009; Moll et al., 1992; Milner, 2020a; Risko & Walker-Dalhouse, 2007). Drawing from empirical research over the last twenty years, Milner (2020a) conceptualizes OCT as curriculum, instruction, assessment, and relational practices that center and connect with students' dynamic and evolving identities. Milner stresses that OCT rejects stale, dated, predetermined, irrelevant, under-responsive, disconnected, "racially neutral," and opportunity-peripheral practices that fail to meet the needs of and inspire racially diverse students. Opportunity peripheral practices are those outside the full scope and center of what is necessary to build and implement humaning and just educational ecologies.

Tenets of Opportunity Centered Teaching (OCT)

The following five interconnected features allow OCT to disrupt opportunity gaps in pursuit of racial justice both inside and outside of schools:

1. OCT centers and prioritizes relationship-building as a pedagogical, curricular, social, and academic anchor for students in school. Rather than focusing on "tricks" to "get to know" students at the beginning of a school year before moving on to "the real work," OCT embraces the cultivation of relationships as "the real work" throughout the entire year.
2. OCT co-constructs community knowledge to inform practice, embracing the fact that families and communities are assets to the classroom. OCT rejects the idea that teachers are arbiters of knowledge and knowing and rely on community knowledge to guide their thinking and professional judgment. Opportunity gaps increase when teachers act as the main sources of knowledge and knowing, ignoring the enormous range of expertise, insights, history, and brilliance in the community.[1]
3. OCT builds practices to gauge psychological and mental health of both students and teachers; after all, it is hard for teachers to teach when they are not psychologically well themselves. Moreover, the framework advances the notion that mental health of students is deeply connected to their capacity to succeed academically, socially, and otherwise.
4. OCT explicitly and intentionally addresses -isms and biases like racism, sexism, and xenophobia that influence beliefs and practices. Teachers constantly reflect on the content of what they are teaching, how they are teaching it, and why they must consciously address bias in the classroom.
5. OCT converges the curriculum with other aspects of students' experiences. Curriculum convergence merges student identity with innovative instructional practices.

In Pursuit of Racial Justice in Elementary ELA

We have heard elementary teachers teaching in self-contained classrooms worry about how to center and work toward racial justice with younger children. Because opportunity-peripheral teaching practices have systematically maintained racism and anti-Blackness, many teachers do not have a framework for transforming their work. OCT for racial justice requires teachers of elementary ELA to build their professional knowledge and skills for emancipatory judgments to disrupt whiteness in and through curriculum, instructional, assessment, and relational practices. To this end, we recommend the following to build teachers' knowledge and skills for racial justice in classrooms while rejecting the maintenance of a white-centric status quo:

1. Understanding how classroom practices contribute to systemic racism;
2. Acknowledging how curriculum can be a site of racial oppression;
3. Converging curriculum sites to help students build ELA knowledge and tools to dismantle racism; and
4. Soliciting, learning from, and responding to student feedback to build a more racially just ELA space.

Next, we expand on these recommendations by posing guided reflection questions elementary teachers may consider as they pursue teaching for racial justice in ELA classrooms.

How Classroom Practices Contribute to Systemic Racism

Although elementary teachers may not understand or believe their individual practices contribute to systemic racism, evidence suggests otherwise (see, for example, Milner, 2015). Opportunity gaps escalate in education when teachers claim not to "see color," as such a mindset reflects a racially unaware and insensitive way of knowing, seeing, experiencing, understanding, interpreting, and interacting with students.

Examples of systemic racial inequities include the over-referral of Black students to the office and subsequent suspension or expulsion (Skiba, Peterson & Williams, 1997; Milner, 2020b); disproportionately high number of Black students who are referred to special education (Blanchett, 2006); and disproportionately low number of Black students who are referred to gifted education (Ford, 1996). Elementary teachers must understand that these inequities affect students' opportunities to learn within all subject areas, including English language arts.

OCT VIEWS CURRICULUM AS A SERIES OF LEARNING OPPORTUNITIES THAT STUDENTS EXPERIENCE BOTH INSIDE AND OUTSIDE OF FORMAL TEACHING AND STRUCTURED INSTRUCTIONAL PERIODS.

As we pursue racial justice in ELA, we recommend teachers reflect on the following questions to help them build tools and practices to disrupt systemic racial injustice:

- What racial group of students do I most often refer to the office?
- What racial group of students is most often suspended or expelled at my school?
- What racial group of students do I refer most often to special education for reading and writing interventions?
- What racial group of students do I recommend most often for gifted education?
- What racial group of students do I recognize as the most creative interpreters of texts they read?
- What racial group of students do I recognize as especially capable readers and writers?
- What racial group of students do I recognize as especially struggling readers and writers?
- Do I recognize communication assets that all racial groups bring to the classroom?
- Perhaps most important, what role does my own racial background play in my decisions and practices as a teacher?
- What am I willing to change to disrupt racist practices identified?

When students are not in the classroom because they have been suspended or expelled, they are not experiencing curriculum, instructional, and relational practices essential for their academic success (Skiba, Peterson, & Williams, 1997). Such students miss opportunities to build comprehension, reading/writing fluency, or processing speed in the classroom. Thus, elementary school teachers must understand how their decisions and classroom practices can contribute to and perpetuate structural forms of racism.

Curriculum as a Site of Racial Oppression

Elementary teachers must not only focus on gaps in opportunity related to classroom practices that contribute to institutional racism but also think deliberately about *what* students have the opportunity to learn. OCT embraces the reality that the curriculum is dynamic and involves far more than what is mandated and written in a curriculum or pacing guide. OCT views curriculum as a series of learning opportunities that students experience both inside and outside of formal teaching and structured instructional periods: It includes not only classroom work but also whatever is posted in the hallways and lunchroom spaces where students spend much of their time. But when opportunities to learn are centered on whiteness, students may dismiss them as tangential to their worldviews, identities, and experiences. To combat this, we recommend teachers reflect on the following questions:

- What books reflecting racial diversity are available for students to read in the classroom?
- Are the authors of these books racially diverse?
- What racial groups are represented both in the books that students are required to read and in those they are allowed to select from the class library?
- Of what racial background are those who decide what books are included in the class library?
- What is/are the racial background(s) of those who decide what books are covered and taught in the formal curriculum?
- Are people and communities of color significantly represented as protagonists in readings across the curriculum?
- What racial messages are represented on the walls inside our classroom?
- What racial messages are represented on the walls throughout the school building?
- How do I expand my racial lens to better center and represent racial diversity within and through the fabric of the curriculum?

Teachers must ask these essential questions if they are to center racial identity in their classrooms. Racial justice means that race and racial identity are embraced in the ELA curriculum and students of color are deeply embedded in curricular decisions and practices.

Converging Curriculum Sites to Further Both ELA Learning and Racial Justice

Converging curriculum sites allows teachers to bridge student identity with students' interests, practices, and engagement both inside and outside of school, taking into account their community and societal experiences, insights, and understandings. Put another way, in the context of OCT, student identifiers like race, gender, and language are viewed as texts that should converge and align with curriculum practices.

Milner (2020) argues that curriculum sites might include listening to music, participating on a sports team, creating art as well as their experiences, understandings, and engagement in their local communities. It is at the intersection of identity, practices, engagement, and community that OCT reaches potentially racially transformative spaces in classrooms. Here are some examples of community and societal texts concerning racial justice and injustice that teachers might consider as sites for curriculum convergence:

- The disproportionate number of deaths from COVID-19 among Black and Latinx communities
- Police shootings and murders of Black people such as Breonna Taylor, George Floyd, Ahmaud Arbery, Rekia Boyd, and Antwon Rose, Jr.
- Colin Kaepernick's refusal to stand during the U.S. national anthem and the ensuing backlash from fans and the National Football League
- Ongoing national immigration debates over children being taken from their families and placed in cages
- The tainted-water crisis in Flint, Michigan
- The brutal shooting of nine parishioners in a church in Charleston, South Carolina
- The January 6 invasion of the U.S. Capitol by right-wing demonstrators

In pursuit of racial justice, elementary teachers use their professional judgment to address issues such as these in a developmentally appropriate manner. Although elementary teachers may believe young students are not thinking about these types of events, we have found that they often are, especially

TEACHING TIPS

The authors invite educators to engage in the "tenets of opportunity centered teaching." To start this work, they provide a list of assessment questions. Within your professional learning communities, use the assessment questions to assess and engage your "curriculum, instruction, assessment, and relational practices that center and connect with students' dynamic and evolving identities." After completing the assessment questions, collaborate with colleagues and administrators in your context to develop structural as well as classroom-level policies, practices, and relationships.

in upper elementary school. They learn about current events through television and social media and overhear their parents (and teachers) discussing them. We believe literacy teachers have a chance to build OCT practices that help students start to understand aspects of racism at a young age and begin developing tools necessary to disrupt them in their own lives.

We recommend teachers reflect on the following questions to help them converge curriculum sites in pursuit of racial injustice:

- To what degree do I consciously build curricular practices that help my students think about racial injustices such as the killing of unarmed Black people at the hands of law enforcement?
- Do I seek relevant, grade-appropriate texts that deal with racial injustices that students may have heard about or experienced?
- To what degree do I introduce readings to my students that merge their racial identities with societal injustices (e.g., Janae Marks' *From the Desk of Zoe Washington*, Lupita Nyong'o's *Sulwe*, Kelly Yang's *Front Desk*)?
- Do I make intentional moves to bridge the school's expected curriculum with the lived experiences of my students of color? Why or why not?
- How do I build curriculum connections that embrace the racial identity of my students, their interests, and the school's expected curriculum?
- What curriculum practices do I intentionally resist that perpetuate racism, white supremacy, and the status quo? What does my resistance look like?
- To what degree do I create opportunities for students to write about racial justice issues that might serve as a form of healing and restoration?
- Do I collaborate with school counselors, social workers, and psychologists to identify and respond to traumatic experiences of my students?
- How do I build opportunities for students—and students of color in particular—to read about, write about, talk about, and work through issues of racial injustice?

OCT's emphasis on curriculum and instructional convergence encourages teachers to focus on the *so what* of learning opportunities just as they do on the *what* and *how* (Milner, 2020a). Students of all races, but especially Black students, spend countless hours in classrooms experiencing curriculum that does not meaningfully resonate or connect with them. To mitigate this, teachers can merge together aspects of student identity with their interests both inside and outside of school, using community and society as textual possibilities. This convergence of the *who* (students and their identities), *what* (community and societal texts), and *where* (inside/outside school) shepherds students into spaces where they can meaningfully apply what they learn in ways that help shape their current and future lives (Milner, 2020a).

Listen to Students, Learn from Students, and Learn Alongside Students

In pursuit of racial justice, ELA teachers must engage in an evolving, iterative, and ongoing process of soliciting students' feedback, learning from that feedback, and responding to it (Howard, 2020).

As a fifth-grade teacher working with mostly Black and Brown students, Jaleel Howard (a co-author of this article) aspired to have his students fall in love with reading. To learn from and with his students, he decided to conduct a student interest survey (Howard et al., 2020). He posted ten interrelated questions about literacy and received feedback from students that informed later practice and curriculum materials. While reviewing the feedback from students, Howard was struck by the answer that one of his most seemingly disengaged readers provided to the question "What type of books spark your interest?" The student, Taylor, answered "We need more books with pictures" and specified her preference for graphic novels—books that provided visual support to deepen her comprehension.

Although Taylor's response challenged Howard's preconceived notions of what reading should look like in the fifth grade, it clarified what was missing for Taylor and many of Howard's other students. Overall, the feedback from students showed Howard that they did not hate reading itself but rather were not engaged by the specific books they were reading in class. Howard honored this feedback and adjusted his practice accordingly, seeking out as many culturally relevant (Ladson-Billings, 2009) graphic novels as he could find.

The feedback from students, and the influx of graphic novels Howard subsequently brought into the classroom, dramatically changed the sustained silent reading time in the classroom. Howard began to observe wonder, excitement, suspense, and curiosity in his students' eyes as they fervently turned the pages and saw artistic depictions of neighborhoods similar to their own in books such as *Monster* by Walter Dean Myers and *Yummy: The Last Days of a SouthSide Shorty* by Gregory Neri. Howard also observed that his students seemed to love exploring the storyline of faraway places like Wakanda as they read the latest *Black Panther* comic book by Ta-Nehisi Coates.

Over time, graphic novels became a preferred and effective medium for unpacking critical ideas in Howard's class. In the process of trying to get his students to fall in love with reading, Howard learned that students' ability to access and connect to texts was essential to teaching and learning. Howard engaged in curriculum convergence in that he linked curriculum practices and student interests, neighborhood, and identities. When students appear apathetic toward ELA opportunities to learn, teachers must delve more deeply to ascertain root causes rather than assume students are incapable of learning. OCT requires teachers to examine how their own practices may contribute to student disengagement. Had Howard not sought students' feedback, they would have remained disenfranchised from literacy, excluded from claiming individual identities as readers. Learning from his students allowed Howard to change the curriculum and create a more racially just classroom space for them.

We recommend that teachers reflect on the following questions as they work to learn from and alongside students as we pursue racial justice in ELA:

- Do I provide my students the opportunity to give feedback on their experiences and their engagement with classroom materials?
- What opportunities do students have to express unfiltered ideas and thoughts in the classroom about what happens there? How do I use their unfiltered feedback to inform curriculum, instructional, assessment, and relational practices?
- How do I use student feedback to create a more racially just ELA space?
- Do I have books that speak to and illuminate Black and Latinx students' interests, dreams, realities, and wonderings?
- Am I attentive to when and how students of color show joy when engaging with literacy? How do I know this, and how can I build on that joy?
- Do I notice when Black and Latinx students are disengaged from literature? If so, do I aim to engage them?
- How do I build feedback mechanisms (such as student surveys) and conferring practices so that I can learn from students who are most often on the margins of the ELA classroom?

Too often, we fail to realize that our students constantly provide us with feedback in our everyday interactions in the classroom. Warren (2013) argues that students give feedback informally, through social and intellectual outcomes; OCT insists that educators be keenly aware of this feedback and constantly adapt to prevent practices that may harm students.

Getting students to fall in love with reading is not about finding the books we believe they should read; rather, it is about listening to them when they tell *us* what books *they* believe should be read.

Summary, Implications, and Conclusions

Racial justice work in elementary ELA is an ongoing pursuit rather than something you can mark off on a checklist. By using the OCT framework, teachers can maximize their work toward racial justice in the context of elementary ELA. To do this effectively, teachers must (1) understand how classroom practices influence systemic racism, (2) acknowledge how curriculum can be a site of racial oppression, (3) converge curriculum sites to help students build ELA knowledge and tools to dismantle racism, and (4) solicit student feedback, learn from it, and respond to students to build a more racially just ELA space.

As we all grapple with the deleterious effects of racism in America, teachers have a unique opportunity to help equip students with mindsets and practices to fight for justice and equity for all. *This* is what OCT looks like.

CHILDREN'S LITERATURE CITED

Coates, T.-N., & Stelfreeze, B. (2017). *Avengers of the new world.* Panini Publishing.

Marks, J. (2020). *From the desk of Zoe Washington.* HarperCollins.

Myers, W. D., & Sims, G. A. (2015). *Monster: A graphic novel.* HarperCollins.

Nyong'o, L. & Harrison, V. (2019). *Sulwe.* Simon & Schuster.

Neri, G. (2010). *Yummy: The last days of a southside shorty.* Lee & Low Books.

Yang, K. (2018). *Front desk.* Scholastic.

REFERENCES

Au, K. H. (2011). *Literacy achievement and diversity: Keys to success for students, teachers, and schools.* Teachers College Press.

Blanchett, W. J. (2006). Disproportionate representation of African American students in special education: Acknowledging the role of White privilege and racism. *Educational Researcher*, 35(6), 24–28.

Delpit, L. (1995). *Other people's children: Cultural conflict in the classroom.* The New Press.

Edwards, P. A., Paratore, J. R., & Roser, N. L. (2009). Family literacy: Recognizing cultural significance. In L. M. Morrow, R. Rueda, & D. Lapp (Eds.), *Handbook of research on literacy and diversity* (4th ed., pp. 77–96). The Guilford Press.

Ford, D. Y. (1996). *Reversing underachievement among gifted Black students: Promising practices and programs.* Teachers College Press.

Howard, J. R., McCall, T., & Howard, T. C. (2020). *No more teaching without positive relationships.* Heinemann.

Ladson-Billings, G. (2009). *The dreamkeepers: Successful teachers of African American Children.* John Wiley & Sons.

Milner, H. R. (2020a). *Start where you are but don't stay there: Understanding diversity, opportunity gaps, and teaching in today's classrooms* (2nd ed.). Harvard Education Press.

Milner, H. R. (2020b). *Brown* Lecture: Disrupting punitive practices and policies: Rac(e)ing back to teaching, teacher preparation, and *Brown*. *Educational Researcher*, 49(3), 147–160.

Milner, H. R. (2015). *Rac(e)ing to class: Confronting poverty and race in schools and classrooms.* Harvard Education Press.

Milner, H. R. (2013). Analyzing poverty, learning, and teaching through a critical race theory lens. *Review of Research in Education*, 37(1), 1–53.

Moll, L. C., Amanti, C., Neff, D., & Gonzalez, N. (1992). Funds of knowledge for teaching: Using a qualitative approach to connect homes and classrooms. *Theory into Practice*, 31(2), 132–141.

National Assessment of Education Progress. (2019). *NAEP report card: Reading.* https://www.nationsreportcard.gov/reading/?grade=4

National Council of Teachers of English. (2016). *Equity and early childhood education: Reclaiming the child.* https://cdn.ncte.org/nctefiles/equityearlyedbrief.pdf

Risko, V., & Walker-Dalhouse, D. (2007). *Tapping students' cultural funds of knowledge to address the achievement gap. The Reading Teacher*, 61(1), 98–100.

Skiba, R. J., Peterson, R. L., & Williams, T. (1997). Office referrals and suspension: Disciplinary intervention in middle schools. *Education and Treatment of Children*, 20, 295–315.

Warren, C. (2013). Towards a pedagogy for the application of empathy in culturally diverse classrooms. *The Urban Review*, 46, 395–419.

ENDNOTE

1. For good books that expand on some of these ideas see Howard, T.C. (2020). *Why race and culture matters in schools.* Teachers College Press; Delpit, L. (1995). *Other people's children*; Ladson-Billings (2009). *The dreamkeepers.* Jossey-Bass. Love, B. (2019). *We want to do more than survive.* Beacon Press; Milner, H. R. (2020a). *Start where you are, but don't stay there.* Harvard Education Press.

H. RICHARD MILNER IV is Cornelius Vanderbilt Distinguished Professor of Education at Peabody College, Vanderbilt University. Milner is an elected member of the National Academy of Education, and he is a Fellow and President-Elect of the American Educational Research Association. Milner was a high school English teacher in an almost all-Black school. As a university researcher and professor, he has studied successful literacy practices among teachers in urban and suburban schools. In teacher education, Milner also works with pre-service and in-service teachers in elementary language arts. He is author of *Start Where You Are, but Don't Stay There* (2020), *These Kids Are Out of Control* (2018), and *Rac(e)ing to Class* (2015). He can be reached at rich.milner@vanderbilt.edu.

JALEEL HOWARD taught fifth grade in a self-contained classroom. Currently, he is a doctoral student in urban schooling at UCLA. He can be reached at jaleel.howard@gmail.com.

TEQUILA CORNELIOUS is a literacy coach in a middle school and a doctoral student in literacy leadership at Concordia University, Chicago. Previously, she was an elementary school teacher, reading interventionist, and elementary literacy coach. She can be reached at crf_corneltn@cuchicago.edu.

BRYANT O. BEST is a former education policy associate who served national associations in both K–12 and higher education. Currently, he is a doctoral student in the Department of Teaching and Learning at Vanderbilt University. He can be reached at bryant.o.best@vanderbilt.edu.

LAURA FITTZ is a former high school English teacher and restorative practices coordinator. Currently, she is a doctoral student in the Department of Teaching and Learning at Vanderbilt University. She can be reached at laura.l.fittz@vanderbilt.edu.

This article originally appeared
in *English Education* 53.3

WHAT'S IN A NAME? Language, Identity, and Power in English Education

GRACE MYHYUN KIM

This article discusses activities and actions for English language arts (ELA) educators to engage in antiracist praxis and humanizing pedagogy through unpacking the common activity of classroom name introductions. The author highlights how learning students' names can involve honoring nondominant histories of racially minoritized communities. Implications of this (re)active praxis include the potential to sustain marginalized students in ELA classrooms by promoting broader racial and linguistic justice.

IN THE FIRST CLASS of a graduate literacy course last year, I wrote my name on the board: Grace 미현 Kim. I then shared an origin story of my name to begin an activity in which students share their names, pronouns, and any story they wish about their name. Next, a student introduced herself and explained that she and her sisters share the same name—a common practice among families she knows in her home country, Costa Rica. Other name stories followed, some humorous, some poignant.

I have tried variations of this activity in English language arts (ELA) teacher education courses as well, followed by debriefing of its purposes. In this essay, I unpack this pedagogical activity and its implications for ELA teacher and K–12 education. Moreover, through (re)active praxis related to this activity, I argue that there is a critical need to invite diverse names—and the languages and cultural histories they may honor—into ELA classrooms.

A Name's Genealogy

After writing my name, I explained Korean names are usually two syllables, although some are single syllable. According to tradition, boys receive a family designated name, a "syllable" carried across all men of one generation. For example, a friend once shared a memory of the only Asian students in his high school: four brothers, each named Jay. He recalled jokes made about the four Jays. I wondered if their names were distinct from each other but had been truncated to Jay for U.S. schools. My father's name is 재철 (Jay Charl), but he often goes by Jay in the United States. His brother and male cousins' names begin with 재 too, each followed by a different second syllable. Generational naming, along with name selection informed by the fortune-telling of a saju expert, is no longer widely followed, yet some families in Korea and across its diaspora still adhere to the practice. I am reminded of it during ritual visits to familial tombstones that catalog patrilineal descendants into the current century. Despite this tradition, my mother determined my sister and I would inherit part of her name, 현주. Just as my name includes 현, so too does my sister's name, 소현.

Names have always been important to my mother. I grew up hearing stories of Korean names forcibly changed under Japan's assimilation policies to erase Korean language and culture (Pak & Hwang, 2011), and the Japanese names she and her siblings assumed at school. Annually, she reminds me of National Liberation Day, the end of Japan's colonial occupation of the Korean peninsula, or the end of World War II. Stories from this history, her childhood, and her pride over bequeathing me part of her name inhere in my name—her careful deliberation over the meanings of the Chinese characters embedded in its Hangul syllables.

It may be the hauntings of the colonial period into which my parents were born that have led my mother to call me 미현 in all communications with me. Although I do not hear 미현 "in school," writing and seeing it in educational contexts—albeit Romanized and arranged between a surname that appears last rather than first—traces the lyrical joy of my mother's voice, her rendition of the Korean alphabet song through which I learned Hangul. Inserting 미현 into my academic life is a reminder that I largely owe my love of language and literacy to a multilingual childhood enriched by my mother's singing and storytelling.

Students' Names

Last year, during her first week of classes, Phuc Bui Diem Nguyen, a student at Laney College in California, received an email from her professor, Matthew Hubbard, asking her to "Anglicize" her name (Taylor & Morales, 2020). After explaining it means "happiness blessing," she received the repeated request with this rationale: "I understand you are offended, but you need to understand your name is an offensive sound in my language." Even if this college of 16,000 students were not almost 30 percent Asian, Hubbard's reply is unequivocally offensive and imposes a redaction of her ancestral identity. In addition to the dehumanizing rejection of the student's name, his request suggests Asian Americans are foreigners in his myopic definition of U.S. society, as well as in the broader American imaginary. Within their exchange, his ownership of the discourse and her exclusion from it are laid bare in his use of "my language." Not only does his communication demean Vietnamese, it precludes the possibility for the student to claim or inhabit English as her language as well.

INSERTING 미현 INTO MY ACADEMIC LIFE IS A REMINDER THAT I LARGELY OWE MY LOVE OF LANGUAGE AND LITERACY TO A MULTILINGUAL CHILDHOOD ENRICHED BY MY MOTHER'S SINGING AND STORYTELLING.

During the initial months of the COVID-19 pandemic, racist slurs and harassment directed at Asian Americans increased, with 26 percent reporting fear of being threatened or physically attacked (Ruiz et al., 2020). At the time of finalizing this manuscript for publication, reported anti-Asian hate crimes in the 16 largest U.S. cities had increased almost 150 percent from 2019 to 2020 (Center for the Study of Hate and Extremism, 2021). This violence is not an inchoate anti-Asian sentiment birthed from racist rhetoric related to the pandemic, although characterizations of it as a "Chinese virus" or "Kung flu" foment xenophobia. Treating Asian Americans as "forever foreigners" (Tuan, 1998) is steeped in a long history of "yellow peril" legislation targeting Chinese immigrants and Asian peoples. Hubbard's need to "Anglicize" a student's name contributes to this history of systemic racism through an expectation for her to assimilate to a dynamic that accommodates his convenience and power. A Texas lawyer's 2009 House testimony on voter identification legislation in which he argued Asian voters should adopt names "easier for Americans to deal with" (Ratcliffe, 2009), like Hubbard's request, upholds Western imperialism and White supremacy.

Asian American students report "language rejection" of their home language(s) due to experiences of accent ridicule and xenophobic comments (Hinton, 2009). U.S. schools do not have policies mandating name changes, yet we must interrogate how the rejection or repeated mispronunciation of the names of students of color maintains Eurocentrism within educational settings, as do implicit social rules that may circumscribe students to accept Anglicized or abbreviated names against their wishes or those of their families. Not learning how to say someone's name, regardless of race and ethnicity, is a social solecism in any context. In school, however, dismissal or repeated mispronunciation of the names of students of color can be especially harmful. Subtle experiences with racism can have lasting effects on their worldview and sense of personhood (Kohli & Solórzano, 2012).

NOT LEARNING HOW TO SAY SOMEONE'S NAME, REGARDLESS OF RACE AND ETHNICITY, IS A SOCIAL SOLECISM IN ANY CONTEXT. IN SCHOOL, HOWEVER, DISMISSAL OR REPEATED MISPRONUNCIATION OF THE NAMES OF STUDENTS OF COLOR CAN BE ESPECIALLY HARMFUL.

Names and Colonial Histories

My mother's memories of the colonial occupation of the Korean peninsula are entwined with the experiences of Japanese families in the United States during the same period: the characterization of Japanese people under Executive Order 9066 as "enemy aliens," including those who were U.S.-born, and the forced removal from their homes into "detention centers" to be guarded by barbed wire and guns. These histories are different from yet also overlap with social justice and human rights issues in the histories of many other communities who have endured institutional violence in assimilating racial and ethnic minority or indigenous groups, such as the material, cultural, and linguistic dispossession of Native American and Mexican peoples dating back to the eighteenth century (Ferg-Cadima, 2004; Zitkala-sa, 1921).

The stories that students engage with during class affirm or deny the experiences of students from racially minoritized groups (Solórzano & Yosso, 2002). Building on this view, the stories that ELA educators support or neglect concerning names contribute to opening or constricting the classroom space for a variety of histories, languages, and worldviews. ELA has privileged a Eurocentric canon and English as the only medium of instruction, yet it is a subject replete with opportunities for encouraging multilingual expression and exploring issues of power related to language use. Affirming culturally diverse names—and the varied tonal systems, phonemes, and writing systems they may involve—is consonant with a U.S. society in which students of color compose 51 percent of K–12 schools (Snyder et al., 2019) and one-quarter of school-age children have at least one parent born outside of the United States (Lou et al., 2019). Refusing to pronounce the names of students of color contributes to the historical role of schools in enforcing the dominant culture (Kohli & Solórzano, 2012) and global histories of assimilating racially and ethnically minoritized communities into colonized ways of speaking and being.

American Names

The racialization of names can invoke nativist notions of who belongs in U.S. society by interpolating "foreignness" into the intersection of race and language. In 2019, President Donald Trump commented that four women of color, Alexandria Ocasio-Cortez, Ilhan Omar, Rashida Tlaib, and Ayanna S. Pressley, should go back to the countries from which they came. Notwithstanding the fact that three of these congresswomen are U.S. born, casting out people of color with names considered "foreign" excludes cultural, linguistic, and religious diversity.

As ELA educators, we can interrupt this reproduction of Whiteness by working toward school cultures in which no name is "too difficult to pronounce," and more broadly, a society in which all names are considered American. Writing Grace and 미현 in U.S. academe is a claim to both names as American. I hope this small act invites my students to draw from their cultural and linguistic repertories in the classroom. I hope they will extend this invitation in visible ways to their ELA students, too. I have certainly made and continue to make mistakes pronouncing names, yet I hope that concerted, patient efforts to learn students' names are mutually beneficial. Within a humanizing pedagogy—including the humanization of educators (Freire, 1972)—what more fundamental act of recognition is there than to learn someone's name?

Decolonial education requires recognizing students as experts of their own identities and histories. Such efforts involve care not to presume others' cultural identities, especially given increased migration, as well as multiracial, multiethnic, multilingual, and multifaith families. As examples, my former students have included an ethnically Chinese tenth grader born and raised in Brazil; Portuguese was her home language. Another student, an ethnically Japanese

TEACHING TIPS

During the pandemic, anti-Asian violence increased in the US by an estimated 150%. Have you, your school, or institution acknowledged this harm with your students? How so? Are you satisfied with this acknowledgement? If not, then what would have been a more appropriate response? Decolonial education, Kim articulates, in part, requires recognizing students as experts of their own identities and histories. Give students opportunities to share their naming genealogies and histories, which may or may not be enmeshed in racial, ethnic, and xenophobic trauma. Kim invites us to avoid asking students to change or shorten their names to fit an imagined American identity: "dismissal or repeated mispronunciation or the names of students of color can be especially harmful." Instead of making assumptions about who students are, be sure to ask them about their backgrounds, as well as their preferences and experiences. Be sure to include multilingual, multicultural, and multiethnic texts in your ELA classrooms to welcome and honor multiple identities.

twelfth grader who grew up in Mexico, spoke Spanish at home. Students adopted by parents of a different race or ethnicity might also have names that challenge assumptions related to race, ethnicity, and language. We must also bear in mind that students of color do not invariably have "exotic" names with meanings to be mined, just as explaining cultural diversity should not be a burden placed on them. Individual identities are also dynamic; therefore, the name(s) any student identifies with may shift over time and in different contexts.

In the aforementioned activity, like students' names, the choice of name story must also be left wide open and reside with each storyteller. For example, students may have recent or distant experiences of trauma associated with histories related to their name. Pressuring students to relive what may be painful memories through writing, speech, or any other mode—even in the service of community building or teachers' desire to get to know their students—cannot be deemed culturally responsive teaching. Students enter classrooms with varying levels of preparation and ease sharing personal stories and family histories (Luke, 2019).

Language Matters in English Education

As we model pedagogies for future teachers, even seemingly prosaic activities such as name introductions can pose important implications for language ideologies embedded in education, generally, and English education, specifically. Inviting the use of minoritized languages, in particular, may be beneficial in challenging the racism underlying linguistic hierarchies often present in schools (Kim, 2020).

Despite the colonial history of Western alphabetic literacy, ideologies of standard English that pervade U.S. schools and society, and the symbolic power of English (Kim, 2016b), as ELA teacher educators, we are well-positioned to model pedagogies that welcome language diversity into the classroom. For example, we can ensure that in courses, the first whole-class text incorporates a language other than English. Continual text selections that include everyday use of diverse names and minoritized languages, including varieties of English other than the "standard," demonstrate a critical pedagogical stance for future ELA teachers. Practices like these communicate to future ELA educators, and the students they will teach, that the ELA classroom need not be an English-only space.

A favorite memory of a secondary English education course I taught last year is the student writing left on the whiteboard before and after each week's class. A student who identifies as African American informally wrote greetings and the day of the week in Japanese or Korean, languages she began learning as an anime fan. Sometimes, when I walked into class, she was deep in consultation with a classmate who is from Taiwan. This student's dominant language is Mandarin, and she knows some Japanese and Korean too. Unlike historically Eurocentric and monolingual ELA curriculum and instruction, students' out-of-school lives show globalized social practices in online spaces that traverse boundaries of nation, race, and language in complex, multilingual, and multiliterate ways (Kim, 2016a, 2016b). By designing curricula that invite out-of-school language and literacy practices, we can open up ELA education in ways that promote multilingualism and may also help to change monolithic perceptions of cultural identity based on race, ethnicity, or place.

Alongside efforts to recruit and sustain more ELA teacher educators and teachers of color from diverse migration and language backgrounds (Kim, 2020), we can all work to sustain and promote linguistic diversity, sometimes starting with something as simple as a name activity. This work is critical for developing a next generation of ELA teachers who will disrupt an English-only norm of ELA education and support multilingualism as an asset for literacy learning.

ACKNOWLEDGEMENTS

I would like to thank 오현주, Estrella Torrez, Rick Ayers, *English Education*'s editor, Melanie Shoffner, and three anonymous reviewers for their support and feedback on this article.

REFERENCES

Center for the Study of Hate & Extremism. (2021). FACT SHEET: Anti-Asian Prejudice March 2020. https://www.csusb.edu/sites/default/files/FACT%20SHEET-%20Anti-Asian%20Hate%202020%203.2.21.pdf

Ferg-Cadima, J. (2004). *Black, white and brown: Latino school desegregation efforts in the pre- and post-*Brown v. Board of Education *era.* Mexican American Legal Defense and Educational Fund.

Freire, P. (1972). *Pedagogy of the oppressed* (M. Ramos, Trans.). Penguin.

Hinton, L. (2009). Loss of heritage languages in the United States. In A. Reyes & A. Lo (Eds.), *Beyond yellow English: Toward a linguistic anthropology of Asian Pacific America* (pp. 331–346). Oxford University Press.

Kim, G. M. (2016a). Transcultural digital literacies: Cross-border connections and self-representations in an online forum. *Reading Research Quarterly*, 51(2), 199–219.

Kim, G. M. (2016b). Practicing multilingual identities: Online interactions in a Korean dramas forum. *International Multilingual Research Journal*, 10(4), 254–272.

Kim, G. M. (2020). Challenging native speakerism in literacy research and education. *Journal of Literacy Research*, 52(3), 368–375.

Kohli, R., & Solórzano, D. G. (2012). Teachers, please learn our names!: Racial microaggressions and the K–12 classroom. *Race Ethnicity and Education*, 15(4), 441–462.

Lou, C., Adams, G., Bernstein, H., Baird, C., Feng, A., Hagerman, L., & Lei, S. (2019). *Part of us: A data-driven look at children of immigrants.* Urban Institute. https://www.urban.org/features/part-us-data-driven-look-children-immigrants

Luke, A. (2019). *Educational policy, narrative and discourse.* Routledge.

Pak, S. Y., & Hwang, K. (2011). Assimilation and segregation of imperial subjects: "Educating" the colonised during the 1910–1945 Japanese colonial rule of Korea. *Paedagogica Historica*, 47(3), 377–397.

Ratcliffe, R. G. (2009, April 8). Lawmaker defends comment on Asians. *Houston Chronicle*. http://www.chron.com/news/houston-texas/article/Texas-lawmaker-suggests-Asians-adopt-easier-names-1550512.php.

Ruiz, N. G., Horowitz, J. M., & Tamir, C. (2020, July 1). Many Black and Asian Americans say they have experienced discrimination amid the COVID-19 outbreak. *Pew Research Center*. https://www.pewsocialtrends.org/2020/07/01/many-black-and-asian-americans-say-they-have-experienced-discrimination-amid-the-covid-19-outbreak/

Snyder, T. D., De Brey, C., & Dillow, S. A. (2019). Digest of education statistics 2017, NCES 2018-070. *National Center for Education Statistics.*

Solórzano, D. G., & Yosso, T. J. (2002). Critical race methodology: Counter-storytelling as an analytical framework for education research. *Qualitative Inquiry*, 8(1), 23–44.

Taylor, D. B., & Morales, C. (2020, June 21). Professor who asked student to "Anglicize" her name is put on leave. *New York Times*. https://www.nytimes.com/2020/06/21/us/phuc-bui-diem-nguyen-laney-college.html

Tuan, M. (1998). *Forever foreigners or honorary whites?* Rutgers University Press.

Zitkala-sa. (1921). *American Indian stories*. Hayworth Publishing House.

GRACE MYHYUN KIM is an assistant professor of language and literacy studies at the University of Texas at Austin, where she is also a faculty member of the Urban Teachers program and the Centers for Asian American and East Asian Studies. A 2016-2018 fellow of NCTE's Cultivating New Voices among Scholars of Color (CNV) program, she has been a member of NCTE since 2000.

This article originally appeared in
Research in the Teaching of English 56.1

IN DIALOGUE: Transnational Childhoods

In this issue's In Dialogue, our three contributing scholars offer generative ways to foreground the subject of transnational childhoods in the literacy field. Though writing from different areas of expertise, the authors are united in their calls for critical, justice-oriented engagements with transnational childhoods in the literacy field.

MARILISA JIMÉNEZ GARCÍA,
FIKILE NXUMALO
& LEILANI SABZALIAN

Transnational Childhoods in US Literacies

Centering transnational childhoods in literacy and literary studies is an especially important undertaking for scholars and scholarship in the United States for a few reasons. First, many scholars, perhaps trained in English departments and colleges of education focusing on English "classics," regardless of their commitments to racial, gender, and social justice, might have little experience with comparative methodologies. Even though the US academy may say that they train scholar-teachers on and for multiple literacies, languages, and cultures, the normative perspective is on the US as a monolingual nation of immigrants, settled by the British, and there is little (if anything) beyond that kind of founding mythology that is valued as knowledge. *Transnational* asks us to question the very foundations of what we consider childhood and knowledge—what we might consider foreign or international. Even the reality of multiple settler colonies and languages on Indigenous lands is something many scholars in the US are only beginning to awaken to.

The racial, cultural, and linguistic divisions in the academy have shaped how we imagine, count, and reward literacies, and therefore have also shaped how we imagine aesthetics and knowledge production as a whole. As a graduate student and now professor interested in youth literature and culture, I have confronted phrases like "the ideal reader" and "the child," thinking: "Whoever decision-makers and other people in power think *that* 'reader' or 'child' is will affect whether certain children are even seen as *children* and *child readers*, especially children of color." These conceptions affect every place where literature and literacy are visibly valued, such as schools, bookstores, and libraries.

Much of my research journey for my book *Side by Side: US Empire, Puerto Rico, and the Roots of American Youth Literature and Culture* (University Press of Mississippi, 2021) was about understanding what got counted as literacy and literature by the Spanish Empire during its 400-year reign in Puerto Rico and by the *Norteamericanos* when they invaded Puerto Rico in 1898. What the empires considered literature and literacy also dictated what they counted as historical records and books. US officials had the nerve to say at the turn of the twentieth century that there weren't any books or written accounts in Puerto Rico's history. Indeed, well-known elites such as Eugenio María de Hostos and even Lola Rodríguez de Tió had published books and accounts. But they weren't in English and, just like that, the officials crafted a tale of illiterate, docile Puerto Ricans with no history.

To consider transnational childhoods at the heart of the literacy project in the US is to reward the legacies of literature and literacy represented by multiple childhoods, and hopefully, to reflect this understanding in our literature and literacy classrooms. *Transnational* is also important as opposed to simply *international*. In the field of children's and young adult literature, *international* often means engaging with other English-dominant countries—Canada, Australia, Britain, etc. However, this practice reinforces the idea that there is no other source of history or knowledge beyond Britain for US childhood scholars. There is also a denial of the US's own position as an empire and colonizing force.

Yet, beyond the concept of multiple nations, *transnational* also opens us up, as a field, to admitting how nations, at this point, have bifurcated and otherwise affected each other. Indeed, to confront these ebbs and flows is often an encounter with colonial violence. Yet it is also an opportunity to see and value how new literacies have formed around these moments in multiple areas, and how they remain in conversation. Ultimately, a move to center transnational childhoods is a move away from deficit discourses.

MARILISA JIMÉNEZ GARCÍA is an associate professor of English and Latino Studies at Lehigh University. She is also the founding director and principal investigator at the Institute of Critical Race and Ethnic Studies (https://wordpress.lehigh.edu/cres/). Jiménez García's research on Latinx literature have appeared in *Latino Studies*, *CENTRO: A Journal of Puerto Rican Studies*, *The Lion and the Unicorn*, and *Children's Literature*. Her new book, *Side by Side: US Empire, Puerto Rico and the Roots of American Youth Literature and Culture* (University Press of Mississippi, March 2021) examines the history of colonialism in Puerto Rico through an analysis of youth literature and culture both in the archipelago and the diaspora. Jiménez Garcia has worked on projects with Teaching for Change, The Children's Defense Fund, and Sesame Street.

Centering Place in Early Childhood Literacies: Thinking with Black Geographies

There is ongoing urgency to find ways to disrupt deficit views of Black children's learning. In my field of early childhood education, Developmentally Appropriate Practice (DAP) remains the dominant mode of engaging Black and other racially marginalized children's learning, despite decades of critical scholarship. This scholarship has shown the epistemic and material injustices of DAP in positioning normal childhood as "middle class, White, monolingual, heterosexual, [and] able-bodied" (Pérez & Saavedra, 2017, p. 6). In early literacy, the dominance of DAP materializes in ways that include a narrow, Eurocentric view of what counts as literacy and the marginalization of the rich multiple literacies of racially and culturally minoritized children (Souto-Manning & Yoon, 2018). As Jiménez García (this issue) powerfully describes, what counts as literacy is bound up with ongoing legacies of colonial empire-building.

In this essay, I turn toward the geographic as one orientation that can be generative for the field of literacy. I discuss some of the ways in which critical attention to place in early childhood literacies brings a generative *otherwise* to the Eurocentric DAP gaze on young Black children and their literacy practices. More specifically, I offer the proposition that Black geographies can bring important disruptions to the normativity and universalism of DAP and its anti-Black formations. Working from the premise that "Black matters are spatial matters," Black geographies make visible the spatialization of anti-Blackness (McKittrick, 2006, p. xiv). In addition, and of particular focus in this essay, Black geographies bring attention to the ways in which place is a site from which to enact and make visible how Black life continuously subverts and resists anti-Blackness. In other words, Black geographies offer possibilities to foreground place as a site of liberatory possibility, where place includes the material, the discursive, and the imaginary (Hawthorne, 2019).

The expansive views of place in Black geographies mean that there are multiple possibilities for interrupting normative early childhood education practices (Nxumalo et al., 2021). For instance, intentional engagement with stories that disrupt discourses of Black unbelonging in outdoor places and spaces is an important part of place literacies that are anticolonial, antiracist, and nonanthropocentric (Nxumalo, 2019; Nxumalo & Rubin, 2018). I purposefully bring together coloniality, anti-Blackness, and anthropocentrism as important sites of disruption through place literacies for two key reasons. The first is to underline the standpoint that relations between

Black, Indigenous, and Black-Indigenous peoples are a necessity for collective world-building against settler colonialism (Habtom & Scribe, 2020). Therefore, decolonial world-building necessarily includes an "ethic of responsibility to Indigenous peoples' sovereignties, their relations to lands and waters, and the multiple nations they sustain" (Sabzalian, this issue). Such world-building matters at multiple scales, including in small, everyday pedagogical encounters between educators, children, and the more-than-human world. Another reason for attending to coloniality, anti-Blackness, and anthropocentrism together is that a necessary part of decolonial world-building is figuring out what it might mean and look like to disrupt the human-centered, capitalist extractivism that has resulted in current conditions of environmental precarity. Put another way, decolonial world-building requires pedagogies of relational reciprocity with human and more-than-human coexistents. A focus on what such relational place-attuned pedagogies feel like, look like, and sound like situates early childhood literacies within current conditions of ecological precarity.

Black geographies disrupt deficit constructions of Black children by attending to storied Black place relations and Black place-making practices. These place stories enact Black "liberation as praxis of rebellious subversion" (McKittrick, 2016, p. 87). So, what might place stories inspired by Black geographies entail? Black geographies attend to the transmodal ways in which Black life is expressed spatially. This means that thinking with Black geographies includes creative, speculative, and performative narratives of Black life that can take visual, textual, and sonic forms. For example, Black geographies scholars have attended to the ways in which discursive and material engagements with fiction, visual art, photography, poetics, and music—among several other forms—are sites of spatialized and cartographic expressions of Black life (McKittrick, 2016).

Brought to the context of early childhood education, Black geographies open up early childhood literacies to the potential of visual, textual, performative, and sonic Black place stories. These place stories can be co-created with children. While it can be challenging to find stories that are situated within local geographies, educators can also seek out Black place stories. For example, working in the context of British Columbia, Canada, I have written about how the story of Hogan's Alley, a Black place in Vancouver's history, can act to disrupt erasures of Black Canada (Nxumalo, 2019). Educators can also create place stories to share with children or to deepen their own understandings of what it means to center Black places in liberatory early childhood literacies. For instance, my dear friend and colleague kihana ross and I (2019) have experimented with speculative storytelling as a mode of unsettling absences and deficits relating to Black children in environmental science and place-based education. We created a place-based science story that affirms Black childhoods, enacts an ethos of radical relationality with the more-than-human world, and dreams of futurities where Black and Indigenous people's relationships include collaboration on design of land-based pedagogies for young people. Importantly, through a grounding in a conceptualization of Black space in education, our speculative storytelling enacts refusals of DAP as the primary mode of understanding Black children's relational learning.

The focus of the Black geographic thought that I have discussed in this short essay is the African diaspora. It is important to consider what early childhood literacies inspired by Black geographies might look like beyond the African diaspora. This requires a consideration of the ways in which contours of coloniality, anti-Blackness, and anthropocentrism are both situated and globalized. For instance, DAP continues to have a firm hold in early learning contexts on the African continent (Burman, 2020). In closing, it remains ever more important to seek out geographically situated liberatory early childhood literacies. Black geographies offer one such orientation that is filled with creative possibilities for thinking and doing childhood literacies otherwise.

REFERENCES

Burman, E. (2020). *Developments: Child, image, nation*. Routledge.

Habtom, S., & Scribe, M. (2020, June 2). *To breathe together: Co-conspirators for decolonial futures*. Yellowhead Institute. https://yellowheadinstitute.org/2020/06/02/to-breathe-together/

Hawthorne, C. (2019). Black matters are spatial matters: Black geographies for the 21st century. *Geography Compass*, 13(11), Article e12468.

McKittrick, K. (2006). *Demonic grounds: Black women and the cartographies of struggle*. University of Minnesota Press.

McKittrick, K. (2016). Rebellion/invention/groove. *Small Axe: A Caribbean Journal of Criticism*, 20(1), 79–91.

Nxumalo, F. (2019). *Decolonizing place in early childhood education*. Routledge.

Nxumalo, F., Odim, N., & Smith, A. (2021). Black geographies in early childhood studies. In N. J. Yelland, L. Peters, N. Fairchild, M. Tesar, & M. Pérez (Eds.), *The SAGE handbook of global childhoods*. SAGE Publications.

Nxumalo, F., & ross, k. m. (2019). Envisioning Black space in environmental education for young children. *Race Ethnicity and Education, 22*(4), 502–524.

Nxumalo, F., & Rubin, J. C. (2018). Encountering waste landscapes: More-than-human place literacies in early childhood education. In C. R. Kuby, K. Spector, & J. Johnson Thiel (Eds.), *Posthumanism and literacy education: Knowing/being/doing literacies* (pp. 201–213). Routledge.

Pérez, M. S., & Saavedra, C. M. (2017). A call for onto-epistemological diversity in early childhood education and care: Centering global south conceptualizations of childhood/s. *Review of Research in Education, 41*(1), 1–29.

Souto-Manning, M., & Yoon, H. S. (2018). *Rethinking early literacies: Reading and rewriting worlds*. Routledge.

FIKILE NXUMALO is an assistant professor in the Department of Curriculum, Teaching and Learning at the Ontario Institute for Studies in Education, University of Toronto. Her work is centered on environmental and place-attuned early childhood education that is situated within and responsive to children's inheritances of settler colonialism, anti-Blackness, and environmental precarity.

Indigenous Internationalism: Land-Centered Literacies and Education for Resurgence

Transnational frameworks have been useful in critiquing the ways "settler nationalisms" and "transnational regimes of exploitative and oppressive power" disproportionately harm Indigenous peoples (Bauerkemper & Stark, 2012, p. 4). Transnational theories of education meaningfully intervene into normative constructions of childhood, and call for childhood studies theories and practices that are rooted in "the brilliance of children of color" (Pérez & Saavedra, 2017, p. 1) and their "everyday embodied experiences" (p. 12). Despite these important interventions, some Indigenous studies scholars remain skeptical of theories that decenter nationhood, particularly when Indigenous peoples continue to advocate for themselves "as *nations*" (Deloria, as cited in Bauerkemper & Stark, 2012, p. 4). Here, in line with Pérez and Saavedra's (2017) "urgent call for recentering global south perspectives" in early childhood education (p. 20), I wish to more specifically center Indigenous theories and consider how they might complicate and enrich transnational childhood studies and literacy education.

Indigenous studies scholars have thoughtfully reframed transnational theories to "acknowledge the mobility and multiple interactions of Indigenous peoples, cultures, histories, and texts" (Allen, 2012, p. xiv); foreground Indigenous understandings of lands, waters, nationhood, and borders (Simpson, 2017); and attend to the "*diasporic* experiences" of urban Indigenous peoples who traverse the borders between their Indigenous nations and the nation-state (Ramirez, 2007, p. 23). Trans-Indigenous scholarship (Allen, 2012), Indigenous internationalism (Bauerkemper & Stark, 2012), and Nishnaabeg internationalism (Simpson, 2017) are just some of these important interventions.

Nishnaabeg internationalism, for example, recognizes the long-standing intellectual and diplomatic practices of Nishnaabeg peoples, which include "complex ways of relating to the plant nations, animal nations, and the spiritual realm" and recognize "the bush as a networked series of international relationships" (Simpson, 2017, p. 56). Indigenous internationalism, including tribally specific iterations, compels transnational theories to begin from an ethic of responsibility to Indigenous peoples' sovereignties, their relations to lands and waters, and the multiple nations they sustain.

Supporting literacies that facilitate respectful Indigenous international relations requires rethinking childhood studies and literacy education through a lens of Indigeneity.

Centering Indigeneity would compel childhood studies and literacy education to foreground Indigenous lands, languages, nations, and knowledge systems, as well as Indigenous aims of freedom and resurgence—that is, Indigenous children's capacity to embody Indigenous intelligence, practices, and ethical processes (Simpson, 2017). With resurgent education as a framework, the goals of literacy education move beyond supporting Indigenous children's literacy, fluency, and success in settler education systems and society, to also cultivating Indigenous children's capacity to "think and live inside their own intelligence systems" (Simpson, 2017, p. 81).

Centering Indigeneity would call for "sovereign pedagogies" (Goodyear-Ka'ōpua, 2013) that prepare Indigenous children to critique colonial relations of power and knowledge, while also becoming literate and fluent in their own languages, practices, and knowledge systems. Literacy education would be broadened to include "land-centered literacies that attend to the health of the environmental systems of which we are a part" (Goodyear-Ka'ōpua, 2013, p. 246). Children would be encouraged to gain literacy of their genealogies, which "can serve as anticolonial tools" (Goodyear-Ka'ōpua, 2013, p. 45), and to embody Indigenous literacies as decolonizing praxis (Jacob, 2013).

The aforementioned theories and practices are imperative for Indigenous children; however, non-Indigenous children also need literacies that support them in seeing past the "denial of the US's own position as an empire and colonizing force" (Jiménez García, this issue). Non-Indigenous children need literacies that disrupt their presumed innocence "and center accurate Indigenous perspectives" (Templeton & Cheruvu, 2020, p. 14), that challenge their affiliations with the nation-states in which they reside, and that help them think about what it means to live responsibly in diaspora (Haig-Brown, 2009). They, too, need support in unlearning the "deep structures of the colonialist consciousness," which socialize them into a sense of superiority and separation from land and other communities (Grande, 2015, p. 99). Sovereign pedagogies can be generative for both Indigenous and non-Indigenous children (Goodyear-Ka'ōpua, 2013), and all children benefit from literacies that are localized and anchored around "place-based Indigenous politics" (Aikau, as cited in Aikau et al., 2015, p. 86).

Unfortunately, "many early childhood educators are unfamiliar with indigenous culture, traditions, values and languages, making it difficult for them to make literacy learning relevant to the lives of indigenous children" (Hare, 2012, p. 395). Too few are versed in "critical Indigenous literacies" (Reese, 2018) or able to recognize Eurocentric education and literacies of dominance as practices of epistemic supremacy. Fortunately, theories and practices of critical culturally sustaining/revitalizing pedagogies (McCarty & Lee, 2014) foreground Indigenous children's experiences and foster literacies that advance educational sovereignty. Moreover, recent scholarship draws attention to the urgent need for early childhood education that unsettles settler logics and decolonizes children's relations with land and the more-than-human world (Nxumalo, 2019). Nxumalo's description (this issue) of Black childhood literacies rooted in radical relationality and Black and Indigenous futurities offers a beautiful model of land-based literacy pedagogy that can facilitate "decolonial world-building."

Though a comprehensive analysis of how Indigenous theories might inform transnational theories of childhood and literacy education is beyond the scope of this brief, here are a few implications and starting points:

- **Rethink transnational childhood studies through Indigenous feminist theories,** which offer fluid conceptions of education, land, Indigeneity, nationhood, and sovereignty that defy colonial categories and cartographies.
- **Broaden literacy education** to include land-centered literacies (Goodyear-Ka'ōpua, 2013) and literacies that foster radical resurgence (Simpson, 2017).
- **Actively work to recruit and prepare Indigenous educators,** who are more likely to be versed in land-centered literacies, and can help Indigenous children gain the "knowledge and skills required for protecting, promoting, and preserving Indigenous people, language, culture, and land" (Shirley, 2017, p. 168).
- **Utilize digital technologies that empower Indigenous youth** to use technology in service of Indigenous self-determination, and that give Indigenous children living in diaspora access to "local indigenous vocabularies and literacies" (Rigney, 2019, p. 1040).
- **Engage in meaningful collaborations with Native families and communities,** as family engagement and collaboration are key to fostering everyday resurgence (Bang et al., 2019).

Echoing Pérez and Saavedra's (2017, p. 21) urgent call, I will end by turning the question to you: "What role will you play in literacy education that fosters Indigenous resurgence?"

TEACHING TIPS

The authors describe impacts of colonial violence on Latinx, Black, and Indigenous communities in the US, Puerto Rico, and Canada. Learning about the transnational experiences of youth and communities is beneficial for all. Have you explored these colonial histories from the perspectives of people in Latinx, Black, and Indigenous communities? Has your school, district, or institution acknowledged these perspectives? What, if any, structural supports and policies are in place within your teaching context to support transnational youth and communities? Brainstorm micro- and macro-levels of supports to support the literacies of transnational youth (or the study of transnational youth literacies, if you do not have transnational youth in your context).

REFERENCES

Aikau, H. K., Arvin, M., Goeman, M., & Morgensen, S. (2015). Indigenous feminisms roundtable. *Frontiers: A Journal of Women Studies*, 36(3), 84–106.

Allen, C. (2012). *Trans-Indigenous methodologies for global native literary studies*. University of Minnesota Press.

Bang, M., Montaño, N., & McDaid-Morgan, N. (2019). Indigenous family engagement: Strong families, strong nations. In E. A. McKinley & L. T. Smith (Eds.), *Handbook of Indigenous education* (pp. 789–810). Springer.

Bauerkemper, J., & Stark, H. K. (2012). The trans/national terrain of Anishinaabe law and diplomacy. *Journal of Transnational American Studies*, 4(1), 1–21.

Goodyear-Kaʻōpua, N. (2013). *The seeds we planted: Portraits of a native Hawaiian charter school*. University of Minnesota Press.

Grande, S. (2015). *Red pedagogy: Native American social and political thought* (10th anniversary ed.). Rowman & Littlefield.

Haig-Brown, C. (2009). Decolonizing Diaspora: Whose traditional land are we on? *Cultural and Pedagogical Inquiry*, 1(2). https://doi.org/10.18733/C3H59V.

Hare, J. (2012). 'They tell a story and there's meaning behind that story': Indigenous knowledge and young indigenous children's literacy learning. *Journal of Early Childhood Literacy*, 12(4), 389–414. https://doi.org/10.1177/1468798411417378

Jacob, M. M. (2013). *Yakama rising: Indigenous cultural revitalization, activism, and healing*. University of Arizona Press.

McCarty, T., & Lee, T. (2014). Critical culturally sustaining/revitalizing pedagogy and Indigenous education sovereignty. *Harvard Educational Review*, 84(1), 101–124.

Nxumalo, F. (2019). *Decolonizing place in early childhood education*. Routledge.

Pérez, M. S., & Saavedra, C. M. (2017). A call for onto-epistemological diversity in early childhood education and care: Centering global south conceptualizations of childhood/s. *Review of Research in Education*, 41(1), 1–29.

Ramirez, R. K. (2007). *Native hubs: Culture, community, and belonging in Silicon Valley and beyond*. Duke University Press.

Reese, D. (2018). Critical Indigenous literacies: Selecting and using children's books about Indigenous peoples. *Language Arts*, 95(6), 389–393.

Rigney, L.-I. (2019). Defining culturally responsive digital education for classrooms: Writing from Oceania to build Indigenous Pacific futures. In E. A. McKinley & L. T. Smith (Eds.), *Handbook of Indigenous education* (pp. 1031–1048). Springer.

Shirley, V. J. (2017). Indigenous social justice pedagogy: Teaching into the risks and cultivating the heart. *Critical Questions in Education*, 8(2), 163–177.

Simpson, L. B. (2017). *As we have always done: Indigenous freedom through radical resistance*. University of Minnesota Press.

Templeton, T. N., & Cheruvu, R. (2020). Childhood innocence for settler children: Disrupting colonialism and innocence in early childhood curriculum. *The New Educator*, 16(2), 131–148. https://doi.org/10.1080/1547688X.2020.1734264

LEILANI SABZALIAN (ALUTIIQ) is an assistant professor of Indigenous studies in education and co-director of the Sapsik'ʷałá (Teacher) Education Program at the University of Oregon. Her research focuses on creating spaces to support Indigenous self-determination in public schools, and equipping educators to challenge colonialism in curriculum, policy, and practice.

This article originally appeared
in *English Journal 110.4*

THE KID IN THE BACK OF THE CLASS

AISHA SAEED

GROWING UP, school was not a safe space. Surrounded by the same bullies from first grade onward, I focused less on learning academics and more on learning how to survive. I shouldered taunts on the playground, shoves in the hallway, and snide notes slid into my desk, telling me I was stupid and worthless and ugly.

As the years went on, they became a second voice thrumming within me. I tried as best I could to shrink. I stayed quiet. Feigned indifference. I wanted more than anything to become invisible. Maybe then, they'd lose interest and leave me alone. It never worked, but all through elementary and junior high, I kept trying.

Trying to survive an abusive environment left little room to focus on my studies, and my grades reflected this reality. I learned to forge my parents' signatures for the failing quizzes and tests I needed signed and returned. I studied the floor when teacher after teacher lectured me on my lack of focus and not completing my assignments.

The truth was, I hated school, but I loved learning. On the weekends and after hours, I couldn't wait to escape into a book. My parents took me to the public library each Saturday and I borrowed as many books as I could. I read every chance I got. No topic was uninteresting. I also loved writing. I filled spiral notebook after spiral notebook with stories.

Aisha Saeed is nine in this photo as she plays in her backyard. Photo courtesy of the author.

But at school? I shut down. None of my teacher's words reached me because when school is linked to trauma, it is impossible to succeed. Eventually, my teachers determined me unreachable and gave up.

Ink Marks

In ninth grade, though many of my childhood schoolmates had dispersed into the much larger school system, I remained wary. I also had absorbed all those years of abuse. When you've spent a lifetime being told you are stupid and unworthy, the words have a way of sticking to you and defining how you see yourself.

In my creative writing class, in ninth grade, we were assigned to write a poem. The prompt was open-ended. We could write about anything we wished. I watched my classmates writing furiously. Discarding page after page of drafts as they searched for the right words. Me? I wrote a short, six-verse stanza and quickly turned it in.

The next day, my teacher, Ms. Fleming, asked to speak to me after class. I knew what she'd say. The poem was too short. The descriptive words lacking. Maybe she'd suggest I drop out altogether. Instead, with tears in her eyes, Ms. Fleming told me my poem was beautiful. The most touching poem she'd ever read.

It was the first time a teacher told me I'd done something wonderful. I was thrown off. Stunned.

Aisha Saeed is in tenth grade in this photo from 1995. Photo courtesy of the author.

I'd never been praised by a teacher before. But even though Ms. Fleming liked my poem, I knew better than to take it personally. The ink marks of "dummy" written along my arms may have faded, but the message remained ingrained. I appreciated the praise, but that poem? It was a one-time fluke. And maybe, it wasn't good at all. Perhaps, I thought, Ms. Fleming was just taking pity on me.

Survival

The summer before tenth grade, my father sat us down at the dinner table and announced that his job relocated him from Miami, Florida, where I'd been born and raised, to a city one hundred miles north. Perhaps some would think this was good news. A chance to start over away from those who haunted my days and my dreams. Instead, I was devastated. I'd learned how to navigate my life at school safely by now. I had only three years to go. Just like that, I'd have to figure out how to survive in another system.

Ms. Bruno was my tenth-grade English teacher that fall. On the first day of school, she asked us to write an essay about our summer. I don't remember what I wrote. But I remember, the next day, how she stood in front of the classroom and said there was one essay in the bunch that stood out from the rest. Where the words flowed beautifully. She felt compelled to share it with all of us.

I remember the skip in my heart when she began reading and I realized it was *my* essay. My essay! I waited for snickers in the audience. I waited for someone to raise their hand and question Ms. Bruno's judgment. But no one snickered. They listened to my essay, the teacher smiled at me, and class continued on.

I am sure my expression that morning was stoic. I had spent a lifetime building up the art of appearing indifferent. Showing feelings and emotions were a surefire way to trigger taunts and insults. I'd learned to bottle up. Had Ms. Bruno seen my face that day and decided to judge who I was from it, she'd have written me off as a sullen teenager in the back of the class. She would never have learned that, beneath my practiced indifference, there was a

TEACHING TIPS

Saeed reflects on her schooling years. Bullying prevented her from full participation in schooling, until a teacher intervened. Do you have students who seem to be withdrawn, either in person or within your remote learning community? If so, reach out those students to ask if there is anything you can do to support their participation. Let them know that teaching and learning can and should happen in supportive environments.

child whose very sense of identity had been shaken. I wondered: If two teachers said my words had worth, maybe it wasn't a fluke?

Throughout the school year, Ms. Bruno would leave notes in my assignments. Kind words in the margins. Hearts around a phrase she particularly loved. Encouraging messages at the bottom of each paper. I cherished those words, and I cherished her class. I began stopping by before school to chat with her. I dropped in during my lunch period, too. I realize now, I was probably cutting into her planning period, but she never made me feel unwelcome, she always made time for me. I began to draw up the courage to share my poems with her. My stories. She took my work seriously.

Aisha Saeed is in twelfth grade in this photo from 1997. Photo courtesy of the author.

Ms. Bruno helped me push away the negative self-talk I'd absorbed over the years simply by consistently believing in me. She helped me learn new ways to identify.

Words Matter

Thanks to Ms. Bruno's words of encouragement, I joined the school's literary magazine. I remember the terror my first day walking into the extracurricular space. How was I actually voluntarily staying after school? But Ms. Bruno was the advisor. She sat in the back, unobtrusively grading papers, and I felt safe. In that club, I met kids who also loved the written word. We exchanged our own poetry and delighted in selecting submissions. I did not make lifelong friends there, but I learned to unclench my jaw and to breathe at last, surrounded by likeminded peers and a teacher who made me feel safe.

Over time, I made friends. I stopped hiding out in Ms. Bruno's room for lunch. My grades began to improve. And Ms. Bruno remained in my life the rest of my time I was in high school. She helped me redefine myself. She showed me my words had value. She didn't give up on me. And in doing that, she taught me not to give up on myself. I graduated from William T. Dwyer High School in 1997.

Years later, I became a teacher. I taught second grade and saw for myself the different ways children process trauma. Some handled it just like me. I don't have the words for what it felt like to pay back Ms. Bruno, by doing what she did for me, for my students: believing in them even when they did not believe in themselves.

Ms. Bruno kept reaching out to that kid in the back of the class and told her that her words mattered and that *she* mattered. She told me so over and over again. Eventually, I heard her.

Teachers can be an incredible force in the life of a child: they lay down foundations for a future they typically never get to bear witness to. Since becoming a published author, I've tried to find Ms. Bruno, to share with her what ended up becoming of the kid she reached out to all those years ago. She no longer teaches at that high school. There's no sign of her on social media.

I wish I could see Ms. Bruno again. Tell her how much her kindness shifted the trajectory of my future by showing that sullen kid in the back of the class that her words—and she—mattered. I truly believe it made all the difference.

AISHA SAEED is the award-winning and *The New York Times* bestselling author of books for children and young adults. Her works include *Amal Unbound, Bilal Cooks Daal, Written in the Stars, Yes No Maybe So* (coauthored with Becky Albertalli), and *Once Upon an Eid: Stories of Hope and Joy by 15 Muslim Voices* (coedited with S. K. Ali). She lives in Atlanta, Georgia, with her husband and children. Visit her online at www.aishasaeed.com.

This article originally appeared
in *Voices from the Middle* 27.1

FROM RAPPORT TO RELATIONSHIPS: Shifting Our Practice from Classroom Management to Community

MATTHEW HOMRICH-KNIELING

THE BEGINNING OF A NEW SCHOOL YEAR is such a special, important time: meeting new students and catching up with former students, refining our curriculum and trying out new pedagogic strategies. Our lesson plans are written and our classrooms and desks are likely as clean and as organized as they will be all year. There's a distinct sense of possibilities and opportunities.

Often, as a new school year begins, we hear a lot about the importance of getting to know our students through icebreakers, community-builders, and fun activities. This is, no doubt, a critical component to the beginning of the school year. We need to create a foundation of community and relationships from which to build throughout the year.

However, these conversations often position community-building practices as something we do at the start of the year before we dive into the important work: our academic content. Educators usually refer to this as "building rapport," which is most often framed as a classroom management technique. This is deeply problematic. We cannot meaningfully build relationships and community with our students if our primary purpose is control and authority of our classrooms. This creates inauthentic, surface-level relationships; it undermines our students' agency, as our community-building is limited to preplanned activities; and it can reproduce oppressive structures.

We live in a society of isolation and hypercompetition, of hate and division, of violence and oppression, and I believe that, as educators, we can play an integral role in transforming this society. We need to reject the notion of building relationships as an item we can check off our beginning-of-the-year to-do list and instead ask ourselves how to meaningfully center relationships in our classrooms, in our pedagogy, and in our practices, not as a classroom management technique but as a way to foster empathetic, democratic, and supportive community. By centering relationships and community in our classrooms, we are practicing visions of justice and liberation that we can then bring into our relationships and communities outside of our classrooms.

In this column, I will tell part of my own story navigating relationships and community in my first year of teaching, reflect on my practices that center relationships and community in my current teaching position, and share insights from my students on this topic.

What's the Answer? A Personal Story

I drove to my school on my first day of teaching as a newly graduated educator full of optimism, enthusiasm, and, of course, anxiousness. I drove home from that first day of teaching as a newly graduated classroom educator in tears.

My first year of teaching was hard. Really hard. I taught sixth grade English language arts in a mid-sized city in New England, where the majority of people struggled to find stable, good-paying jobs. This systemic instability, which often carries traumas, showed up in my school under the guise of "misbehavior." The school's approach to discipline was highly punitive, exclusionary, and dehumanizing. I knew in my heart that the school's practices were wrong, but I didn't know how to do it right. As Carla Shalaby tells us in her book, *Troublemakers: Lessons in Freedom from Young Children at School* (2017), "It is difficult to build classrooms in the image of a freedom that we have not yet authentically seen in the world" (p. 174).

I HAD TO LEARN THAT I NEED TO INVEST IN MY RELATIONSHIPS WITH MY STUDENTS; I NEEDED TO INVEST MY TIME AND ENERGY IN THE COMMUNITY OF MY CLASSROOMS AND IN THE COMMUNITY OF MY STUDENTS.

I had so much love and respect for my students, and I felt myself stuck between an oppressive system and my own values. While I tried to create classroom systems and processes that honored my students' humanity and dignity, I was also seriously struggling with disruptive behavior and a chaotic environment.

I remember getting home from school after the first few weeks and frantically doing research on classroom management techniques, community-building practices, restorative justice . . . I was trying desperately to find the solution to creating a safe, humanizing classroom in a highly punitive, unsafe institution: What is the pedagogy that I need to implement? What is the system or the structure I need to use? How *exactly* should I respond to disruptive behavior?

Eventually, I had to learn that the answer to these questions does not exist. There is no pedagogy or structure or curriculum that can automatically create humanizing classrooms. To believe such is to undermine the complexity of our students as humans.

Instead, I had to learn that I need to invest in my relationships with my students; I needed to invest my time and energy in the community of my classrooms and in the community of my students; I needed to recognize that relationships are messy and so teaching and navigating conflicts and building community is and will always be messy. I had to learn that "it isn't the behavior of the children that threatens community; it is the response to that behavior, the use of exclusion, that threatens community" (Shalaby, p. 162).

I share this experience to acknowledge that the practices I describe are not meant to be seen as a tutorial for building community or solutions to problems and conflicts in your classrooms; rather, I hope these practices will highlight a way of being in our classrooms that shifts our focus away from classroom management and toward community.

Practicing Community

DAILY CHECK-INS

With the increase of high-stakes accountability and testing, teachers are often pressured to feel a sense of urgency. We are asked to follow strict pacing guides, prepare students for standardized tests, and move through our curriculum quickly, all of which, I know from experience, can limit our capacity to invest in our classroom community.

Deciding to resist this sense of urgency and the ways in which it can dehumanize our students, I now start every class period, every day, by doing a group check-in. I ask my students: *How are you, really? What'd you do after school? Do you have any life updates you want to share?* We try to follow the "one mic" rule (one person talks at a time) as students share. I, too, share stories/updates from my own life. Our check-ins generally last anywhere from 2 to 5 minutes.

This sounds simple, and it is. However, this intentional time to slow down and ask our students about their lives, to share stories from our own lives, and to listen as a community, is a practice that runs contrary to shifts we're seeing toward scripted, fast-paced curricula. The impact this routine practice has had on my classroom communities has been powerful: students feel more connected to one another, supported by one another, and comfortable in class.

COMMUNITY AGREEMENTS AND MEETINGS

Toward the beginning of the school year, my students and I often reflect on our experiences of schooling and education. I ask my students to think about times in schools/classrooms when they felt unsafe, unrecognized, or unheard. Then I ask them to think about what practices or behaviors caused them to feel that way. Finally, I ask them to imagine what could have prevented that from happening.

We use those reflections and discussions to develop a set of community agreements to work toward creating a safer space. I intentionally frame these as agreements, not rules, recognizing that we will each make mistakes and that that's ok. The purpose of these agreements is to set an intention as a class to work together in building a safer community, not to punish each other when we mess up. When I asked my students how we can support each other in our agreements, they had the idea of community meetings.

At least twice a month on Fridays, we arrange the desks into a big circle for our student-led community meeting. The purpose of the meetings is to reflect openly on how we're doing with our agreements and on our classroom community. These meetings generally last 8 to 10 minutes. The students set the agenda, but it generally looks something like this:

- **Opening**: Each student around the circle answers a question (e.g., "What is one interesting fact about you?").
- **Centering purpose:** The student-leaders remind their peers that this is a space where they can/should be honest and participatory.
- **Reflecting:** The student-leaders guide us through a reflection on how we've done on our agreements the past week (e.g., "What agreements do we feel like we've really kept this week? Is there anyone in particular we want to celebrate? What agreements do we need to focus on?")
- **Choosing a focus:** Based on that discussion, the student-leaders will choose one or two agreements to focus on for the next week.
- **Anything else:** The student-leaders will often open it up for their peers to share any other thoughts/feedback on our classroom community.
- **Closing**: The student-leaders will then evaluate the meeting (e.g., "We're going to go back around the circle and have everyone share one word to describe this meeting.").

Though our community meetings were initiated by my students, as we've prepared for meetings, I have brought in practices from restorative or talking circles (Bintliff, 2014). And while our community meetings have had challenges (e.g., students can be reluctant to share), they have also helped create a culture of shared power, student leadership, and honesty.

TEACHING TIPS

The author directs educators to invest time in building student relationships, not just at the beginning of the year but throughout the year. If you center relationships and community in your classroom, Homrich-Knieling argues, you are practicing visions of justice and liberation that can sustain relationships and communities outside of your classroom. Because of the community-centered relationships Homrich-Knieling built with his students, the students developed an after-school activism club: the Student Action Club. A major accomplishment of the Student Action Club was to develop a student-led professional development for teachers and staff about how to create positive relationships and communities in classrooms. As you build substantive relationships with your students throughout the year, seek and facilitate trauma-informed and healing-centered leadership opportunities for students that extend beyond your classroom.

Insights from Students: Student-Led Professional Development

During the 2017-18 school year, a group of students and I started an after-school activism club: The Student Action Club. We tell stories, identify shared challenges, and work toward solutions and action. One of the Student Action Club's proudest accomplishments was our student-led professional development (PD) session for our school's teachers and staff. The PD was centered around how to create positive relationships and community in classrooms.

My students identified care and respect as foundational to relationships and community in classrooms. As part of the training, in order to help educators foster care and respect, my students offered a list of practices to avoid, as well as a list of practices to embrace. I'll share a few items from each list.

Practices to Avoid:

- Pointing out a minor "negative" behavior publicly in order to "make an example" of that person, instead of talking to that student one-on-one.
- Using data walls with individual markers (even if they are anonymous), because it can make students feel uncomfortable, ashamed, and not smart.
- Not allowing students to have normal conversations in Spanish with their friends. We acknowledge that not all teachers speak Spanish, and this can make them feel uncomfortable, but Spanish is part of our culture.
- Coming to school in a bad mood or not feeling well and taking it out on students, instead of explaining that you're having a bad day.
- Yelling when there are disruptions, because that only causes more negativity.

Practices to Foster:

- Asking students (one-on-one) if they're okay if they look down.
- Getting involved in the community (outside of school functions).
- Joking around.
- Understanding some people don't feel comfortable sharing an answer out loud, so don't force it; talk with them one-on-one about why they're uncomfortable.
- Taking time to know the students' stories and talking about themselves personally—be yourself, be vulnerable.

It's important to note that the majority of my students are first- and second-generation Latinx immigrants and that their cultural practices influence their experience of community and relationships in the classroom. This, too, demonstrates the importance, especially for people like me—a white educator teaching in a community of color—of building classroom community as a means of "sustaining the cultural ways of being of communities of color rather than eradicating them" (Paris & Alim, p. 2).

Conclusion and Daily Affirmation

I recognize that as the school year progresses, it will become easy to lose sight of the ongoing work of centering relationships and community in our classrooms. In closing, then, I will offer a daily affirmation that I wrote and try to read to myself every morning to help me stay grounded in my values of social justice through education. I encourage you to write your own affirmation that reflects your values.

My students are brilliant, brave, and special. They are not defined by data, test scores, or learning objectives. They are worth so much more than that. Take time to appreciate them, to center their humanity, and to listen to them. Resist the sense of urgency, slow down, and take care of your students and yourself.

REFERENCES

Bintliff, A. (2014, July 22). Talking circles: For restorative justice and beyond. Retrieved from https://www.tolerance.org/magazine/talking-circles-for-restorative-justice-and-beyond

Paris, D., & Alim, H. S. (2017). *Culturally sustaining pedagogies: Teaching and learning for justice in a changing world*. New York, NY: Teachers College Press.

Shalaby, C. (2017). *Troublemakers: Lessons in freedom from young children at school*. New York, NY: The New Press.

MATTHEW HOMRICH-KNEILING is an ELA teacher and restorative justice coordinator in Detroit. He's a co-founder of MIStudentsDream, a coalition of educators, students, and community members organizing and advocating at the intersection of immigration and education justice. His work has appeared in *Learning for Justice*, *Voices from the Middle*, and *Education Week*. His teaching and organizing focuses on community-based, culturally-sustaining, & abolitionist pedagogies, youth organizing, and transformative justice. The views expressed in his chapter do not necessarily reflect the views of his employer.

This article originally appeared in *College English* 83.3

ACCESS FATIGUE: The Rhetorical Work of Disability in Everyday Life

ANNIKA M. KONRAD

> **Pressure is hard to notice unless you are under pressure. A system can put some bodies under pressure without that pressure being experienced, let alone witnessed by others who are not under that pressure.**
>
> —SARA AHMED 28

> **And you get to a point where you get so tired of trying to explain to someone that you just don't go into detail, you just don't bring up the subject, you just don't make an issue out of it and it's not that you're trying to hide, it's just that you don't want to get into that debate where people are wondering, "Well, are you . . . ?" "it can't be that bad," or the comment, "Gee, I didn't know it was that bad." They change their whole viewpoint and you're able to see how that's changed when you've told people, when you've fully disclosed versus the ones that you don't say anything to.**
>
> —ETHAN,[1] STUDY PARTICIPANT

WHY IS IT SO HARD to communicate about disability? This is a question that has been sitting in the pit of my gut since I was diagnosed with a blinding disease at age fourteen. This question stayed with me through a graduate course in disability studies and a doctoral dissertation focused on the rhetorical experiences of people who are blind and visually impaired. The gulf that lies between disabled and non-disabled people is so wide and deep I'm not sure I'll ever answer this question, but every time I read Ethan's account above, I am reminded of one reason why it is hard to communicate about disability—every time people with disabilities disclose or show up in public space, they have to confront how we all think and feel about disability, and it is usually not positive. Like Ethan explains, people are confused, sad, surprised, and mostly, they don't know how to react—and disabled people have to deal with the consequences. Not only is it difficult to explain, especially when one does not appear disabled (as Ethan says, people wonder what your status is and say, "Well are you . . . ?"), but it is also taxing to watch people walk through their discomfort about disability and, as Ethan points out, change their opinions of a person's capacities. As a result, as Ethan puts it, "You get so tired of trying to explain to someone that you just don't go into detail, you just don't bring up the subject, you just don't make an issue out of it. Sometimes you just don't say anything at all." The exhaustion that Ethan describes illustrates a concept I call *access fatigue*, which names the everyday pattern of constantly needing to help others participate in access, a demand so taxing and so relentless that, at times, it makes access simply not worth the effort.

And yet, access often depends on one's ability to communicate. A recent and rich body of scholarship at the intersections of disability studies and rhetoric studies has shown how seeking access depends on the difficult and risky rhetorical work of navigating power relationships and institutional barriers. While findings from my study of the rhetorical experiences of people who are blind and visually impaired demonstrate a similar phenomenon, my findings also reveal how the need to help others participate in access is an everyday pattern that can accumulate to the point of giving up on access altogether. Developed from twenty-two interviews with people who are blind and visually impaired, several rounds of qualitative data analysis, and reflection on my own personal experience, the concept of access fatigue theorizes access through the lens of fatigue, demonstrating how access requires constantly taking care of one's self while taking care of others. The stories of access fatigue shared in this essay show how seeking access necessitates that disabled people constantly toggle between self-invention and self-preservation because inventing a self that is suitable for public engagement requires confronting how other people think and feel about disability, which in turn can re-inform one's own sense of self. Practically speaking, then, not every exchange is worth the effort, and participants in my study described having to weigh the value of each exchange. In an attempt to curtail these demands, participants in my study attempt to teach skills of access they hope others will transfer to future situations, but this pedagogical work, too, is fatiguing.

One might assume that people with disabilities automatically or instinctively know how to—or always want to—advocate for their own access. People with disabilities are often encouraged to advocate for their own access without consideration for the mental and emotional labor required to do so. For example, in a seminar titled, "Talking about Low Vision: Language and Vocabulary to Explain Your Experience to Family, Friends, and Community," a vision rehabilitation teacher and visually impaired person named Dr. Linda Fugate suggests that people with low vision respond to discomfort and unease by adjusting their own personal affect: "If they see that you have a lighter approach to your vision, that you're okay with it, then they can be okay with it" ("Low Vision Focus"). While strategies like Fugate's might be an effective way to quell discomfort surrounding disability, logics that motivate disabled people to be independently responsible for their own access often do not take into account how confronting and managing how others think and feel about disability is a mentally and emotionally exhausting activity that is, at times, simply not worth the effort.

And yet in the public imagination, access is largely a procedural matter—one that happens by procuring resources for qualified individuals in the appropriate times and places or, as disability scholars Elizabeth Brewer, Cynthia Selfe, and Remi Yergeau call it, "consumptive access" (151). A recent and rich body of scholarship at the intersections of disability and rhetoric studies has shown us that access is a deeply rhetorical act for which disabled people carry the heavy burden (Kerschbaum; Kerschbaum et al; Price, *Mad at School*; Yergeau; Dolmage; Simpkins; Cedillo; Brueggemann; Wood). While these scholars continue to advocate for collective, interactive, and dynamic approaches to access that involve everyone—not just disabled people—it remains uncommon to encounter such a dynamic approach to access in daily life (Price et al.). Accessibility remains an afterthought and disabled people are, as sociologist Tanya Titchkosky puts it, "justifiably excludable" (78). Disability scholarship published in *College English* re-theorizes writing, rhetoric, and literacy through the lens of disability (Brueggemann; Ceraso; Heilker and Yergeau; Miller; Mossman; Rinaldi; Vidali), but as Lauren Obermark points out in her recent article, in practice, accessibility is often brushed aside—what she calls the "disability bypass"—allowing people to excuse themselves from the situation of access. The dilemma that lingers, then, is that we have theoretical understanding of access as a collaborative, interactive process but no structure of habit for practicing collective access in everyday life. To work toward building a structure of habit for collective access in everyday life—that *already* and *always* involves everyone and their own multiple forms of identification—in this article I offer the concept of access fatigue as a framework for noticing the habits that need to change to support more inclusive public life.

While experiences of fatigue were common across all twenty-two life history interviews, participants' rhetorical experiences were never *only* about disability. The ways each individual musters energy and navigates feelings of fatigue are intertwined with axes of oppression and privilege. For example, Roberto's experience advocating for his own access in each of his careers was shaped by each professional field's expectations and normative workplace commonplaces (a concept developed from this study that I explore in "Reimagining Work: Normative

Commonplaces and their Effects on Accessibility in Workplaces" published in *Business and Professional Communication Quarterly*). In addition to the particular standards of each professional field, gender shaped his rhetorical experience. For instance, when his friends and family members suggested he settle for a job in telemarketing, he wondered how, as a father, he could provide for his family on a telemarketer income. As a blind man, the pressure to be the breadwinner for his family felt especially heavy. Similarly, Ethan described switching seats with his wife in the car before pulling up to a friend's house so that it would appear that he was driving. On the other hand, privilege might aid in seeking access in certain situations. For example, Roberto's male gender could have aided his ability to build his credibility as a blind auto mechanic. The rhetorical work of access and its fatiguing nature as explored in this article are intimately intertwined with a multitude of identity and context factors that shape each person's experiences of privilege and oppression.

Below I demonstrate how paying attention to fatigue in the rhetorical work of access reveals how minute requirements for access accumulate and interact with other forms of privilege and marginalization and can result in the loss of access itself. First, I explain how access fatigue builds upon concepts from critical race studies, intersectional feminist studies, and disability studies by bringing these conversations together through a new framework that reveals how rhetorical demands for access can accumulate and make the pursuit of access fatiguing. Then I explain how utilizing a rhetorical life history interview method allowed me to uncover the accumulation of rhetorical demands in lived experiences of people who are blind and visually impaired. In my analysis of participant accounts, I share four interconnected dimensions of negotiating access that I found make the work of access fatiguing: Access requires (1) inventing a disabled self that is suitable for public engagement, an activity that can involve (2) confronting audience reactions to disability, which can re-inform a disabled person's own sense of self and be so taxing that they need to preserve their own energy by (3) weighing the value of each exchange and (4) teaching others how to participate in access. I end by explaining how scholars and teachers across disciplines can release some of this pressure on disabled people by developing a structure of habit for access in everyday life.

Accumulation in the Rhetorical Work of Access

Access fatigue builds upon previous scholarship in critical race studies and intersectional feminist studies that has shown the impacts of accumulation in everyday experiences of oppression. Access fatigue extends this conversation by bringing attention to the specific rhetorical demands required for accessibility—an activity that often requires the involvement of others and teaching audiences to do things in new and more collaborative ways. The concept of microaggressions (Sue) has drawn attention to how subtle, everyday behaviors, whether intentional or not, can go unnoticed and accumulate to the point of harming marginalized people (Sue et al.). While the stories shared in this article may contain accounts of microaggressions, the concept of access fatigue draws attention to the specific labor of involving others in accessibility, which, similar to microaggressions, often unearths how people think and feel about disability. While microaggressions have become part of public discourse, most people are less familiar with microaggressions stemming from ableism, and few studies of microaggressions have focused on people with disabilities (Olkin et al. 757). Rather than raise awareness about specific microaggressions stemming from ableism, the concept of access fatigue reveals how a lack of familiarity with disability and practices of accessibility places pressures on disabled people to teach others how to participate in access.

The concept of "the Black[2] tax," as theorized by rhetoric scholar Cedric Burrows, provides a foundation for understanding why the labor marginalized people need to perform to participate in the dominant society is especially taxing. Burrows explains that since African-Americans have historically been viewed as a problem, they are taxed with the burden of working twice as hard to prove their respectability in white society. This pressure is especially taxing because, Burrows explains, it requires being constantly viewed through the lens of whiteness. Like the Black tax, access fatigue reveals how access depends on performing forms of disability acceptable for other people—in other words, access fatigue demonstrates how access is just as much about other people and their thoughts and feelings about disability as it is about disabled people's own needs. And the process of being rhetorical about access can be especially taxing because, like the Black tax, it exposes disabled people to how others think and feel about disability, which can then re-inform their own sense of self. While there are important distinctions between the ways racialized bodies and disabled bodies have been viewed as problems—and have faced different forms of violence and oppression—access fatigue outlines the specific demands placed on disabled people to teach others how to participate in access while at the same time confronting their thoughts and feelings about disability.

The concept of access fatigue also builds upon intersectional feminist scholar Sara Ahmed's concept of "hammering," which refers to the work that non-gender-conforming people have to do to be accepted in social space. According to Ahmed, hammering is a labor that non-gender-conforming people must perform in social space: "If you do not conform to an idea of woman—of who she is, how she comes to be, how she appears—then you become a diversity worker in both senses. For to exist as a woman would require chipping away at the walls that demarcate who resides there, who belongs there" (32). Like hammering, access fatigue demonstrates how seeking access necessitates a kind of diversity work, a rhetorical pedagogy of interdependence in this case, in which disabled people have to constantly teach and re-teach non-normative ways of being and moving in social space. Ahmed explains that institutions erect walls that only exist in front of those who fall outside the boundaries of their norms. These walls, she argues, are "experienced as hard and tangible by some [but] do not even exist for others" (32). Through a practice of hammering, a tool for chipping away at these walls, diversity workers can make these walls visible to everyone who implicitly participates in hardening them. Access fatigue participates in the project of hammering by providing a framework for noticing the everyday habits we all hold that make the work of seeking access so mentally and emotionally taxing for disabled people.

Disability scholars have shown how rhetorical acts characteristic of disability experience, like disclosure and accommodations requests, require navigating power relationships and accommodating other people. Stephanie Kerschbaum argues that disability disclosure requires that both speaker and audience understand disability as identity—not as a deficiency—which is rare among the general public (69). Seeking individual accommodations, too, can require managing how other people feel about disability (Jung; Simpkins; Womack; Wood). Disability justice activist Mia Mingus uses the term "forced intimacy" to describe the emotion work disabled people have to do to gain access: "[D]isabled people have to build and sustain emotional intimacy and relationships with someone in order to get access—to get safe, appropriate, and good access" ("Forced Intimacy"). Feminist bioethicist Jackie Leach Scully argues that such relationships are unethical, calling attention to the "hidden labor" of disability, or the pressure for disabled people to manipulate audience expectations and perceptions. Through attention to accumulation, the concept of access fatigue builds upon prior attention to the power relationships that shape disability access by naming the everyday pattern of constantly needing to help others participate in access and shows how access depends on both self-invention and self-preservation.

Through access fatigue, we can see how marginalization and oppression are experiences of simultaneously acting out and drawing in, speaking out and staying quiet, showing up and staying home, because the logics that structure our habits for engagement with difference depend on individuals' own rhetorical activities and ability to cope with the consequences of doing so. Access fatigue attunes us to the ways everyday demands for rhetoric accumulate and cause moments of engagement and disengagement, which shows how both self-invention and self-preservation are required for responding to logics of individual responsibility for access. By building upon previous scholarship of race, gender, and disability, access fatigue participates in the imperative to better understand the societal conditions that pressure disabled people to rely on their own self—rather than all people and their complicit participation in systems of power that create inaccessible spaces. Rather than rely on people with disabilities to continue accommodating audience expectations, access fatigue provides a means to identify the habits and structures that need to change to support more inclusive public life.

A Life History Method for Everyday Rhetorical Experience

I originally set out to understand the role of rhetoric in everyday life with disability. To do so I elected to use a life history method for gathering interview data because I wanted to understand how duration shapes rhetorical experience, something that I believe ultimately led me to the concept of fatigue.

I knew from personal experience and experience in the community that disability is not static, and as Margaret Price advises in "Disability Studies Methodology: Explaining Ourselves to Ourselves," the embodied status of both researcher and participant should be treated as ever-evolving. Life history is a qualitative research method that aims to undersand life experiences over time in the greater context of people's lives (Cole and Knowles), which provides a useful framework for understanding how a person's relationship to rhetoric and disability evolves over time within the greater context of their lives. I used Deborah Brandt's literacy life history interview protocol as a guide for how to structure an interview that investigates the development of linguistic experience over the course of a lifespan (208–210). While Brandt's interview protocol focuses on literacy, I used its organization as a model for designing a life history interview that investigates the forces that shape rhetorical experience over a lifespan.

The protocol was divided into three life stages (early childhood through teenage years, mid-life, and middle adulthood through later adulthood) and seven contexts in which I hypothesized individuals might communicate about disability (school, work, family life, community, social life/leisure, medical contexts, and social/political advocacy). I also asked participants questions about their general relationship to disability at each of their life stages in order to understand the relationship between the development of disability identity and communication experiences. Interviews were semistructured to allow participants to describe the communication experiences and strategies most meaningful to them.

Participants were recruited through a community-writing project and my own involvement in local blind and visually impaired community activities. The majority of participants were blind and visually impaired individuals, but I also interviewed one parent of a blind child and two blindness professionals, one of whom is also visually impaired. Participant ages at the time of the interviews ranged from 21 to 72, and they represented people who identify as blind, visually impaired, and low vision, though many participants use these labels interchangeably. Participants included those who have been blind or visually impaired since birth and those who began experiencing vision loss in childhood and adulthood.

To allow participant narratives to drive the meaning-making process, data were collected and analyzed using a grounded theory approach (Charmaz), a qualitative research method that emphasizes making meaning from the ground up through multiple rounds of reiterative coding to discover common themes across interviews. I observed that while participants described times when they engage in rhetorical activity, they also described many times when they chose not to. And in fact much of the data were not about what I call "external rhetorical experience," but instead about "internal rhetorical experience," or their internal processes of invention and coping with the demands to be rhetorical. I conducted a second round of more focused coding to understand the relationship between "external" and "internal" experiences of rhetoric. While I found it difficult to distinguish between the two, it was through this process that the theme of fatigue emerged, and another round of coding was performed to identify evidence of exhaustion or fatigue. These narratives were then sorted into four categories that describe some of what makes the rhetorical labor of access fatiguing: Access requires (1) a performance of self, (2) confronting audience reactions, (3) a value exchange, and (4) a rhetorical pedagogy. For this article, I selected those examples that most clearly exemplify the above four defining features of access fatigue.

While I focus on the experiences of people who are blind and visually impaired to develop the concept of access fatigue, many aspects of identity and embodiment shape this phenomenon, as the disabled self cannot be understood in isolation from other forms of privilege and marginalization. Most notably, I found that gender, race, age, and use of assistive technology are important factors in how individuals experience the rhetorical situation of access. There are, of course, particularities to blindness and visual impairment that shape participant experiences of public engagement—blindness is one of the most feared and mythologized disabilities (Kleege; Bolt; Rodas). At the same time, there is great diversity among blind and visually impaired people—blindness is a wide spectrum, and appearing blind is not the same as being visually impaired and having no markers of disability. Conclusions from this study cannot be generalized to all people with disabilities, but my conclusions about what makes the work of access especially fatiguing are likely resonant across disability experiences. In each narrative below, I discuss how multiple identifications—not only disability—shape experiences of access fatigue.

Why Is Access So Fatiguing?

On its surface, access fatigue describes the physical and mental exhaustion that results from the work of seeking access. When examined through a rhetorical lens, however, paying attention to fatigue helps us see how access depends on how we all think and feel about disability. In order to navigate audience thoughts and feelings about disability, participants have to practice both rhetorical self-invention and self-preservation. I found four interrelated components of negotiating access that contribute to its fatiguing nature. First, access requires that disabled people perform a disabled self that is suitable for public engagement, which can involve managing their own personal affect, even when being denied access. Second, being rhetorical about access can expose disabled people to audience thoughts and feelings about disability, which can then re-inform their own sense of self, affecting their willingness to continue engaging. Third, given the high levels of mental and emotional energy required for this work, access requires weighing the value of each exchange to determine whether it is worth the effort. Fourth, in response to these intensive demands, some participants described developing pedagogies they can use to teach better access behavior to others so they can preserve some of their own energy, but this pedagogical work, too, is fatiguing.

ACCESS REQUIRES A PERFORMANCE OF SELF

The rhetorical labor of access involves making disability and inaccessibility "okay" for other people, which often involves performing a disabled self that helps others feel more at ease. Mingus explains that disabled people know well that their access depends on their invention of a friendly disabled self: "[A]s disabled people know all too well, able bodied people will not help you with your access unless they 'like' you" ("This is Why Consent"). The following two examples demonstrate how material and social forms of access rely on disabled people's abilities to make others feel better about disability, and these pressures are deeply intertwined with axes of oppression and privilege shaped by gender, race, age, and use of assistive technology.

Candace's narrative was marked by feelings of social isolation and difficulty finding a job for years after college. Candace is a white woman in her thirties who travels with a guide dog and recently relocated for a new job. She lives alone and has no family members in town. Having recently moved to the city, she spent a lot of time learning the bus system and how to navigate various public spaces she needs to traverse on a regular basis. It takes Candace an hour or more to get to and from work every day, while it would take twenty minutes to travel the same distance by car. At the time of our interview, she was working in data entry at a company that receives government subsidies to employ people who are blind and visually impaired. She described multiple instances in her lifetime when she encountered a communication barrier—in college she felt like no one would sit near her in classrooms or stop by her dorm room to socialize. More recently, she feels like people avoid saying hello to her in public places like at bus stops. She also described the paternalistic way that people attempt to help her navigate by grabbing or pulling her dog's harness, insisting that they know where she wants to go. When I asked her how she responds to these situations, she described trying to remain polite—a pressure that in at least one instance accumulated to the point of removing herself from the situation.

At one particular grocery store she has been repeatedly denied access to help from a store shopper, an accommodation that is supposed to be available at grocery stores and something she learned to ask for in her orientation and mobility training. When she was repeatedly told at one particular store that they were too busy to help her, Candace described remaining polite and smiling: "I mean I don't really show them my frustration. I just try to smile but inside I'm at like a hundred degrees." Candace explained that the frustration she feels and the pressure to remain polite have caused her to stop shopping alone at that particular grocery store. She encountered this barrier so many times that she simply gave up, which means she can only shop there when a friend or family member can accompany her. Given the time and energy she has to spend traveling around the city by bus searching for a grocery store where someone will help her, it is evident how needing to expend extra energy to get help simply becomes not worth the effort. The public rhetorical work of inventing a polite disabled self has emotional and material consequences for Candace, important factors in causing her to stop advocating for her own access and allowing ableist and normative practices to prevail.

Nadine, an African-American woman in her twenties who travels with a white cane, recently graduated college and moved away from home to pursue a graduate degree. Her narrative was marked by the overwhelming burden of having to deal with the discomfort that people feel in her presence. Although Nadine has different styles of white canes to match different outfits, she described finding it difficult to move through public space without causing discomfort:

> It's a huge announcement and I've talked to my friends and I've said it's difficult because sometimes you don't want everyone to look at you when you walk into a room. Sometimes you just want to sneak in and go, especially if your hair's not done or you're just not feeling good, anything that any other woman is dealing with, that you're just like I just want to blend in.

To cope with this burden, Nadine shared advice from a friend: "My friend told me in a very beautiful way, she said, 'You're not built for that. You're not built to just blend into the background. That's not who you are, that's not who you've ever been. And so you're going to have to step into who you are.' And that's just all there is to it."

While she has worked hard to "step into" who she is, Nadine emphasized the amount of time and energy she has to expend getting people comfortable with her. Nadine described how access often depends on her ability to display her own comfort in the world: "Sometimes I spend more time getting people comfortable with the fact that I'm comfortable." She went on to describe how aspects of her physical embodiment influence the ways people interact with her. Her facial expressions, she explained, influence how others talk to her: "If I have an expression on my face where I am very anxious, very confused, or very nervous, people will talk down to me often. I get this reaction on average whereby they speak, 'Ma'am do you know where you're going? Are you okay?' [speaking like speaking to a child]. I get that often." In contrast, if she has a relaxed expression on her face, people react differently: "But if I am very laid back, or I feel very confident, my expression is one of relaxation and comfort and if I'm okay in that sense people react to me differently." At the same time, she finds that she needs to respond to the anxiety and discomfort people bring to their interactions. Nadine said, "I'll often be the one calming them down." Projecting a comfortable, friendly disabled self, even in the face of paternalism, is often a requirement for engaging audiences in access.

Candace and Nadine's narratives demonstrate how the rhetorical work of access depends on the performance of an "okay" disabled self. Candace feels a pressure to remain polite while Nadine needs to calm people in order for them to engage. In this way these examples show how access is just as much about their audience's thoughts and feelings in the presence of disabled bodies as it is about the interdependence they need. Candace finds times when this demand is so fatiguing that she withdraws, and Nadine's account hints at the constant burden she feels at never being able to "sneak in and go," and she stresses the time she has to spend convincing people that she is comfortable ("Sometimes I spend more time . . . "). They each encounter different forms of discomfort, denial, and confusion. While Candace feels pressured to remain polite, even in the face of access denials, Nadine feels that she needs to calm people down in order to get them to help her. Both Candace and Nadine are female-identifying participants who might experience greater pressure to remain nice in the face of access refusals, while male-identifying people may feel more comfortable taking a more assertive stance. In addition to gender, race can compound access fatigue, contributing to the level of discomfort a person with a disability encounters (or does not encounter) and the amount of energy they need to put toward calming others down. Modalities, like the use of a white cane versus a guide dog, for example, are received differently in public space; guide dogs can incite controversy, while white canes often make people confused. What is clear in both instances is that the pressure to perform a particular kind of disabled self—one that makes other people feel better, whether about disability, race, gender, assistive technology or all four—is fatiguing, and the pressure can be so overwhelming that sometimes people give up.

ACCESS REQUIRES CONFRONTING AUDIENCE REACTIONS

As the above examples demonstrate, performing a disabled self for others can mean confronting how people think and feel about disability, which is exhausting because it can influence a person's own sense of self and their willingness to engage. Participant accounts below demonstrate how being rhetorical about disability exposes people to audience ideas about disability and accessibility, which can in turn shape one's own sense of self. These examples show how a requirement for the rhetorical work of access is a belief in yourself as a being with agency.

Like many other participants, Lisa's narrative centered around her lifelong process of coming to terms with her own disability, which she explained coincided with her process of learning to communicate about it. Lisa is a visually impaired white woman who travels with a white cane. Looking back on her experiences, Lisa explained that over time she learned that if she does not feel positive or confident about herself in the moment, then she cannot communicate as effectively with others. Lisa described that her internal sense of self and experiences communicating about disability exist in a "dynamic loop" in which the ways she perceives herself and the ways others react to her constantly re-inform one another. Lisa's narrative demonstrates how access requires confronting audience reactions to disability, which, in the example below, sometimes involves confusing and inaccessible information, which requires that Lisa spend time and energy redirecting people and teaching them how to help.

Lisa described a time when an audience reaction would have required so much extra labor in a moment when she wasn't feeling confident that she lost the will to continue engaging. After a long day of being guided around an unfamiliar campus, she told her friend that she didn't need directions back to her dorm, but when she walked out of the building, she discovered that she had no idea how to get back to her dorm, so she asked a stranger for directions. Lisa describes the stranger's response: "[T]hey're like, 'they're right over—': the infamous 'right over [there],' which is so not useful." Lisa explained that given this response, which did not provide her the information she needed in a way that is accessible to her, and given that she was already exhausted, she withdrew from the task of teaching her interlocutor how to respond: "And at that point I was so undone and so tired and so overwhelmed. The usual thing I would say is, 'Well can you please, can you describe that to me because I don't see where you're pointing.' I couldn't even do it. I was like okay, I'll figure it out. I'll go in that general direction. I'll figure it out." Reflecting upon this situation, Lisa described a direct connection between how she feels internally and her ability to perform the public rhetorical work of access:

> I was really aware that the more fatigued I am or feeling unconfident or whatever else is going on when I ask for help and someone doesn't give good directions, then it's just like, now it's another layer of having to ask and sometimes it's just like, forget it. I'll figure it out. Back to that old thing [referring to a period in her life when she did not ask for help] because it's now more exhausting to ask you for more directions than it is to just figure it out.

Lisa makes it clear that sometimes, it is so exhausting to teach people how to help her that it is more beneficial to her own self-preservation to disengage.

Similarly, Nadine described a time when an audience reaction to her blindness affected her self-perception and prevented her from eating at her school cafeteria. One day in college, Nadine entered the cafeteria and heard a peer refer to her as "the blind girl": "And it just threw me so hard I don't even think I ate my dinner after that, or my lunch. It hit me so hard, like a ton of bricks . . . It was just such a blow to me, and I didn't go back to that cafeteria for some time." In this example an audience reaction to her disabled self as one-dimensional caused Nadine to withdraw from public engagement. Nadine did not return to that cafeteria for months, which affected how she acquired food. She began asking her mother to take her on more trips to the grocery store so she could eat meals in her dorm, but eventually her mother figured out that something unusual was going on. Instead of advocating for herself, Nadine turned to her mother: "I didn't have the strength to do that when you just have so much other stuff going on." This moment stood out to Nadine as a time when her audience's reaction to her embodied presence stifled her rhetorical abilities. In this instance she relied on her mother to call an authority at the school and explain the importance of teaching students to refer to Nadine by name. This example demonstrates how the self-invention and self-preservation of access are intertwined—while access requires self-invention, it also requires coping with audience reactions to that disabled self, which in turn, re-inform one's own sense of self and willingness to engage. As Ethan described in the passage shared in the epigraph, he spent decades avoiding disclosure because it exposes him to how people think about disability: "They change their whole viewpoint and you're able to see how that's changed when you've told people, when you've fully disclosed versus the ones that you don't say anything to."

Some people with disabilities, like Ethan, have the privilege of deciding whether or not to disclose. For others with visible disabilities or who carry assistive technologies, disclosure is not optional—what does this mean, then, for the amount of labor they have to perform for access? Like Burrows' concept of the Black tax, access fatigue reveals how being rhetorical as a disabled person—whether through disclosure or simply showing up—turns up how other people view people with disabilities. In Nadine's experience of showing up in the cafeteria, she had to confront how people think of her as a label ("the blind girl"), a fatiguing experience that prevented further engagement. When Lisa asked for directions but did not disclose her disability, she was faced with inaccessible information that required her rhetorical energy for teaching her audience how to reshape their response in a way that would help her. Both these examples show how access requires confronting how people respond to disability, often in negative, confusing, or denigrating ways, which at times can cause people with disabilities to shut down, even at the expense of access itself.

ACCESS REQUIRES A VALUE EXCHANGE

On a daily basis, individuals with disabilities must input intellectual and emotional energy into rhetorical situations in hopes that they will receive something, like help from a grocery store employee or directions to a specific location. In this way, access is a value exchange, and participants described needing to calculate whether each exchange is worth the effort. At times, the sheer volume and frequency of the rhetorical demands of access make seeking access simply not worth the effort. The value of access is also intertwined with other forms of inclusion and requires weighing access against the labor required for dealing with multiple forms of violence and oppression.

Roberto, who was previously introduced, assesses the value of each exchange based on the potential outcomes. When a school district claimed that Roberto cannot be a teacher after a long career teaching in another US state because he cannot "monitor" students, he had to weigh the value of the exchange: "I've worked for all these years. I'm like an old plow-horse. I miss being in the harness, but it's one of those things where it's an ongoing battle, you have to know when to pick your battles. You have to know when to pick them and when to just walk away." Roberto chooses his battle based on how many people he thinks the access barrier might affect. In the case of advocating for his ability to work in the school district, Roberto thought about all the other blind and visually impaired people who want to teach: "I look at it like all the blind people that are going to come after me that are going to get education and aren't going to be able to get a job teaching because they tell them you're blind and you can't monitor." In this instance, then, he decided to take the case to court and spent several years in a legal battle that he ultimately lost. In other instances, Roberto rationalized that the rhetorical work of access was not worth his effort, or as he put it, "this is not a hill to die on."

Assessing the value of each exchange can also involve weighing access against other forms of inclusion. Nadine explained that she has to "figure out which battles to fight" because she has to weigh access against racial inclusion: "I'll find people who are very helpful to me with certain things related to my disability, with helping me get around, get my food at a buffet, but I also will hear some of those individuals say some things that are just really racially insensitive or just ignorant." Nadine went on to explain that in these instances, she has to pick and choose her battles and sometimes she prioritizes the immediate accessibility need over respect for other aspects of her identity: "And figuring out which one of those things do you deal with. And so that can be challenging, and again it's unfortunate but trying to discern, do you challenge and potentially get into an argument or do you ensure that you're going to get home safely tonight?" Nadine's example demonstrates how access work has physical consequences, too. In this situation her physical safety is at risk in at least two ways—if she challenges the interlocutor on an issue related to race, she risks losing a ride home, but if she accepts a ride home, she could risk her safety because of her race. For some individuals, the rhetorical labor of access involves not only assessing how much energy is required but also weighing access against other forms of violence and oppression. For Nadine, it is not only a question of preserving her energy, but also a question of protecting her safety.

Other participants noted the sheer volume and frequency of the rhetorical work of access. Walter, a professional who teaches orientation and mobility skills to people who are blind and visually impaired, has observed that there are so many decisions to make even within a single interaction—and so many interactions within a single day—that you have to pick and choose. He said, "You got to go through a value, a rating system, how much is this worth?" The weight of each exchange, however, is shaped by multiple identity factors. Nadine has to weigh access related to disability against racial violence, placing higher demands on individuals who have to pick and choose between different types of inclusion and oppression. Needing to negotiate multiple forms of inclusion may mean individuals are worn down from fighting battles on other fronts, too. The self-preservation that is required for access cannot be isolated from other rhetorical burdens that result from oppression and marginalization.

ACCESS REQUIRES RHETORICAL PEDAGOGY

By now it should be apparent that access often requires teaching others how to engage. Rhetorical pedagogies of access involve teaching specific habits and ways of thinking so that people can participate in creating access. This teaching can be quite repetitive and is sometimes needed multiple times throughout the course of a single interaction. Given that single interactions can require multiple pedagogical moves, some participants described pedagogical strategies they developed for teaching access-oriented behaviors that they hope will transfer to future situations. In other words, the public rhetorical work of access can be so repetitive that some participants have developed pedagogies they hope will curtail demands for their rhetorical efforts.

Curtis, a white male in his fifties who travels with a guide dog, described a deep commitment to educating the public about disability and accessibility. Curtis navigates through access denials by teaching audiences about their responsibilities for access. He described doing so by "arming them with information."

When he is denied access to public places because of his guide dog, which he said has happened "30, 35, 40, 45" times, he combines a "cool, calm, collected" demeanor with specific information about his rights and the responsibilities of the business owner. For example, he has memorized the state's public accommodations law, Americans with Disabilities Act (ADA) Title Three, and the exact phone number for the ADA hotline and the URL for ADA guidelines website, all of which he recited in our interview:

> [In a very soft, sweet tone] I'd love to tell you more about what the [State] Public Accommodations law and the Americans with Disabilities Act say, and what they provide for you as a business owner, as well as for me as a person with a legitimate service animal, service dog in this case.

Even when being denied civil rights, Curtis finds it important to educate his audiences about their responsibilities for access because he is aware of all the guide dog users who might come after him. He wants to make a positive impression to encourage future engagement while educating the public about their role in access. He believes that changing people's attitudes might help improve how the public engages with disability and wants to avoid shutting down future interactions by reacting with hostility. The ease and authority that Curtis brings to these access denials, however, stands in contrast to those of participants like Candace and Nadine, who have to spend considerable amounts of time and energy managing their own personal affect to perform a "nice" disabled self. While Curtis employs a dose of niceness in his pedagogy, his gender, age, and racial privilege might make it more possible for him to take an authoritative approach.

Abigail, a blind white woman who travels with a guide dog, told a narrative of developing a rhetorical strategy over time that evolved from what she called "it's the law" to "how can everyone win here?" In other words, she remembers that she used to try to navigate through inaccessibility by leaning into her legal rights, but over time she has learned that it is more effective to frame access as something that benefits everyone. She noted the difficulty, though, of getting people to practice access on their own without her prompting them.

For example, she described that she has been trying to teach people in her church community how to break what she calls the "isolation bubble" that surrounds people with disabilities. "Mix and mingles," she explained, are difficult for her because she cannot take food from a buffet line without assistance and she cannot spot a friend to sit by unless they are talking loudly. Abigail has taken a multimodal approach—verbally providing tips for interaction during meetings, writing in church publications, writing for a statewide storytelling project, and recording a story for the state's public radio station. Despite her multimodal approach to teaching access, she remarked that it is a long process that requires stamina: "To keep putting myself in those spots, because I'm on the parish council, people have obviously voted me in, but then at the same point when it comes to a mix and mingle it's ugly for five minutes and then it's all fine." Here, Abigail refers to the repetitive nature of the work ("to keep putting myself in those spots") and how it requires re-entering situations where she has not made much progress ("it's ugly for five minutes"). Abigail commented on how repeating the rhetorical work means that she might make only marginal progress: "To keep doing those things and know that next time we might get it down to 4.3 minutes or—that's the hard stuff." Finally, Abigail notes that teaching people to actually uptake the rhetorical work of access without her prompting them is even harder: "Because you can educate and you can give them five tips or they can see it in their bulletin or wherever, it's on the Catholic Digest for November, but to translate that into, 'Can I help you through the line?' That's a long process."

TEACHING TIPS

People who live with disabilities require more than procedural and policy efforts to live a fulfilling life with minimal trauma. One might assume, Konrad explains, "that people with disabilities automatically or instinctively know how to—or always want to—advocate for their own access." Access has at least four requirements: (1) performance of self; (2) confronting audience reactions; (3) value exchanges; and (4) a rhetorical pedagogy. Therefore, Konrad theorizes the concept of access through the lens of fatigue. "Access fatigue" provides a framework for understanding the daily patterns of mental and emotional rhetorical labor that is both taxing and relentless for people who depend on access. To mitigate harm, arrange a conversation with your local disability resources office. Familiarize yourself and your students about micro- and macro-level disability resources available in your teaching context. Use available disability access resources as a guide to revise your teaching, curriculum, course policies, and practices accordingly.

Toward a Structure of Habit for Access in Everyday Life

In this article, I have drawn from life histories shared by blind and visually impaired people to offer a concept of access fatigue that builds on a body of work in disability studies, critical race studies, and intersectional feminism that shows how everyday rhetorical actions accumulate and contribute to fatigue. By theorizing access through the lens of fatigue, I have shown how both rhetorical self-invention and self-preservation are necessary for the demands of access. The above examples show how access requires managing how we all think and feel about disability—a demand that necessitates constant toggling between showing up and staying home, speaking up and staying quiet, turning on and shutting down. By treating moments of disengagement as sites of action rather than inaction, we can see how access is a rhetorical experience that requires a great deal of mental and emotional energy, which are not unlimited resources. Logics that construct disabled people as independently responsible for their own access place unexamined pressures on people with disabilities to say more, perform more, and do more for their own access, ignoring the mental, material, and emotional costs of doing so.

Understandably, readers always want to know what they should do. Ironically, this leaves me with the additional burden of teaching other people how to do access. This is a burden that I, and others in my study, at times accept because there is often no other option for changing systems of power and oppression. With knowledge of the concept of access fatigue, however, I want to urge readers to take on the critical internal work of unraveling our thoughts and feelings about disability to develop everyday habits of access. There are of course many pragmatic ways to facilitate access in our communities—for example Universal Design and Universal Design for Learning offer frameworks for incorporating access into the design of spaces and experiences. While it is important to meet the needs of disabled people through the design of accessible spaces and experiences, access fatigue demonstrates the additional need for a structure of habit for access in everyday life.

Habits for access in everyday life are essential because, as the above narratives show, the rhetorical work of access does not only occur during momentous rhetorical events—it happens on the fly, on the ground, over the course of a lifespan, and it occurs even when we least expect it—sometimes simply by showing up. These habits, however, should not be practiced out of obligation or without care. A structure of habit for access in everyday life requires the critical internal work of examining how we think and feel about disability, so we can approach the work of access through relationships structured around care and interdependence. Based on the four qualities of access that contribute to fatigue outlined above, a structure of habit for access in everyday life should include habits for inviting engagement with difference, embracing unfamiliar relationality, exercising a notion of agency that includes disability and use of assistive technology, and uptake and transfer of access-oriented practices from one situation to another.

While the concept of access fatigue as it is theorized in this article only partially explains why it is so hard to communicate about disability, naming the everyday experience of constantly needing to say more and do more for access personally brings me some relief. Ethan said, "People often say that I'm in denial," referring to the way people blame him for not disclosing or making his disability apparent to other people. "But I always say I'm in defiance," he said, by which he meant that by choosing not to communicate about his disability he is strategically side-stepping the pressures to be openly disabled because he knows there are high mental, material, and emotional costs of doing so. By naming the experience of fatigue—and demonstrating how it originates not from within disabled individuals themselves but from outside pressures we all perpetuate that construct disabled people as independently responsible for access—we can relieve some of the pressure. Rather than making disability okay for other people, access fatigue instead makes it okay at times to say nothing at all.

NOTES

1. All study participants are referred to with pseudonyms.
2. While Burrows did not originally capitalize "Black" in "the Black tax," I have chosen to do so in solidarity with the Black Lives Matter movement and to follow the style choice adopted by major news organizations in summer 2020.

WORKS CITED

Ahmed, Sara. "An Affinity of Hammers." *Transgender Studies Quarterly*, vol. 3, nos. 1–2, 2016, pp. 22–34.

Bolt, David. *The Metanarrative of Blindness: A Re-Reading of Twentieth-Century Anglophone Writing*. U of Michigan P, 2013.

Brandt, Deborah. *Literacy in American Lives*. Cambridge UP, 2001.

Brewer, Elizabeth, et al. "Creating a Culture of Access in Composition Studies." *Composition Studies*, vol. 42, no. 2, 2014, pp. 151–54.

Brueggemann, Brenda Jo. *Lend Me Your Ear*. Gallaudet UP, 1999.

———. "On (Almost) Passing." *College English*, vol. 59, no. 6, 1997, pp. 647–60.

Brueggemann, Brenda Jo, and Stephanie Kerschbaum. "Disability: Representation, Disclosure, Access, and Interdependence." *How to Build a Life in the Humanities*, edited by Greg Colón Semenza and Garrett A. Sullivan, Jr., Palgrave Macmillan, 2015, pp. 183–92.

Burrows, Cedric. "Writing While Black: The Black Tax on African American Graduate Writers." *Praxis: A Writing Center Journal*, vol. 14, no. 1, 2016, pp. 15–20. praxisuwc.com/burrows-141

Cedillo, Christina. "What Does It Mean to Move?: Race, Disability, and Critical Embodiment Pedagogy." *Composition Forum*, vol. 39, 2018. compositionforum.com/issue/39/to-move.php

Ceraso, Steph. "(Re)Educating the Senses: Multimodal Listening, Bodily Learning, and the Composition of Sonic Experiences." *College English*, vol. 77, no. 2, 2014, pp. 102–23.

Charmaz, Kathy. *Constructing Grounded Theory: A Practical Guide through Qualitative Analysis*. SAGE Publications Ltd., 2006.

Cole, J. Gary, and Ardra L. Knowles. *Lives in Context: The Art of Life History Research*. AltaMira Press, 2001.

Dolmage, Jay Timothy. *Disability Rhetoric*. Syracuse UP, 2014.

Heilker, Paul, and Remi Yergeau. "Autism and Rhetoric." *College English*, vol. 73, no. 5, 2011, pp. 485–97.

Jung, Julie. "Textual Mainstreaming and Rhetorics of Accommodation." *Rhetoric Review*, vol. 26, no. 2, 2007, pp. 160–78.

Kerschbaum, Stephanie L. "On Rhetorical Agency and Disclosing Disability in Academic Writing." *Rhetoric Review*, vol. 33, no. 1, 2014, pp. 55–71.

Kerschbaum, Stephanie, et al. *Negotiating Disability: Disclosure and Higher Education*. U of Michigan P, 2017.

Kleege, Georgina. *Sight Unseen*. Yale UP, 1999.

Konrad, Annika. "Reimagining Work: Normative Commonplaces and their Affects on Accessibility in Workplaces." *Business and Professional Communication Quarterly*, vol. 81, no. 1, March 2018, pp. 123–41.

"Low Vision Focus @ Hadley Presents: Talking about Low Vision." *Seminars@Hadley*, 21 Jan. 2016.

Miller, Elisabeth. "Literate Misfitting: Disability Theory and a Sociomaterial Approach to Literacy." *College English*, vol. 79, no. 1, 2016, pp. 34–56.

Mingus, Mia. "Forced Intimacy: An Ableist Norm." *Leaving Evidence*, 6 Aug. 2017. leavingevidence.wordpress.com/2017/08/

———. "This Is Why Consent Doesn't Exist for Disabled Folks." *Everyday Feminism*, 20 Aug. 2017. everydayfeminism.com/2017/08/consent-doesnt-exist-disabled/

Mossman, Mark. "Visible Disability in the College Classroom." *College English*, vol. 64, No. 6, 2002, pp. 645–59.

Obermark, Lauren. "Making Space for the Misfit: Disability and Access in Graduate Education in English." *College English*, vol. 82, no. 2, 2019, pp. 173–203.

Olkin, Rhoda, et al. "The Experiences of Microaggressions against Women with Visible and Invisible Disabilities." *Journal of Social Issues*, vol. 75, no. 3, 2019, pp. 757–85.

Price, Margaret. *Mad at School: Rhetorics of Mental Disability and Academic Life*. U of Michigan P, 2011.

———. "Disability Studies Methodology: Explaining Ourselves to Ourselves." *Practicing Research in Writing Studies: Reflexive and Ethically Responsible Research*, edited by Katrina Powell and Pamela Takayoshi, Hampton Press Inc., 2012, pp. 159–86.

Price, Margaret, et al. "Disclosure of Mental Disability by College and University Faculty: The Negotiation of Accommodations, Supports, and Barriers." *Disability Studies Quarterly*, vol. 37, no. 2, 2017. dsq-sds.org/article/view/5487

Rinaldi, Jacqueline. "Rhetoric and Healing: Revising Narratives about Disability." *College English*, vol. 58, no. 7, pp. 820–34.

Rodas, Julia Miele. "On Blindness." *Journal of Literary & Cultural Disability Studies*, vol. 3, no. 2, 2009, pp. 115–30.

Scully, Jackie Leach. "Hidden Labor: Disabled/Nondisabled Encounters, Agency, and Autonomy." *International Journal of Feminist Approaches to Bioethics*, vol. 3, no. 2, 2010, pp. 25–42.

Simpkins, Neil. "Towards an Understanding of Accommodation Transfer: Disabled Students' Strategies for Navigating Classroom Accommodations." *Composition Forum*, vol. 39, 2018. compositionforum.com/issue/39/accommodation-transfer.php

Sue, Derald Wing. *Microaggressions in Everyday Life: Race, Gender, and Sexual Orientation*. Wiley, 2010.

Sue, Derald Wing, et al. "Racial Microaggressions in Everyday Life: Implications for Clinical Practice." *American Psychologist*, vol. 62, no. 4, 2007, pp. 271–86.

Titchkosky, Tanya. *The Question of Access: Disability, Space, Meaning*. University of Toronto Press, 2011.

Vidali, Amy. "Performing the Rhetorical Freak Show: Disability, Student Writing, and College Admissions." *College English*, vol. 69, no. 6, 2007, pp. 615–41.

Wilkinson, Eleanor, and Iliana Ortega-Alcázar. "The Right to Be Weary? Endurance and Exhaustion in Austere Times." *TIBG: Transactions of the Institute of British Geography*, vol. 44, no. 1, 2019, pp. 155–67.

Womack, Anne-Marie. "Teaching Is Accommodation: Universally Designing Composition Classrooms and Syllabi." *College Composition and Communication*, vol. 69, no. 3, 2017, pp. 494–525.

Wood, Tara. "Rhetorical Disclosures: The Stakes of Disability Identity in Higher Education." *Negotiating Disability: Disclosure and Higher Education*, edited by Stephanie L Kerschbaum, et al., U of Michigan P, 2017, pp. 75–93.

Yergeau, Remi. *Authoring Autism: On Rhetoric and Neurological Queerness*. Duke UP, 2018.

Yergeau, Remi, et al. "Multimodality in Motion: Disability and Kairotic Spaces." *Kairos: A Journal of Rhetoric, Technology, and Pedagogy*, vol., 18, no. 1, 2013. kairos.technorhetoric.net/18.1/coverweb/yergeau-et-al/

ANNIKA M. KONRAD is a senior lecturer in the Institute for Writing and Rhetoric at Dartmouth College, where she teaches writing courses focused on rhetoric of disability and accessibility. She recently coedited a special issue of *Composition Forum,* and her writing has been published in *Business and Professional Communication Quarterly*, *Reflections*, and *Best of the Journals in Rhetoric and Composition.*

This article originally appeared
in *Language Arts* 96.2

ADDRESSING HOMELESSNESS IN OUR SCHOOLS AND LANGUAGE ARTS CLASSROOMS

In this column, the authors examine how to address child homelessness in American and Canadian language arts classrooms and suggest ideas for advocacy, literacy teaching, research, and policy.

THERESA ROGERS & ROWAN SHAFER

"Living in the car was the worst . . . we had everything in there and there wasn't enough room to sleep."

"Every time we moved I had to make new friends and lose the old ones."

"I don't think kids should have to deal with [homelessness]."

HOMELESS CHILDREN, IN THEIR OWN WORDS (2010)

IN THE CONTEXT of increasing economic inequality in North America, it is important for educators to understand poverty and homelessness and how it impacts children in our schools. In particular, we need to reject deficit models and look toward systemic causes so that teachers can be knowledgeable advocates for young people experiencing homelessness. In this article, we draw on this premise, on our combined experience working extensively on literacy projects with youth who are homeless (Rogers, 2016; Rogers, Winters, Perry, & LaMonde, 2015), and on our teaching in elementary schools from an activist position (Shafer, 2017). We argue that as language arts educators, we can and should become knowledgeable about homelessness and about the related policies and reform efforts that affirm the rights of children. We can then take on activist roles by advocating for and implementing practices and policies in classrooms and schools to support children in this situation. We can also help all learners to understand that child homelessness is not the fault of any given individual or family but a failure of our society.

In keeping with the consequential policy themes that have been recently covered in this column, we consider how to address child homelessness in its various forms in our schools and particularly in language arts classrooms. We begin by briefly discussing the ways deficit discourses in the media and popular culture can lead to misunderstandings of the structural forces that lead to the persistence of poverty and homelessness. We then share key statistics and related policies and discuss productive reform efforts for schools, classrooms, and, in particular, language arts educators.

Definitions and Statistics: Child Homelessness in North America

Over time, the media has produced and reflected a discourse that ascribes homelessness less to economic issues and more to individual attributes, thus working to maintain the material conditions of poverty. That is, there has been a tendency to blame the victim (Ryan, 1971). In the 1980s, for instance, news articles in the United States began to attribute homelessness to individual characteristics such as alcoholism, mental illness, laziness, and other personal failings.

As Pascale (2005) argues, this erasing of structural economic causes serves to naturalize the capitalist system. Even when economic conditions worsened due to various welfare, wage, and housing policies (Duffield, 2001) and forced more people into homelessness, they were referred to as the "new homeless" in the media to distinguish them from other people who were homeless (Pascale, 2005, p. 255). One way literacy educators can work toward social justice in this and other domains of inequality, then, is to understand the phenomenon of homelessness in our society and to reformulate how we convey our understandings of others and ourselves in the world through our language.

In the United States and Canada, many children live in poverty—as many as 1.3 million in Canada ("Just the facts," 2018) and 15.5 million in the United States ("Child Poverty," 2018), or about one in five children in each country. In any given year, estimates of children in the United States who experience homelessness range from 1 million to 1.4 million (Ingram, Bridgeland, Reed, & Atwell, 2017). In Canada, the figure is harder to establish (Aleman, 2016; "Just the facts," 2018), although it is likely well over 35,000 a year.

Estimates of children who experience homelessness will vary depending on how it is defined and the methodology used. For instance, analyses based on numbers of people who are homeless on a given night will differ from the numbers who experience homelessness in a given year. In addition, definitions vary, given the often fluid or transient state of being housed, and may include those who are precariously housed in temporary arrangements (e.g., emergency shelters) as well as those with no shelter (e.g., Tierney, Gupton, & Hallet, 2008).

Determining the number of children experiencing some form of homelessness in our schools is even more difficult to assess given the phenomenon of the "hidden homeless." For instance, the authors of the report entitled "Hidden in Plain Sight" (Ingram et al., 2017) note that in the United States, it is estimated that there were more than 1.3 million students identified as homeless during the 2013–2014 school year, based on a report by NCHE Federal Data Summary School Years 2011–2012 to 2013–2014 ("Education for homeless children," 2018). Yet they also acknowledge that many students hesitate to identify themselves because of embarrassment, fear of stigma, or concern that informing school officials of their precarious circumstances may lead to intervention that could result in breaking up their families (Duffield, 2001; Ingram et al., 2017).

For all these reasons, it is difficult to name or definitively count children who are experiencing some form of homelessness. In this article, we include in our definition both the children who may be homeless and those who may be precariously housed, many of whom may be "hidden." Ultimately, as Kozol (1988) reminded us in his book, *Savage Inequalities*, "We would be wise . . . to avoid the numbers game. . . . There is no acceptable number" (pp. 12–13).

Educational Policies Addressing Homelessness among School-Age Children

Education alone cannot solve social problems such as poverty and homelessness (Berkshire, 2017), given that among children, they are largely the result of many factors, including the egregious and increasing structural inequities resulting from the socioeconomic systems at work in North America. These factors also result in most of these children attending poorly resourced schools that are located in districts with high rates of poverty (Anyon, 2014). The situation is exacerbated when poverty, like homelessness, is described in terms of individual and family deficits, or the need for children to develop more grit and resilience (Tierney, 2015), rather than focusing on structural inequities.

ONE WAY LITERACY EDUCATORS CAN WORK TOWARD SOCIAL JUSTICE IS TO UNDERSTAND THE PHENOMENON OF HOMELESSNESS IN OUR SOCIETY.

However, some research suggests that there are many productive approaches to supporting these students in our schools. These approaches rely on educators who understand the larger structural aspects of homelessness as well as the various governmental policies, outlined below, that speak to these resulting inequities and that guide the approaches educators can implement. As Duffield (2001) points out, "[A] major challenge to the education of homeless students is the continuing lack of awareness of homelessness, and of homeless students' educational rights, among school personnel and communities" (p. 332).

LEGISLATION: ACKNOWLEDGING STRENGTHS AND WEAKNESSES

The United States government established the McKinney-Vento Homeless Assistance Act in 1987 and provided an amendment in 2001 (see

McKinney-Vento Act, 1994). Now a federal law, the McKinney-Vento Act was created to reduce barriers related to housing, records, immunization, guardianship, and transportation for homeless children who are accessing education. The law provides for the immediate enrollment and educational stability for children and youth experiencing homelessness, and also provides federal funding to states and school districts for the purpose of supporting these children and youth. Under this law, for instance, children are allowed to remain in the schools they were attending when they became homeless ("Institute for Children and Poverty," 2003).

The McKinney-Vento Act provides some infrastructure to help address the challenges faced by youth and their families and resulted in an increase in school enrollment of children and youth experiencing homelessness, up to 88% by 2002 (Duffield, 2001). The recent passage of the Every Student Succeeds Act (ESSA) further strengthens existing supports, requires states, districts, and schools to disaggregate graduation rates by students who are homeless, and affirms the urgency and importance of addressing homelessness for the future of our young people (Ingram et al., 2017). However, the persistently high percentages of children in our schools who may be homeless indicates much work still remains in order to address this issue in the United States, especially for literacy educators who seek to support their students.

In Canada, there is no corresponding government policy related to children in schools who experience homelessness; however, in 1999, the Canadian government launched the National Homeless Initiative (now called the Homelessness Partnering Strategy), which allotted funds to communities to invest in initiatives that encourage governments and local agencies to find solutions. Many of these initiatives seek to support students who face barriers related to accessing education (Aleman, 2016).

Children experiencing homelessness face many barriers to education, such as chronic absence and transience in schooling (Tierney & Hallett, 2012). Tierney and Hallett (2012) also note that children who are homeless may suffer from various illnesses, including asthma, ear infections, stomach problems, speech problems, anxiety, depression, and hunger, in disproportionate numbers. Not surprisingly, therefore, these children are also much more likely than others to have learning challenges.

Children who experience homelessness may also be dealing with a lack of space to study and high rates of mobility, both of which lead to disruption in schooling, and they frequently have to repeat a grade (Duffield, 2001). The situation is often amplified by school policies and practices (e.g., residency requirements, delays in the transfer of school records, transportation policies) that can keep children from even enrolling in or attending school (Duffield, 2001). As a result, children experiencing homelessness and those who live in poverty are also the least likely to complete school and to attend college or university (Tierney & Hallett, 2012).

REFORM EFFORTS TO ADDRESS CHILD HOMELESSNESS IN SCHOOLS

One way that literacy teachers can become knowledgeable experts is to understand the various advantages and disadvantages of current reform efforts, including those implemented as supplemental supports, in all types of schools: transitional, modified-comprehensive, and mainstream (Mawhinney-Rhoads & Stahler, 2006). Supplemental support services include after-school programming, but can also include in-school counseling; transitional schools are often attached to a shelter for the purpose of helping students transition to mainstream schools; and modified-comprehensive schools are transitional educational settings structured to emulate mainstream schools and provide extensive support services such as mentoring, tutoring, counseling, food programs, and physical/mental health services. A survey of more than 40 segregated classrooms or schools found that these separate programs provide inferior educational opportunities (National Law Center on Homelessness & Poverty, 1995, as cited in Duffield, 2001, p. 334).

Mainstream schools, described as the "preferred educational reform" site under the McKinney-Vento Act, integrate students into current school structures (Mawhinney-Rhoads & Stahler, 2006, p. 295). However, given that most of the research-based literature we found discusses practices for supporting students outside of mainstream schools, it brings into question the extent to which the needs of students are being met. Indeed, given the claim that schools have often not adequately provided the additional assistance needed for children experiencing homelessness (Mawhinney-Rhoads & Stahler, 2006), there is much work to be done.

Educators as Activists in School-Based Reform Efforts

As Oakes (2015) argues, academics and teachers can become allies in educational reform efforts and approach their work with "a mix of strong social theory, evidence, and activism" (p. 117) that is open and participatory, blending local and expert knowledge. For instance, prevalent stereotypes may prevent educators from even recognizing children in their classrooms who may be experiencing homelessness. Therefore, becoming experts and actively creating awareness through professional development, community meetings with homeless service providers, and other activities are ways that schools can better understand and serve these students (Duffield, 2001; Oakes, 2015).

While the research specific to what language arts teachers can do remains limited (see below), discussions of reform approaches at the school policy and program level can have significant effects on the language arts classroom. We located two approaches to school-level reform that affirm the rights of students experiencing homelessness by encouraging collaboration with communities and emphasizing and empowering staff as activists: 1) professional development that empowers teachers as experts and advocates, and 2) the development of coordinated services.

EMPOWERING TEACHERS AS KNOWLEDGEABLE EXPERTS AND ACTIVISTS

While a large body of literature focuses on teachers' deficit perceptions of students and families experiencing homelessness (MacGillivray, Ardell, & Curwen, 2010; NCHE & Moore, 2013; Powers-Costello & Swick, 2011), it is also widely acknowledged that teachers can make a significant difference in the lives of these students (Popp, Grant, & Stronge, 2011; Powers-Costello & Swick, 2011; Rafferty, 1998). Thus, developing teacher advocates and activists constitutes one of the most influential activist policies and practices school systems can invest in for students who are homeless.

Schools can provide meaningful professional development training and experiences that heighten all educators' understanding of the unique lives and needs of their students who are homeless. For instance, academics and schools might collaborate in teacher professional development that encourages activism through serving the local community (e.g., Oyler, 2017). In this way, teacher professional identities become defined, in part, by their understanding of and experience in these communities (Rogers, Marshall, & Tyson, 2006), and they become part of the stakeholder groups that provide the much-needed support of students experiencing homelessness. As the authors of the report *Hidden in Plain Sight* (Ingram et al., 2017) note:

> Schools are a central touch point for students and their families, with deep roots and connections to the communities they serve. These institutions can function as a hub for quickly identifying homeless students, and connecting them and their families to the organizations and agencies that have the capacity and resources to provide housing, transportation, mental health care, and other tangible and emotional supports that will help students persist in school during these difficult times. (p. 4)

Specifically, professional development opportunities for teachers may include workshops, readings, or even time for teachers to collaborate with shelters or other community organizations. In order to truly develop teachers as experts who are empowered to advocate on a student's behalf, schools can also support teachers' engagement in reflection that challenges preconceived notions of homelessness. For example, Powers-Costello and Swick (2011) studied a teacher-created critical reflection group that sought to understand how to better support their students. They found that professional development targeted toward services for youth experiencing homelessness can benefit a wide range of students; teachers "gained confidence and insight, which enhanced their teaching of all their students but in particular those who are facing extreme obstacles based upon their race, class, and gender" (Powers-Costello & Swick, 2011, p. 4).

While we caution against putting the main responsibility on teachers to support students who are homeless, we note that teacher professional development that aims to deepen educators' understanding of homelessness as a systemic problem rather than an individual deficit better prepares these teachers, including developing their expertise and ability to advocate for their students and to develop sophisticated approaches to teaching *about* these issues to all students in their classrooms.

ENGAGING IN COORDINATED SERVICES

Teachers who are knowledgeable advocates can also partner with communities to access various resources and coordinate services for students who are homeless. One of the apparent differences between mainstream schools and other educational models is the ability to coordinate those services to address educational barriers, including transportation, residency, adequate food, clothing, school supplies, mental and physical health needs, time, transience, and continuity in schooling (Hanning, 1996; Mawhinney-Rhoads & Stahler, 2006). Given that none of the reviewed studies document a mainstream school providing such coordinated services, the significant need for school-based reforms that address the needs of students where they most frequently reside is underscored.

While the breadth of ways schools can address these barriers is beyond the scope of this article, we want to emphasize that streamlining such efforts at the school or district level through coordinated policies, such as waiving residency requirements to provide continuity in schooling and providing health clinics in schools, can work to make mainstream schools more accessible for this population. However, we do not encourage a one-size-fits-all approach. As Oakes (2015) suggests, the unique needs of local contexts should determine what and how school practices are implemented. For example, Powers-Costello and Swick (2011) suggest creating action teams or an office responsible for developing goals and overseeing implementation of policies and programs aimed at supporting students who may be experiencing homelessness.

THROUGH COLLABORATION, SCHOOLS AND COMMUNITY ORGANIZATIONS CAN WORK TOGETHER TO SUPPORT THE EDUCATION AND AFFIRM THE RIGHTS OF STUDENTS WHO ARE HOMELESS.

Since homelessness is a systemic issue, teachers are better able to support students and address larger systemic issues when working in partnership with community organizations. Mawhinney-Rhoads and Stahler (2006) offer the example of the innovative J. Pappas School in Arizona as a model modified-comprehensive school. The school district provides services such as food, transportation, and mental health support; a health clinic, dental clinic, and play therapy are offered through community professionals who volunteer their time; and a donation center, tutoring, and mentoring are made possible by partnering with local nonprofits. Powers-Costello and Swick (2011) further suggest the establishment of school liaisons who are responsible for developing and maintaining relationships with other organizations, shelters, and government offices. Such examples demonstrate that through collaboration schools and community organizations can work together to support the education and affirm the rights of students who are homeless.

Coordinated academic services also work to support the education of children experiencing homelessness. As these students may attend several schools in the course of a year, efficient ways to share pertinent records between schools are important. Implementing procedures to quickly gather information about a new student, such as an intake meeting, can allow school teams to develop a support plan and thus reduce the loss of instructional time (MacGillivray et al., 2010; National Center for Homeless Education & Moore, 2013).

Classroom Practices That Support Homeless and Precariously Housed Children

In conjunction with addressing the unique, school-level challenges experienced by children facing homelessness, we found three broad approaches to shifting classroom practices to better assist students: a focus on classroom culture, on academic expectations, and on support systems. Notably, these practices do not work to support only students who may be homeless; in fact, teachers may not even know which of their students are homeless at any given time. Therefore, we offer practices that can benefit all students and are tantamount to good teaching. Following this, we explore practices specific to the language arts classroom that cultivate a positive literacy culture, and we discuss using children's literature to address homelessness with all students.

CREATING A POSITIVE CLASSROOM CULTURE

Many scholars emphasize the importance of creating a welcoming, accommodating classroom culture for children who are homeless. This includes considering not only the physical environment of the classroom, but also classroom procedures, expectations, and perhaps most important, relationship building. In a research summary of teaching and classroom strategies for homeless and highly mobile students, the National Center for Homeless Education ("Education for Homeless Children," 2018) emphasizes the need for classrooms to provide a sense of stability for this population of students. For students and families who may not have the control to structure their lives outside of school, the predictability of consistent classroom routines and organization can provide the security needed to promote learning (NCHE & Moore, 2013).

In a study of effective teachers of at-risk and highly mobile students, Popp et al. (2011) suggest that effective classroom management be structured and calm. Recognizing that these children may come to school with unique worries or needs, teachers can work to cultivate a classroom culture that students view as a safe place to learn and decompress (Walker-Dalhouse & Risko, 2008, p. 83). This includes having snacks on hand for students who may not have had breakfast, providing opportunities for quiet time—possibly a peaceful transition to the school day (MacGillivray et al., 2010; Walker-Dalhouse & Risko, 2008)—and communicating in words and actions that establish the classroom as a home for all (MacGillivray et al., 2010).

As with all good teaching, demonstrating interest, compassion, and investment in students' lives is central to creating a positive learning environment (Walker-Dalhouse & Risko, 2008). Indeed, positive relationships may be a condition for academic success (Popp et al., 2011). Students are more likely to disclose that they are homeless to teachers they trust. Teachers who know their students well are also able to identify their needs—such as adequate meals, quiet time, or counseling—and can act as advocates in the school system (Popp et al., 2011). We argue that building such positive relationships also necessitates cultivating trusting, respectful relationships with families as co-contributors to the child's well-being.

Since these children may change schools many times in a single school year (Mawhinney-Rhoads & Stahler, 2006), teachers might consider how they can ameliorate the distress and anxiety of entering a new classroom before new children arrive. NCHE and Moore (2013) suggest creating orientation packages that include information about classroom policies and procedures, but also materials to get them settled without having to worry about what they might not have. Moreover, as MacGillivray et al. (2010) point out, teachers need to be mindful of their own assumptions about classroom expectations that may not be readily apparent to students who join their classes after the year is underway. Communicating each classrooms' unique norms and behaviors through personal attention or an assigned peer buddy can help to ease these transitions and allow students to feel more relaxed and able to focus on learning. Additionally, considering how to equitably share resources among students from the beginning of the year is an activist stance that teachers can take to address inequalities among many students of differing or unknown socioeconomic status.

MAINTAINING ACADEMIC SUPPORTS AND HIGH EXPECTATIONS

Informed, holistic academic and emotional supports can also be significant to these or any child's success. Ongoing assessment can inform teachers' planning and instruction, including planning for differentiation that can fill any identified gaps in student knowledge (NCHE & Moore, 2013; Popp et al., 2011). Given the high rates of transience among this population, teachers should be empowered to use informal assessments to determine strengths and advocate for needed supports instead of losing instructional time waiting for formal assessments to be conducted for new students (NCHE & Moore, 2013). Berliner (2013) suggests creating a holistic portfolio that highlights students' strengths and illuminates weaknesses, so that in case a student has to transfer again, the next teacher will be able to "pick up where the student left off" (as cited in NCHE & Moore, 2013, p. 10).

It is also important that teachers maintain high expectations for their students, no matter the challenges they face; housing-related challenges should not be viewed as a rationale for lowered standards (Noll & Watkins, 2003). However, best teacher practices measure and communicate success outside of standardized assessments and recall; for instance, the most effective teachers in Popp et al.'s (2011) study "emphasize making meaningful connections over memorizing disjointed facts" (p. 286).

Shifting the deficit perception of students experiencing homelessness includes maintaining high expectations without precluding the recognition and accommodation of the unique needs of this group. Teachers can be flexible with due dates, ways to complete out-of-school assignments or projects that need additional materials, and topic assignments that may be exclusive (such as writing about vacation or drawing a home), all while encouraging high-quality work (MacGillivray et al., 2010; NCHE & Moore, 2013). Clearly, such flexibility and modifications necessitate that teachers know their students well enough to anticipate the need for such flexibility.

Much of the literature also discusses academic supports that benefit students who are homeless, such as one-on-one instruction (MacGillivray et al., 2010; Sinatra, 2007; Willard & Kulinna, 2012), tutoring, and mentoring. However, while such supports would be valuable to most students, it is very difficult for classroom teachers to provide such consistent, individualized instruction. And while many authors discuss the value of summer school (Sinatra, 2007; Willard & Kulinna, 2012) or after-school tutoring (Hanning 1996; NCHE & Moore, 2013; Walker-Dalhouse & Risko, 2008), and some discuss teachers as "human resources" that can provide workshops in homeless shelters and volunteer their time (Walker-Dalhouse & Risko, 2008, p. 8), we are reticent to endorse such suggestions wholeheartedly. Although these measures may greatly benefit students and parents, we need to find sustainable solutions to systemic problems that do not focus on only one student or group of students at a time.

What Language Arts Teachers Can Do

While there is limited research that discusses general teacher practices to support students who are homeless, current literature with specific strategies for literacy and language arts teachers is even more scarce, and what is available focuses primarily on reading practices. Many scholars have focused on literacy programs and practices that take place outside of mainstream schools, such as the Brownstone School after-school program (Hanning, 1996; Walker-Dalhouse & Risko, 2008), The Reading Connection community organization (Hanning, 1996), or summer school programs at various locations (Sinatra, 2007; Willard & Kulinna, 2012). While we draw on this work to extrapolate relevant practices for mainstream literacy teachers' classrooms, we also raise concerns about the lack of literacy research on mainstream schooling practices for children experiencing homelessness.

Relying on out-of-school programs to meet the crucial literacy needs of students who are homeless or precariously housed may do little to address the systemic nature of the problem. We advocate for the investment in school-wide literacy support systems and practices that support all students' unique needs. Within classrooms, we encourage teachers as knowledgeable advocates to support the literacy needs of students who may be homeless, and to actively support all learners to understand the systemic nature of homelessness.

DEVELOPING A POSITIVE LITERACY CULTURE

One of the most useful practices we have found is cultivating a positive literacy culture that includes fostering reading identities, providing access to books and other literacy materials, and collaborating with families. Several of the studies we have cited in this article highlight the effectiveness of one-on-one or small-group lessons, additional tutoring, and/or mentoring, but we have also identified the related difficulties of implementing such programs consistently in schools. That being said, we believe that encouraging a positive relationship to literacy is not only well within the scope of a general education teacher's capacity, it can have profound effects on all students.

One practical strategy is for teachers to ensure all students have access to books and other materials, such as journals and pencils, that can "go home and stay home" (Walker-Dalhouse & Risko, 2008, p. 84). Ensuring that all children have self-selected, high-interest books in their home environments, even when families may not have the disposable income to supply them, supports positive relationships to literacy and can foster identities as "readers" (Hanning, 1996; The Ohio State University, 2017; Walker-Dalhouse & Risko, 2008). Teachers might find ways to gift books to students based on their interests or invite them to select books to keep from the classroom library. In conjunction with school library book giveaways and novel study books that students can keep and write in, teachers can provide students with several books each year to call their own. We are aware there are costs associated with such initiatives. As we argue for solutions that move beyond individual actions, we encourage school districts to financially support such teacher activism so that these efforts are not contingent upon individual fundraising or spending.

Literacy practices are not only influenced by the classroom, but by home environments as well. Contrary to the common deficit perceptions that may be ascribed to parents of children who are homeless, we strongly encourage teachers to view families as partners in cultivating a child's literacy experiences. In their study examining the perceptions of children experiencing homelessness and literacy practices of families in homeless shelters, MacGillivray et al. (2010) found that they had much to learn from the ways mothers and children living in a shelter employed literacy practices during a time of upheaval. Their research highlights some of the ways living in a homeless shelter can hinder literacy practices, but also how it can catalyze the creation of new practices. For instance, mothers often passed notes to children at dinner to keep conversations private, took them to the public library for activities and to borrow books, and discussed books with them. The children made Mother's Day cards, decorated their rooms with Bible verses, and used flash cards to study. What MacGillivray's team reveals is that lack of knowledge about homelessness may impede teachers from both recognizing strengths of students and cultivating productive working partnerships with families for their children's literacy success.

Teachers can play an active role in promoting collaboration between families and schools by demonstrating that family members are essential to the learning process (Walker-Dalhouse & Risko, 2008). Parents and caregivers can share essential knowledge about children's out-of-school literacy practices and behaviors while teachers can provide the same regarding in-school settings, thus working together toward shared goals of the child's success (MacGillivray et al., 2010). When trust is built, teachers can make educational meaning of the child's various literacy engagements and provide guidance for families to support their child's literacy development outside of school (Hanning, 1996).

One way to do this is to cultivate such partnerships through a readers and writers survey that students complete outside of school. Child-friendly questions include, "Do you consider yourself a reader/writer? Why? Do you like to read/write? Why? Where do you get ideas for writing?" Students might also be asked what kinds of reading and writing they do at home in an effort to extend their lists beyond typical children's book genres to magazines, comics, grocery lists, and writing activities for a range of practical purposes. Children have the option to complete this with any family member (who could also do the writing for them), and families are invited to share additional information or ask questions in the last section. While this activity requires reading and writing from adults as well as children, this is one way to develop cultures of literacy as a collaboration between home and school, and to communicate that different forms of literacy practices and relationships to reading and writing are valued. The use of these surveys to conference with students also helps teachers to pick out high-interest books for each child.

USING CHILDREN'S LITERATURE TO ADDRESS HOMELESSNESS

Children's literature about homelessness, or with characters who are experiencing homelessness, can provide teachers with unique opportunities to address this systemic issue with all students. Literature can play a central role in children's lives as a means to make sense of their own experiences, to connect to the experiences of others, or to temporarily evade hardships of real life (Noll & Watkins, 2003). In their use of book discussion groups with homeless and housed students, Noll and Watkins (2003) provided opportunities for children to make connections between their own lives and those of the characters through examining characters' motivations, engaging in collaborative meaning making, and expressing their understandings through multimodal activities. These activities allowed students to work on needed skills and to reveal their strengths in a literacy-rich environment.

These uses of literature can be a rich learning experience for all students and are especially useful to children in times of crisis (MacGillivray et al., 2010). Broadening the representations of families, homes, and living situations in classroom libraries and the curriculum is also a way teachers work against discourses that blame the individual and instead re-situate homelessness within the community—important lessons for all students.

As Mary Cowhey (2006) notes:

> One might argue that the realities of homelessness, poverty and hunger are too much for young learners. I haven't found that to be the case. . . . young children are capable of amazing things, far more than is usually expected of them. . . . [They] understand fairness and are deeply moved and highly motivated by the recognition of injustice. (p. 18)

We caution that discussions should not include identifying students as homeless, as many students would like to keep this private; instead, these

TEACHING TIPS

Before and during the pandemic, homelessness among students has been an important issue. As many educators shifted to remote instruction, students who struggled with the precarity of homelessness across the US missed out on instruction. Also, special accommodations had to be made for college students who relied on college dorms for stable housing. As Rogers and Shafer explain, "homelessness is not the fault of any individual or family, but a failure of our society." They also urge educators to learn about the nature of homelessness—and to explore policies that affirm the rights of these students. Discuss local homelessness reform efforts in your teaching context with your fellow educators.

conversations enrich all students' understandings as they work to de-stigmatize homelessness.

Teachers must be discerning about how diverse characters are portrayed in order to avoid stereotypes or tokenizing representations of homelessness that perpetuate misconceptions. As Rogers and Marshall (2012) point out in their study of cultural texts about homelessness, "Textual and visual representations are important to analyze as the discourses about homelessness within them are tied to material effects that influence the everyday lives" (p. 725) of young people. Our intention here is to offer language arts teachers a similar approach to addressing issues of homelessness with all elementary students through children's books. We propose a set of questions teachers can ask themselves when reviewing and teaching books that challenge deficit discourses of homelessness:

- Does this book broaden representations of families, homes, and living situations?
- To what extent does the book acknowledge systemic inequalities as the problem rather than blaming the victim? Is homelessness represented as a community issue or an individual failure?
- How does the book communicate the various forms of homelessness (including precariousness and transience) and its relationship to poverty?
- What is the relationship of children experiencing homelessness to school and to literacy in the book? Does the book acknowledge rights of children to education without barriers?
- Does the book portray people experiencing homelessness as in need of saving or as agential?
- What representations of activism to combat the systemic nature of homelessness are present?

See the sidebar for a list of books we have identified as meeting different aspects of this list. While not every book will meet all criteria, considering these questions can lead to productive classroom discussions.

Conclusion

Addressing homelessness in our schools is a complex problem in all the ways we have discussed—including the difficulty of identifying the students experiencing it. But given our economic system, it is likely to be an ongoing concern for all of us. We call for a continued focus on students' rights to a quality education, particularly within mainstream schools. We argue that the approaches and practices we recommend—becoming knowledgeable experts, taking an activist approach, and advocating for and enacting supportive practices—serve to benefit all students. These practices also include collaboration among schools as well as between schools and other community organizations, professional development for teachers, and creating positive literacy classroom cultures for all of our students, whether housed, precariously housed, or homeless.

REFERENCES

Aleman, A. (2016). Education and homelessness. Retrieved from http://homelesshub.ca/blog/education-homelessness

Anyon, J. (2014). *Radical possibilities: Public policy, urban education, and a new social movement* (2nd ed.). New York, NY: Routledge.

Berkshire, J. (2017). Education can't fix poverty. So why keep insisting it can? Interview with H. Kantor. Retrieved from http://haveyouheardblog.com/thepovertyfix

Berliner, D. (2013). Effects of inequality and poverty vs. teachers and schooling on America's youth. *Teachers College Record*, 115, 1–26.

Child poverty in the U.S. (2018). Children international. Retrieved from https://www.children.org/global-poverty/global-poverty-facts/facts-about-poverty-in-usa

Cowhey, M. (2006). *Black ants and Buddhists: Thinking critically and teaching differently in the primary grades.* Portland, ME: Stenhouse.

Duffield, B. (2001). The educational rights of homeless children: Policies and practices. *Educational Studies*, 32, 323–336.

Education for Homeless Children and Youths (EHCY) Program. (2018). National center for homeless education. Retrieved from https://nche.ed.gov/downloads/ehcy_profile.pdf

Hanning, E. (1996). The reading connection: Literacy development and homeless children. *Journal of Children and Poverty*, 2(2), 5–21.

Homeless children, in their own words. (2010). Homeless hub. Retrieved from http://homelesshub.ca/resource/homeless-children-their-own-words

Ingram, E. S., Bridgeland, J. M., Reed, B., & Atwell, M. (2017). *Hidden in plain sight: Homeless students in America's public schools.* Retrieved from http://civicenterprises.net/MediaLibrary/Docs/HiddeninPlainSightOfficial.pdf

Institute for Children and Poverty. (2003). Miles to go: The flip side of the McKinney-Vento Homeless Assistance Act [Fact sheet]. Retrieved from https://www.issuelab.org/resource/miles-to-go-the-flip-side-of-the-mckinney-vento-homeless-assistance-act.html

Just the facts. (2018). Canada without poverty. Retrieved from http://www.cwp-csp.ca/poverty/just-the-facts//

Kozol, J. (1988). *Rachel and her children: Homeless families in America.* New York, NY: Three Rivers Press.

MacGillivray, L., Ardell, A. L., & Curwen, M. S. (2010). Supporting the literacy development of children living in homeless shelters. *The Reading Teacher*, 63, 384–392.

Mawhinney-Rhoads, L., & Stahler, G. (2006). Educational policy and reform for homeless students: An overview. *Education and Urban Society*, 38, 288–306.

McKinney-Vento Act, 42 U.S.C. § 11301 (1994). Retrieved from https://www2.ed.gov/policy/elsec/leg/esea02/pg116.html

National Center for Homeless Education, & Moore, J. (2013). *Research summary: Teaching and classroom strategies for homeless and highly mobile students.* Retrieved from https://nche.ed.gov/pr/res-teach-class.php

National Law Center on Homelessness & Poverty. (1995). *A foot in the schoolhouse door: Progress and barriers to the education of homeless children.* Washington, DC: National Law Center on Homelessness & Poverty.

Noll, E., & Watkins, R. (2003). The impact of homelessness on children 's literacy experiences. *The Reading Teacher*, 57, 362–371.

Oakes, J. (2015). Social theory, evidence, and activism: Challenging education inequality in an unequal society. In W. Tierney (Ed.), *Rethinking education and poverty* (pp. 117–136). Baltimore, MD: Johns Hopkins University Press.

Oyler, C. J. (2017). Constructivist resistance: Activist repertoires for teachers. *Language Arts*, 95, 30–39.

Pascale, C. M. (2005). There's no place like home: The discursive creation of homelessness. *Cultural Studies⇔Critical Methodologies*, 5, 250–268.

Popp, P. A., Grant, L. W., & Stronge, J. H. (2011). Effective teachers for at-risk or highly mobile students: What are the dispositions and behaviors of award-winning teachers? *Journal of Education for Students Placed at Risk*, 16, 275–291.

Powers-Costello, B., & Swick, K. J. (2011). Transforming teacher constructs of children and families who are homeless. *Early Childhood Education Journal*, 39, 207–212.

Rafferty, Y. (1998). Meeting the educational needs of homeless children. *Educational Leadership*, 55(4), 48–52.

Rogers, T. (2016). Youth arts, media, and critical literacies as forms of public engagement in the local/global interface. *Literacy Research: Theory, Method, and Practice*, 65, 268–282.

Rogers, T., & Marshall, E. (2012). On the road: Examining self-representation and discourses of homelessness in young adult texts. *Journal of Adolescent and Adult Literacy*, 55, 725–733.

Rogers, T., Marshall, E., & Tyson, C. A. (2006). Dialogic narratives of literacy teaching and schooling: Preparing literacy teachers for diverse settings. *Reading Research Quarterly*, 41, 202–224.

Rogers, T., Winters, K., Perry, M., & LaMonde, A. (2015). *Youth, critical literacies, and civic engagement: Arts, media, and literacy in the lives of adolescents.* New York, NY: Routledge.

Ryan, W. (1971). *Blaming the victim.* New York, NY: Vintage.

Shafer, R. (2017). The (young) people's climate conference: Teaching global warming to 3rd graders. *Rethinking Schools*, 31(4). Retrieved from https://www.rethinking schools.org/articles/the-young-people-s-climate-conference

Sinatra, R. (2007). Literacy success with homeless children. *The Journal of At-Risk Issues*, 13(2), 1–9.

The Ohio State University. (2017). Keep books. Retrieved from www.keepbooks.org

Tierney, W. (Ed.). (2015). *Rethinking education and poverty.* Baltimore, MD: Johns Hopkins Press.

Tierney, W. G., Gupton, J. T., & Hallett, R. E. (2008). Transitions to adulthood for homeless adolescents: Education and public policy. Center for Higher Education Policy Analysis (University of Southern California). Retrieved from https://files.eric.ed.gov/fulltext/ED503645.pdf

Tierney, W., & Hallet, R. E. (2012). Homeless youth and educational policy: A case study of urban youth in a metropolitan area. In C. Campy Yeakey (Ed.), *Living on the boundaries: Urban marginality in national and international contexts* (Advances in education in diverse communities: Research, policy, and praxis [pp. 49–78]). Oxford, UK: Emerald Group Publishing.

Walker-Dalhouse, D., & Risko, V. J. (2008). Homelessness, poverty, and children's literacy development. *The Reading Teacher*, 62, 84–86.

Willard, A. L., & Kulinna, P. H. (2012). Summer literacy intervention for homeless children living in transitional housing. *Journal of At-Risk Issues*, 17(1), 15–21.

CHILDREN'S LITERATURE CITED

Applegate, K. (2015). *Crenshaw*. New York, NY: Feiwel and Friends.

Bunting, E. (1991). *Fly away home* (R. Himler, Illus.). New York, NY: Clarion.

Curtis, C. P. (2012). *Mighty Miss Malone*. New York, NY: Yearling.

de la Peña, M. (2015). *Last stop on Market Street* (C. Robinson, Illus.). New York: G. P. Putnam's Sons.

Gunning, M. (2004). *A shelter in our car* (E. Pedlar, Illus.). San Francisco, CA: Children's Book Press.

Hathorn, E. (1994). *Way home* (G. Rogers, Illus.). London, UK: Andersen Press.

Landowne, Y. (2004). *Selavi: That is life*. El Paso, TX: Cinco Puntos Press.

McGovern, A. (1997). *The lady in the box* (M. Backer, Illus.). New York, NY: Turtle Books.

O'Connor, B. (2009). *How to steal a dog*. New York, NY: Farrar, Straus and Giroux.

Sendak, M. (1993). *We are all in the dumps with Jack and Guy: Two nursery rhymes with pictures* (1st ed.). New York, NY: HarperCollins.

Woodson, J. (2003). *Locomotion*. New York, NY: G. P. Putnam's Sons.

Yang, K. (2018). *Front desk*. New York, NY: Arthur A. Levine.

THERESA ROGERS is a professor in the Department of Language and Literacy at the University of British Columbia in Vancouver, Canada. Her research and many publications focus on youth literacies and young adult literature (see https://ubc.academia.edu/TheresaRogers). She can be contacted at theresa.rogers@ubc.ca.

ROWAN SHAFER is a master's student in the Equity Studies in Education program at Simon Fraser University. A previous elementary school teacher, her research interests include teacher activism and queering children's literature. She can be contacted at rshafer@sfu.ca.

This article originally appeared
in *English Journal 110.5*

THERE'S HOPE FOR US ALL: Transformative Moments

A family member's coming out inspired the author to reconsider her obligation to be a more thoughtful and effective LGBTQ+ ally for the students in her classroom.

HEIDI LYN HADLEY

AT A RECENT POETRY WORKSHOP that I facilitated, a teenaged girl stood up to read her poem. It was about how she can never eat peppermints again, because that's what she was eating on the day that her father explosively reacted to the news that the US Supreme Court had upheld marriage equality. He raged about how ungodly the ruling was, how sinful the gays were, on and on. "I can't eat peppermints," she read with a quavering voice, "because they always taste like bitterness / like knowing I can never tell my Dad / exactly who I am."

When we talk about LGBTQ+ advocacy in the classroom, inevitably we're going to have to talk about American religiosity. There is a vast spectrum of religious practices in the United States, even within Christianity, the most prevalent religion. Within this spectrum, there are religious LGBTQ+ youth who are well cared for, emotionally and spiritually. But there are conservative religious communities that inflict deep emotional and spiritual damage on LGBTQ+ youth, simply because of who these young people are.

Hard Truths Can Be Learned

I want to tell the truths that I have learned, both as a teacher and as a human being, about making our classrooms places of safety and inclusion for LGBTQ+ youth. First, I've come to understand that ELA teachers have the ability to either mitigate that emotional and spiritual damage or add to it. Second, I believe that there's hope (and opportunity) for us to become better advocates for *all* of our students, but that being so requires a commitment to transformative self-inquiry and pedagogy.

I've learned these truths the hard way, admittedly. I entered the classroom without examining my own identity and assumptions, which made me the kind of teacher who compounded emotional and spiritual damage. But, through my own (sometimes painful) metamorphosis, I have realized that we are capable of experiencing and creating transformative moments.

As a new teacher—a proud graduate of my conservative religious community's university and its religiously based curriculum—I taught in a small suburban community mostly populated by people who looked like me, thought like me, talked like me, and worshipped like me. In the early 2000s (so long ago!), I knew of no student who identified as LGBTQ+. My religiously informed view of the world was safe, intact, and unchallenged by the demands of my profession and community.

I ENTERED THE CLASSROOM WITHOUT EXAMINING MY OWN IDENTITY AND ASSUMPTIONS, WHICH MADE ME THE KIND OF TEACHER WHO COMPOUNDED EMOTIONAL AND SPIRITUAL DAMAGE.

In my second year of teaching, my favorite brother—the brother I know and trust more than anyone else in the world—came out as gay. Suddenly, my world upended. Everything that I thought that I knew about gay people was challenged. I had been told that gay people were making sinful choices, letting the devil into their hearts, and acting on perversions. These things—which had always made sense because LGBTQ+ identity was an abstraction that I had never examined as a human quality—were suddenly, simply false. I could look at my brother, and the proof of those beliefs' inaccuracies was right there in front of me. I knew him to be the kindest, best, and most . . . well . . . *Christian*—to put it in the language of my community—of my seven siblings. Suddenly, everything that I had been so *certain* about was absolutely uncertain.

Meaningful Transformation Can Take Time

I'd like to say that my brother coming out was that one transformative moment that I needed, but that's too tidy of a narrative for most human journeys; it certainly is for mine, anyway. It was, however, one moment that opened the doorway to tens and hundreds and thousands of other moments. These moments are important because they give us opportunities to see incongruences between concepts that we were sure we knew and the newly acknowledged realities of the world around us. Admittedly, we don't always understand them as invitations for transformation, and embracing them as transformative doesn't always take away the sting of change and growth.

In full transparency, I've left my faith community or, more accurately, lost religion altogether. I don't think that losing faith is the only option for teachers of faith as they begin examining their own religious identities and how those self-elements contribute to their abilities to affirm LGBTQ+ students in their classrooms. My current research on this topic examines the varied ways that some conservatively religious teachers are working to balance their professional ethics with the sometimes-competing demands of their personal faith identities. I listen often and closely to teachers' stories that reflect deep anguish over making difficult and conflicting choices as they work to responsibly interact with LGBTQ+ youth—stories that are entangled with spiritual, religious, and professional beliefs about our responsibilities to students. I understand the discomfort. However, our professional ethics *require* us as ELA teachers to mitigate harm, to advocate for all students, and to show deep respect for varieties of belief systems—even when they do not align with our own. This is complicated work—too complicated perhaps, for a short column to tackle completely—but as we balance the diverse needs and identities of the students in our classrooms, complications and being off-balance are norms.

TEACHING TIPS

Hadley explains, "I entered the classroom without examining my own identity and assumptions, which made the kind of teacher who compounded emotional and spiritual damage." As an educator who grew up in a conservative religious home and community, Hadley struggled with her capacity to be an ally in the LGBTQ+ community. After a coming-out encounter with a close loved one, she wrestled with her professional ethics as a teacher of all students. Reflect on your personal and professional ethics and ask yourself, what opportunities do you see to mitigate harm among your LGBTQ+ students? What, if any, institutional supports are available to support LGBTQ+ youth in your teaching context?

Self-Interrogation Can Be Important for Allies

In my teaching identity, I am still transforming, and I have to continuously examine my assumptions, language, and practices. I have several questions that I ask myself to self-interrogate how my teaching practice is supporting or harming LGBTQ+ identities, including the following:

- Am I using language that indicates to students that I will allow them to define their gender and sexual expressions and identities?
- Am I using heteronormative and cisnormative assumptions when I have discussions with and build relationships with students?
- Am I creating curricular experiences that are inclusive of multiple sexual and gender identities and expressions—even if I am unaware of these diverse identities in my classroom?

These kinds of questions, among others, remind me to examine my assumptions and experiences—many of which are still deeply informed by my religious upbringing—through a critical lens. These self-interrogations matter because moments of transformation don't always move us to positive change. If we think about the experiences of the young poet I described at the start of this column, we can also see a moment of transformation: a moment when her world became smaller, less kind, less honest, and less open, at a time when she had thought (or hoped) that there might be a space for her—exactly as she was. We need ELA teachers who understand that one of the best parts of teaching ELA is that teaching literature, writing, and language ethically invites us—teachers and students—to make the world bigger, kinder, more honest, and more open. That would be a truly powerful and welcome transformation.

HEIDI LYN HADLEY is an assistant professor and director of the English Education program in the English department at Missouri State University. She previously worked as a language arts and ESOL high school teacher. Her research interests include teacher education, the intersection of religion and education, reading instruction, and community-based youth literacy practices. She has been a member of NCTE for more than a decade.

This article originally appeared in *English Journal* 109.3

TEXTS OF BECOMING: A Parent's Plea for the Inclusion of Trans* Narratives

A teacher educator and parent shares her child's story, recommends literary works, and presents ideas to support students' gender identities.

ANONYMOUS

MY DAUGHTER SUMMER'S (pseudonym) coming out as a transgender girl at the age of seven was not a surprise. Instead, it was a series of moments that led to her proclamation that we had been using the wrong pronouns and name all along. We had assumed since the day of the ultrasound that we had brought a boy into the world, but we were incorrect. In this column, I share how she came into her identity and the role trans* narratives played in her journey in becoming. I use the term *trans** with an asterisk to denote a spectrum of non-cisgender identities including but not limited to transgender, agender, and genderfluid (Miller). In Summer's case, she identified fully with the opposite biological sex and chose to transition socially, and I describe her as transgender. However, in discussing trans* texts, I am including children's and YA literature that represents a wide range of gender identities and expressions.

From the time my toddler could choose toys, he gravitated toward those that were traditionally feminine. (I use the pronoun *he* to mark the time prior to Summer's social transition, and *she* after she transitioned. I made the decision to do this for clarity of writing, as marking the time before and after her transition is relevant to her story.) The first time we went to the Disney Store, he made a beeline to the fairies and excitedly picked out a Fawn doll that he adored. He later collected all fairies and had a series of toy obsessions procured from Target's "girls" aisle. To alleviate any confusion, we explained that toys are for all kids, and boys and girls could play with whatever they want. Our child understood this and rehearsed telling it to the preschool children who might believe otherwise.

This pattern, however, went far beyond toy choices. For instance, there was the ballet class at age four when he dutifully wore the black tights and white T-shirt that boys were expected to wear. He sat sadly on the side while the pink tutu'ed girls pranced happily across the dance floor. He did this normally at home wearing a Hello Kitty tutu. Another example is the time he dressed as the Disney character Merida for Halloween with red curls spilling down his back. When he looked in the mirror, he said, "I am beautiful." He really meant it.

Poring Over the Books

One moment in particular stood out. I remember when he was alone in his room for quiet time. As I peered through the door, I could see him poring over the book *When Kayla Was Kyle* (Fabrikant and Levine).

He was lingering over the pictures and seemingly deep in thought. We had previously read the book aloud together. It tells the story of a child who presents as a boy but who does not identify as such. Ultimately, the child claims an identity as a girl named Kayla. In the book, Kyle (aka Kayla) resists going to school after being bullied. One significant passage reads:

> Kyle pulled the covers over his head, "I'm not going. I can't go. It's not going to work out. . . . I only look like a boy, but I'm not like other boys," Kyle cried. . . .
>
> "Is it because you feel like a girl?" Kyle's mother asked as she pulled down his covers.
>
> Everything stopped. Kyle's room was still. It felt like all the air was gone. Kyle lifted up the covers and his parents scooped him up into their arms and hugged him for a long time. (18)

Kayla's story clearly resonated for our child. Soon after, he asked, "Why did you name me Seth? That's a boy's name."

I responded, "When you were born the doctor told us you were a boy, and we liked that name. But maybe we made a mistake."

He replied, "You did. I want you to call me Summer and call me she."

And so, we did. It was challenging at first, and we slipped into using her old name and pronouns at times. But Summer corrected us. When she saw her cousins, she told them to do the same. And they did. The name *Summer* just started to feel normal as this is who she had been all along.

The Role of Trans* Narratives

There were a variety of factors that paved the way for Summer to come into her trans* identity. I believe it was *When Kayla Was Kyle* and other key books such as *My Princess Boy* (Kilodavis and DeSimone), *Jacob's New Dress* (Hoffman et al.), and *I Am Jazz* (Herthel et al.). These books opened space in Summer's understandings of gender identity and offered other realities. By seeing herself reflected in the story of Kayla, Summer could see that it was possible to push against the boundaries of gender and assert her identity as a girl.

As parents, we made these literary texts available to her. We read them aloud and also left them in her room for her to go back into as she wanted. While we had these texts at home, many families did not. I have seen very few of these books in Summer's classrooms.

My urgent plea to fellow English language arts teachers at all levels is to expand their classroom and school libraries and expose children and adolescents to trans* narratives—fictional stories or memoirs featuring a trans* character. We need trans* texts in classrooms so that students like Summer do not have to hide their identities. Moreover, cisgender students can expand their understandings about gender and become potential allies. Ideally, teachers will engage in whole-class explorations of trans* experiences. For instance, when reading *George* (Gino), the story of a fifth-grade transgender girl who wants to play Charlotte in the school production of *Charlotte's Web* but is told she cannot because she is perceived to be a boy, students could write their own skits portraying varied gender identities.

Another possibility for middle school readers is creating a digital storytelling project based around *Gracefully Grayson* (Polonsky), the story of a transgender tween coming into her identity. Perhaps in high school classrooms teachers might use memoirs about how some students transition such as *Some Assembly Required: The Not-So-Secret Life of a Transgender Teen* (Andrews). If teachers do not feel prepared to design and teach a unit on gender identity, the American Library Association's Rainbow List (glbtrt.ala.org/rainbowbooks/) offers powerful suggestions for texts that can become part of a classroom library.

AS A PARENT, I OPENED THE SPACE FOR SUMMER TO COME INTO HER IDENTITY. I NOW INVITE YOU, HER TEACHERS, TO OPEN SPACES IN YOUR CLASSROOMS.

Research shows the powerful role trans* texts have in our classrooms. In the article "A Queer Literacy Framework Promoting (A)gender and (A)sexuality Self-Determination and Justice," sj Miller encourages teachers to engage in pedagogies that "open up spaces for students to self-define with chosen (a)genders, (a)pronouns, or names" (36). A key aspect of opening spaces is making literature available that represents characters with varied gender identities.

As a parent, I opened the space for Summer to come into her identity. I now invite you, her teachers, to open spaces in your classrooms. As Summer enters middle school next year, I hope that her teachers will offer texts that represent a positive trans* experience. Summer needs to see her identity represented so that she can feel safe to share her own story. Other young people like her might see themselves reflected in the pages of books and find the courage to claim their identities. Children and adolescents have a right to read and discuss literature that represents trans* identities, and teachers have a responsibility to provide it.

Summer Today

Five years later, Summer is a thriving sixth grader who is interested in theater, singing, and socializing. However, she has chosen to keep her transgender identity private since relocating to a new city. In fact, I write this article anonymously because it is too risky to out her, and disclosure is her right. I hope for the day when she is no longer fearful of being bullied or ostracized, and when all children live in a world designed to accept and affirm their identities.

WORKS CITED

Andrews, Arin. *Some Assembly Required: The Not-So-Secret Life of a Transgender Teen*. Simon and Schuster, 2014.

Fabrikant, Amy, and Jennifer Levine. *When Kayla Was Kyle*. Avid Readers Publishing Group, 2013.

Gino, Alex. *George*. Scholastic, 2015.

Herthel, Jessica, et al. *I Am Jazz*. Dial Books for Young Readers, 2014.

Hoffman, Sarah, et al. *Jacob's New Dress*. Albert Whitman and Company, 2014.

Kilodavis, Cheryl, and Suzanne DeSimone. *My Princess Boy*. Aladdin, 2011.

Miller, sj. "A Queer Literacy Framework Promoting (A)gender and (A)sexuality Self-Determination and Justice." *English Journal*, vol. 104, no. 5, 2015, pp. 37–44.

Polonsky, Ami. *Gracefully Grayson*. Disney-Hyperion, 2016.

Rainbow Book List: GLBTQ Books for Children and Teens, 2019 *Rainbow Book List*. Gay, Lesbian, Bisexual, and Transgender Round Table and the Social Responsibilities Round Table of the American Library Association, 2019, glbtrt.ala.org/rainbowbooks/rainbow-books-lists#.

ANONYMOUS is a teacher educator, literacy researcher, parent, and community activist who works toward collectively building a world where student identities are seen and honored in classrooms. They have been a member of NCTE since 2007.

This article originally appeared in
Teaching English in the Two-Year College 48.3

TRAUMA-INFORMED WRITING PEDAGOGY: Ways to Support Student Writers Affected by Trauma and Traumatic Stress

This article argues that two principles of a trauma-informed writing pedagogy grounded in clinical scholarship—instructor as buffering role model and psychologically safer classroom spaces—can support students affected by trauma and traumatic stress. Moreover, when these principles are embedded in course structures using concepts central to universal design, they can support all community college writing students facing adversity.

MELISSA TAYLES

AS COMMUNITY COLLEGE writing instructors, we see glimpses of our students' personal lives as we guide them through the writing process and hold regular one-on-one conferences. We listen as some of our students disclose distressing accounts of overwhelming stress, abuse, suicide, neglect, poverty, racism, homelessness, and war. We also listen as students detail how they have overcome such adversities with resilience and perseverance in order to attend college and pursue their academic goals while struggling and succeeding to manage the demands of being adult learners, employees, caregivers, and parents. Certainly, not all community college students are affected by these stressors and adversities, but the COVID-19 pandemic and recent efforts to address the systemic racism in our society have affected a majority of our students. As a result, trauma, which was once a topic discussed only in isolated pockets of our culture and viewed as consisting only of individual and extraordinary experiences, is now addressed more openly in terms of collective experiences as the world attempts to cope with the challenges of living through the economic, physical, and emotional ramifications of the pandemic and persistent racial inequities.

Even before the COVID-19 pandemic, writing instructors were seeking pedagogical resources—such as those found in a trauma-informed writing pedagogy (TIWP)—to allow them to channel their compassion and empathy in a productive and professional manner. Daniel Gutierrez and Andrea Gutierrez confirmed the need for essential trauma awareness by noting that "students come from all walks-of-life and bring with them a wide array of personal experiences, some of which may be rooted in traumatic experiences before entering college or experiencing trauma during their college experience" (11). Both collective and individual traumas that affect our students continue to motivate college writing instructors to build a trauma-informed lens and discover a TIWP that will help us support students so they may thrive in academic settings.

Anecdotally, community college writing instructors assume that trauma is prevalent among their students based on students' confessions and disclosures. Research on the prevalence of exposure to potentially traumatic experiences in undergraduate populations confirms these suspicions as the majority of studies find that more than half of study participants report exposure to at least one potentially traumatic experience across a lifetime (Anders et al.). More specifically, Anders et al. found that 99 percent of participants had experienced at least one traumatic event in their lifetime and that 70 percent had experienced a traumatic event within a two-month period during the study (453). Most distressing for community college instructors is this study's finding that community college students reported higher percentages of exposure to potentially traumatic events, worse health outcomes as a result of the traumatic events, and lower life satisfaction in response to these exposures to trauma. As noted by Anders et al., “the biggest difference was in terms of being psychologically or emotionally mistreated (74% of the community college sample and 54% of the university sample)” (453). This study confirms the anecdotal evidence and compels us to recognize the pressing need to adopt a TIWP to accommodate the ways in which trauma affects our students.

In another finding, Renae Duncan noted that childhood adversity, a unique form of trauma, correlated directly with students prematurely ending their academic careers:

> The results of the current study suggest that college students with histories of child abuse are less likely than nonvictims of abuse to remain in college. The higher drop-out rates begin almost immediately, with victims more likely than nonvictims to drop out after their first semester in college, though the largest drop in enrollment appears to occur at the end of the freshman year. (993)

Given the prevalence of trauma and Duncan’s findings regarding dropout rates at the end of the first two semesters, community college instructors may be more inclined than ever to adopt a TIWP designed to strategically and comprehensively support students affected by trauma with buffering relationships and safer classroom spaces—two principles that I consider essential to a TIWP.

However, when writing instructors turn to composition theory to shape a TIWP, as I did, they will discover that scholarly voices in the writing as healing (WAH) line of inquiry generally favor a theoretical approach for responding to trauma in the writing classroom that is inadequate when compared with a clinical awareness of trauma. Generally, WAH scholars argue that the writing process can bring closure to or heal students’ psychological pain caused by acute or isolated overwhelming experiences. These scholarly voices and arguments have consistently held a place in the field’s scholarship since the early 1990s, when scholars such as Wendy Bishop started voicing support for WAH; more recently, Marion MacCurdy and Benjamin Batzer have added to WAH discussions. While these scholars and others have brought attention to the need to address trauma in the writing classroom, their contributions have centered on writing’s healing potential rather than on trauma-informed practices designed to support students affected by trauma. Bishop’s work, published in the 1990s, pointed to the composition field’s focus on process over product, response pedagogy, and expressivism as evidence for writing as therapy and addressed how writing instructors might respond to distressing student confessions. MacCurdy has argued that autobiographical writing can help individuals heal from emotional pain and distress; she supports her claim, in part, with anecdotal examples from her work with students enrolled in advanced writing courses as well as generalizations from therapeutic writing experiments. MacCurdy’s work has allowed writing instructors to consider how clinical scholarship might inform composition theory. Meanwhile, Batzer’s work has emphasized the ways in which WAH may be aligned with WPA outcomes for first-year composition and has argued that the writing process and the writing classroom community can empower students who carry the burdens of trauma. Throughout his work, he has drawn parallels between clinical scholarship and composition theory.

COMMUNITY COLLEGE STUDENTS REPORTED HIGHER PERCENTAGES OF EXPOSURE TO POTENTIALLY TRAUMATIC EVENTS, WORSE HEALTH OUTCOMES . . . , AND LOWER LIFE SATISFACTION.

WRITING AS HEALING MAY UNINTENTIONALLY PRESSURE STUDENTS TO CONFESS THEIR PSYCHOLOGICAL PAIN OR PRODUCE PAINFUL AUTOBIOGRAPHICAL WORK.

These arguments have established a framework for TIWP, but the scholarship has relied largely on general parallels between writing and healing rather than on pedagogical practices informed by clinical scholarship and designed to build relationships with and support students who are currently experiencing trauma or have a history of trauma. Additionally, WAH may unintentionally pressure students to confess their psychological pain or produce painful autobiographical work in the context of the classroom. As a result, a student’s sense of safety may be threatened, and the instructor’s ability to objectively evaluate writing may be compromised. Thus, even though WAH scholarship may be readily available for writing instructors who seek pedagogical strategies for addressing trauma in the classroom, this line of inquiry in composition scholarship falls short of informing a comprehensive TIWP.

Michelle Day confirms the need to incorporate clinical scholarship into a solid TIWP:

> The field's current writing pedagogies that address trauma are dissatisfying because they are not comprehensive enough and rely almost exclusively on humanities-based perspectives on trauma (which center on representation and memory) and almost never draw from clinical perspectives from applied fields, such as social work, which work directly with trauma survivors and continually refine best practices for interacting with those survivors. (3)

Rather than privileging the traumatic experience and memory recall as a pathway to healing, as WAH scholarship does, the clinical scholarship referred to by Day focuses on trauma-informed services designed to support survivors by establishing relationships and facilitating safer service environments. Trauma-informed service providers and scholars recognize trauma in terms of complex stress responses and survival instincts that may be defused, at least to some extent, with buffering relationships and role models who are capable of modeling resilience. More specifically, clinical scholarship published from the 1990s to the present by experts such as Maxine Harris and Roger D. Fallot, Stephen Porges, Sandra Bloom, Bessel van der Kolk, Bruce Perry, Peter Levine, and Judith Herman offers in-depth discussion of the importance of increasing safety cues and building supportive relationships in order to reduce the mobilization of the stress response and empower individuals affected by trauma. With its emphasis on evidence-based practices, this scholarship can be used by writing instructors to develop a trauma-informed lens that will ultimately serve as the foundation for a responsible, comprehensive, and supportive TIWP.

A Lens for Trauma-Informed Writing Pedagogy: Inclusive Definitions, Responses, Retraumatization, and Resilience

Even as the world's scientific community scrambled to discover a vaccine for COVID-19, the pandemic's physical, mental, and financial consequences persisted. Social distancing and quarantining measures, as well as devastating losses of wellness and life, have shined a light on the sharp inequities that divide the population and prompted a more complex awareness of trauma that was previously hidden from many Americans. As the consequences of the pandemic are beginning to light a new perspective on trauma for the American population, community college writing instructors have the opportunity to embrace a multidimensional trauma-informed lens that will enlighten and shape a TIWP. A nuanced trauma-informed lens strongly influenced by clinical scholarship can help instructors build the working knowledge and appreciation for trauma responses that they need as a foundation for a TIWP. Key elements include definitions of trauma, the importance of trauma responses, the risk of retraumatization, and resilience.

AN INCLUSIVE DEFINITION OF TRAUMA

Writing instructors may define trauma as the acute traumatic experiences that some students confess or describe in their writings, such as a tragic car accident, the unexpected death of a friend or family member, or a heinous act of violence. However, the full definition of trauma is far more extensive, and writing instructors have the opportunity to shape a more nuanced TIWP when they embrace a more inclusive definition of trauma that more fully represents some community college students' lived experiences. The surge in understanding of trauma that clinicians have gained since the mid-1990s has allowed trauma-informed service providers to appreciate the fact that adverse physical, emotional, and psychological consequences may occur when individuals are exposed either to isolated traumatic experiences or to consistently high levels of adversity, which may be referred to as *chronic*, *toxic*, or *traumatic* stress. Bloom explains that such terms are used interchangeably because "we do not have a word in English that combines 'trauma,' toxic stress,' and 'allostatic load,' so we find ourselves in a language dilemma, repeatedly hastening to explain what we *really* mean when we use the word 'trauma'" (20). Jennings, like most scholars of trauma-informed teaching and learning, approaches *trauma* as an umbrella term with a thorough awareness: "I use the terms *trauma*, *chronic stress*, *traumatic stress*, and *adversity* interchangeably to refer

KEY ELEMENTS INCLUDE DEFINITIONS OF TRAUMA, THE IMPORTANCE OF TRAUMA RESPONSES, THE RISK OF RETRAUMATIZATION, AND RESILIENCE.

to ongoing overwhelming stressors that erode our health and well-being" (9). Using an inclusive definition of trauma allows writing instructors to develop greater appreciation for the ubiquitous nature of trauma in their students' lives.

As community college writing instructors, we are familiar with our students' efforts to manage multiple responsibilities with limited resources; we hear accounts from some students of their efforts to juggle full-time employment, family, and school—all within the context of racial inequities, poverty, and the pandemic. Initially, we may not identify these lived experiences as anything that would fit into a familiar definition of acute trauma, but clinical scholarship may help us understand that these experiences do fall within a more inclusive definition of trauma that encompasses chronic or toxic stress. One approachable way to understand chronic stress as trauma comes from Dr. Nadine Burke Harris, a practicing pediatrician and the California Surgeon General. In *The Deepest Well*, she offers readers an analogy to help explain how the human body responds to a significant threat. She asks readers to consider walking in the woods and encountering a bear. The brain immediately registers the bear's presence as a threat and releases hormones to activate fight, flight, freezing, and/or numbing responses in order to survive a potential attack. Ideally, after the threat passes, the body metabolizes the stress hormones and returns to a state of homeostasis, but Burke Harris asks readers to consider the following: "What happens when you can't experience safety in your cave because the bear is living in the cave with you? . . . For many of my patients, the stress response was activated dozens and sometimes hundreds of times a day" (52). When an individual is deprived of the opportunity to return to homeostasis, stress hormones demand that the nervous system, brain, and body remain in high-alert survival mode. The bear in Burke Harris's analogy represents persistent, more frequently encountered threats in the form of daily life stressors, such as the current pandemic, poverty, racism, and domestic violence. Some of our writing students experience prolonged survival responses as they experience and cope with adversities. When we as writing instructors acknowledge chronic or toxic stress within an inclusive definition of trauma, we can better appreciate why our students may not so easily enter the classroom space focused and ready to abide by academic behavioral norms; moreover, we can better shape a nuanced and supportive TIWP that recognizes and responds to our students' lived experiences.

"WHAT HAPPENS WHEN YOU CAN'T EXPERIENCE SAFETY IN YOUR CAVE BECAUSE THE BEAR IS LIVING IN THE CAVE WITH YOU?"

TRAUMA RESPONSES OVER TRAUMATIC EXPERIENCES

Discussions of trauma typically focus on the experience. Throughout WAH scholarship, emphasis is placed on isolating, narrating, and making meaning out of the experience. The experience is tangible and initially suits the work we do in the writing classroom. However, a trauma-informed lens should look beyond the experience and examine the trauma responses that may threaten a student's success and connection in the writing classroom. Scholarly voices throughout trauma-informed services scholarship offer uniquely worded definitions of trauma, but most share the key components of the Substance Abuse and Mental Health Services Administration (SAMHSA) definition: "experiences that cause intense physical and psychological stress reactions" (xix). This definition places less emphasis on the qualities of the experience and far more emphasis on the effects of the responses associated with the experience; in other words, it values responses over experience. According to this paradigm, trauma-informed writing instructors have an obligation to develop a working knowledge of the stress response, regulation, and dysregulation—not to diagnose or label but to "allow us the ability to recognize signs of trauma in our students" (Gutierrez and Gutierrez 16) and to respond with empathy and nonjudgmental attitudes. Trauma responses are sophisticated and complex reactions that occur within the brain, body, and nervous system; when writing instructors privilege the response over the experience, we more fully appreciate that trauma entails embodied psychological, physical, and emotional responses worthy of accommodation.

WHEN STUDENTS ARRIVE FOR CLASS IN A REGULATED STATE, THEY ARE NOT EXPERIENCING THE RUSH OF HORMONES AND SURVIVAL INSTINCTS.

When students arrive for class in a regulated state, they are not experiencing the rush of hormones and survival instincts just described. Rather, their bodies are relaxed, and their brains more easily access executive functions and maintain the behavioral and emotional control necessary for effective learning. However, when the threats of the pandemic, racism, poverty, or violence continue to influence students' minds and bodies, they enter the classroom in a state referred to in clinical scholarship as *dysregulated*. Common trauma responses include experiencing varying states of hyperarousal (fight or flight) or hypoarousal (freezing or numbing). Unfortunately, in the past, I've quickly judged easily agitated writing students as extreme or hostile. Likewise, I've assumed that students who were sleeping or appearing "checked-out" lacked the motivation and desire to learn. In reality, these students may have been exhibiting a variation of hyper- or hypoarousal. Individuals who have experienced frequent or prolonged mobilization of the stress response will find it difficult to exhibit the signals I look for in engaged, productive, and motivated students. Clinical scholarship investigates these responses in detail and acknowledges that prolonged trauma exposure and dysregulation alter the brain. For example, Bessel Von der Kolk defines trauma as a "fundamental reorganization of the way mind and brain manage perceptions. It changes not only how we think and what we think about, but also our very capacity to think" (21). By recognizing, privileging, and understanding trauma responses, writing instructors can recognize the ways in which trauma and traumatic stress responses may alter students' ability to think, learn, and behave as forms of neurodiversity that deserve pedagogical approaches and practices grounded in appreciation and accommodation of these students' needs.

RISK OF RETRAUMATIZATION

The community college writing classroom is a unique learning environment that promotes community and open discussions about sometimes-challenging topics. As we work on autobiographical, argumentative, and proposal essays, the classroom community could easily engage in discussions of topics ranging from racial inequalities to sexual harassment and many other worthy, complex issues that engage students' interests, activism, and critical thoughts. Students with trauma histories, though, may view such discussions as threatening experiences; therefore, an ideal and nuanced trauma-informed awareness must also include an understanding of retraumatization. Individuals who have experienced adverse responses to traumatic experiences are more likely to be vulnerable to retraumatization, which SAMHSA defines as, "the process of reexperiencing traumatic stress as a result of a current situation that mirrors or replicates in some way the prior traumatic experience" (xviii). Threat signals enter an individual's nervous system, brain, and body through sensory cues and environmental stimuli; an individual who is persistently in a state of hyperarousal or hypoarousal will respond with swift and acute survival responses to perceived threats, and these responses may interfere with the ability to engage in learning in the writing classroom.

ALL ENVIRONMENTAL STIMULI ARE OF CONCERN, AS ARE ASSIGNMENTS.

Therefore, instructors implementing a TIWP should remain mindful and vigilant regarding the risk of retraumatization. All environmental stimuli are of concern, as are assignments. For instance, Carello and Butler warn that well-intentioned writing instructors may be exposing already vulnerable students to retraumatization when writing assignments require autobiographical accounts of painful experiences (158). Awareness of the possibility of retraumatization allows writing instructors to carefully consider and review essential elements of their classroom spaces; certainly, it is impossible to completely eliminate the risk of retraumatization for every student in our classrooms, but appreciating and being aware of how stimuli may lead students to experience trauma responses will allow us to design and implement a supportive and nuanced TIWP.

RESILIENCE

The most rewarding part of my career has been seeing so many of my students rise above so many adversities to reach their academic and personal goals. They use their personal strengths and institutional resources to remain resilient despite the challenges of academic writing, school, and life in general. In fact, resilience is arguably the most crucial area of awareness for a trauma-informed lens . SAMHSA defines resilience as "the ability to bounce back or rise above adversity as an individual, family, community, or provider. Well beyond individual characteristics of hardiness, resilience includes the process of using available resources to negotiate hardship and/or consequences of adverse events" (xviii).

Linda Graham presents a thorough interpretation of resilience as involving strategic choices made after adversity changes the brain's way of thinking and in turn the individual's behaviors and responses. She encourages individuals to be particularly perceptive of both external and internal messages regarding adversity and responses to adversity: "Our capacities for perception and response are among the most important factors determining or predicting our ability to be resilient and regain our balance going forward" (8). Therefore, resilience should be understood as a process of claiming or reclaiming the ability to self-regulate, remain flexible, and acquire healthy coping skills for responding to adversity. Explicit and frequent conversations about the process that Graham describes may be easily integrated into a TIWP, since the work of learning and laboring through the writing process can foster resilience.

In a different view, Karen Gross is critical of the term *resilience* on the grounds that it "presupposes that people can bounce back" (13). Instead, she encourages trauma-informed educators to consider the term *lasticity*, which encompasses five strength-based principles that she argues can support and encourage post-traumatic growth in college students affected by trauma. SAMHSA advocates for a similar strengths-based approach to trauma-informed services. Writing instructors who appreciate resilience and strengths-based models gain an opportunity to emphasize empowering and resourceful approaches to learning and writing. The nuanced trauma-informed lens detailed here enables writing instructors to shape the principles of a TIWP in order to support and serve their students affected by trauma.

Two Foundational Principles: Instructor as Buffering Role Model and Psychologically Safer Classroom Spaces

Fortunately, composition instructors do not need to invent a framework for trauma-informed services. Harris and Fallot set forth five principles to "*serve* survivors of childhood trauma without *treating* them for the consequences of that trauma" (3): ensuring psychological and physical safety, establishing trust, increasing choice and agency, increasing collaboration, and prioritizing empowerment. Using this clinical framework, I have designed a TIWP that includes seven principles—instructor as buffering role model; psychologically safer classroom spaces; trustworthiness and transparency in classroom routine and evaluation; peer support throughout the writing process; regulated and coregulated classroom community collaboration; self-care and the growth mindset as elements of the writing process; and cultural, historical, and gender-based trauma-informed practices—that may be understood as constituting universal design to support all students. There are two foundational principles that I encourage community college writing instructors to consider as initial steps toward a TIWP: the instructor's role as a buffering role model and psychologically safer classroom spaces. These two principles enable writing instructors to do more than show empathy for students dealing with trauma responses; when these two principles are embedded into our courses, we can understand TIWP as universal design (UD). As Anne-Marie Womack has argued, "UD privileges flexibility and redundancy, building accommodations directly into the framework of a system" (498). Based on research noted earlier, as well as anecdotal evidence that writing instructors have collected during their interactions with students, we might agree that enough of the college student population is affected by trauma and traumatic stress, especially during the collective trauma of the current pandemic, that it is responsible and necessary to embed these accommodations into our pedagogical practices in order to support all students. The following two sections detail these two principles, along with my own praxis, thus illustrating how these principles can be understood as UD.

CONSIDER THE ROLE OF A BUFFERING ADULT WHO PROMOTES AND DISPLAYS RESILIENCE AND REGULATION.

WRITING INSTRUCTOR AS BUFFERING ROLE MODEL

In WAH scholarship, the instructor's role lies somewhere on a spectrum ranging from passive or active healer to therapist to writing instructor. In contrast, scholarship on trauma-informed teaching and learning at the K–12 level advocates for instructors to consider the role of a buffering adult who promotes and displays resilience and regulation throughout course instruction, classroom spaces, and interactions with students. Nadine Burke Harris defines a buffering adult as a loving, supportive, and stable adult who serves as an essential ingredient in minimizing trauma responses and adverse consequences of traumatic experiences and chronic stress (53). While working with adults, writing instructors can begin to recognize how they might become a stable role model of regulation and resilience for their writing students, especially if they too were community college students, first-generation college students, or students who benefited substantially from instructors who modeled alternative ways of moving through the world. As Morgenroth et al. define it, "role models have three distinct functions . . . (a) acting as behavioral models, (b) representing the possible, and (c) being inspirational" (2). Acting in the capacity of a buffering role model necessitates that we consider these three functions and appreciate how our words, actions, reactions, and overall presence might mitigate responses to trauma and overwhelming stress while demonstrating flexible coping strategies and strengths-based approaches to writing and learning.

To help community college writing instructors carve out and define a trauma-informed approach as a buffering role model, a combination of K–12 trauma-informed scholarship and clinical scholarship may be useful. Such scholarship highlights that children affected by trauma and traumatic stress struggle to regulate their emotions and behaviors; as a result, they may be marginalized in the classroom and lack secure relationships with their teachers and peers. In response to these dynamics, trauma-informed pedagogy scholar Patricia Jennings discusses work done by Ruzek et al. to identify the ideal qualities for middle and high school instructors who want to build supportive relationships with students, promote regulation, and foster resilience. These qualities include perceived support, utilization, and a sense of relatedness. Perceived support consists of students' perceptions of the instructor's ability to anticipate and respond to their needs; utilization consists of students' inclination to rely on the instructor for support; and sense of relatedness consists of students' sense of belonging in the class (53).

In addition to K–12 trauma-informed scholarship, the buffering role model should also be aware of Stephen Porges's polyvagal theory, first published in 1995. The theory offers a complex model of the human nervous system that cannot be fully detailed here; in short, it posits that humans send and receive involuntary and instinctual social cues through the nervous system, brain, and body during face-to-face communication. These cues signal either safety or threat, and, as Porges describes it in a 2020 article about the pandemic's influence on humans' ability to connect, when the "'other' person projects cues regarding their autonomic state through prosodic voice, warm welcoming facial expressions, and gestures of accessibility," the stress response will downregulate and allow for calm social engagement to take place ("The COVID-19 Pandemic" 132). Awareness of the polyvagal theory enables buffering role models to be particularly cognizant of how their vocalizations and body language influence students' behaviors and interactions.

Using the concept of a buffering adult, the K–12 qualities of a supportive instructor, and the clinical framework for supporting trauma survivors, community college writing instructors can respectfully and responsibly position themselves not as healers or therapists (as WAH composition scholarship may encourage) but as buffering role models for their students. Such a role does not alter our commitment to high-quality writing instruction and to meeting course objectives. Nor does positioning ourselves as buffering role models compromise our respect for professional boundaries. Assuming the capacity of a buffering role model who is equipped with a nuanced awareness of trauma does, however, allow writing instructors to appreciate how our presence in the classroom space may support students affected by trauma.

AS A BUFFERING ROLE MODEL, I MAKE EVERY ATTEMPT TO RESERVE A FEW QUIET MOMENTS BEFORE EACH CLASS SESSION TO PRACTICE SELF-REGULATION.

As a buffering role model, I make every attempt to reserve a few quiet moments before each class session to practice self-regulation so that when I enter the classroom, my tone of voice and facial expressions may immediately send out the cues that Porges discusses as the foundation for increased levels of safety and connection. I have also committed to facilitating explicit and honest conversations about how stress interrupts the critical thinking involved throughout the stages of the writing process. I share with students that invention and revision are particularly stressful for me since they require a significant amount of time, which is a finite resource for all of us, and how stress influences the quality of my writing. Disclosing these adversities ideally shows students that I appreciate the challenges of the writing process and also feel the stressors associated with academic writing. As a buffering role model in the classroom, I also share the ways in which I manage these stressors. I explain how I integrate time for exercise and other self-care strategies into my invention and revision work to help me cope with the challenges I face while brainstorming and substantively altering my writing. I also offer concrete examples of how I budget my time during major writing projects to meet my responsibilities and commitments as a mother, wife, teacher, and student. These efforts have been particularly useful when teaching through the pandemic. I frequently and explicitly acknowledge how the pandemic has disrupted our daily lives and added multiple layers of stress and worry to our lived experiences.

Such honest and explicit discussions about stress, flexible coping strategies, and resilience attempt to normalize the levels of distress and threat faced by all writers; simultaneously, I am attempting to show strategies that my students may have never considered but that they might use to stay regulated and resilient in the face of writing adversities. Furthermore, these discussions are intended to encourage students to know they can speak to me about how to mitigate the stressors of the writing process and of college life in general before missing a series of classes or a major deadline. Overall, assuming this role recognizes the significant ways in which I attempt to support students affected by trauma without the overwhelming weight of attempting to heal or counsel them during one term. Additionally, I am able stay within the limits of my training and expertise, given that I lack the mental health training necessary to engage in therapeutic practices. As I enact the function of the buffering role model, I am able to maintain a keen focus on writing instruction and to model flexible coping strategies that might help students perceive a source of support and observe alternative ways of coping and responding to trauma and stress.

PSYCHOLOGICALLY SAFER CLASSROOM SPACES

Instructors and students must feel some level of safety and security before they can engage in the risky and daunting work of learning and writing. Individuals affected by trauma have a difficult time feeling safe because their stress responses are more sharply and consistently mobilized and because returning to homeostasis is more challenging for them than for those not affected by trauma. Students with trauma histories expend an enormous amount of energy attempting to detect and anticipate threats in their immediate surroundings that may appear completely benign and safe to others; they may find transitions (which register as some level of threat for most people) especially challenging. Therefore, a TIWP must prioritize embedding practices and strategies that contribute to establishing psychologically safer learning spaces, which will ultimately support all students, not just those with trauma histories. Promoting a psychologically safer classroom space may be challenging for instructors who already feel that their class is safe enough and therefore do not perceive potential threats, whether in online, remote, or physical classroom spaces. Fortunately, trauma-informed teaching and learning scholarship offers a framework to begin to appreciate the ways in which writing instructors can facilitate increased levels of psychological safety.

Just as building a complex awareness of trauma is essential for writing instructors interested in adopting a TIWP, so is acquiring a comprehensive definition of psychological safety. SAMHSA explains that ensuring psychological safety is an ongoing process. The organization offers two definitions of safety that are relevant to writing instructors' work in the classroom: establishing environmental safety and preventing recurrence of trauma, or retraumatization (112–13). SAMHSA notes that environmental safety considerations can include "triggers such as lighting, access to exits, seating arrangements, emotionality within a group, or visual or auditory stimuli"; preventing the recurrence of trauma, on the other hand, is concerned with decreasing or, ideally, eliminating the risk of retraumatization (19). Committing to the TIWP principle of increasing psychological safety is an undertaking that is never fully completed. Instead, trauma-informed writing instructors must consistently observe and monitor for potential environmental conditions that may threaten safety and for factors that might increase the risk of retraumatization. Carello and Butler offer the following overview of psychological safety concerns for the classroom: "individual characteristics of students, the content and context of what is taught, the requirements of assignments, aspects of both instructor and student behavior and interaction, characteristics of the classroom setting, and the instruction on and practice of self-care" (269).

Such considerations help shape a nuanced awareness of safer classroom spaces, as does the feminist theory of positionality. Even though safety is widely accepted and encouraged as a foundational principle for trauma-informed services and pedagogical practices, feminist and queer theorists argue that safety is a privilege and is impossible for some identities to experience. Their criticism must be acknowledged in a TIWP since some identities encounter frequent and significant threats in nearly all spaces throughout our culture. Here, the feminist concept of positionality becomes most useful in building safer classroom spaces. In particular, Linda Alcoff's theory of positionality encourages speakers to thoroughly examine their social locations prior to speaking for or about others; her theory calls attention to the fact that all elements of social location—including gender, sexuality, class, ability, religion, education, and race—influence a given message and its potential effects on listeners. Thus, becoming acquainted with and mindful of Alcoff's theory of positionality gives writing instructors a framework for questioning their privilege and social locations before shaping the communication they present to their students. Alcoff advises speakers to "interrogate the bearing of our location and context on what it is we are saying" (25). If instructors complete this form of interrogation prior to writing course policies, assignments, online content, and feedback on student writing, they can make significant strides in creating safer learning environments for their students.

Furthermore, as T. Passwater contends, writing instructors must see the classroom space as far more than a physical location or room and instead view it as consisting of "permeable infrastructural complexes of mobilities" (par. 10). The bodies in the room, as well as the institutional and community forces—such as the collective trauma of the pandemic, racial violence, toxic stressors, and individual trauma histories—gather and "become a knot" (par. 11). As with all concepts, understanding the theoretical view of psychologically safer spaces is far different from practical application, but Passwater offers writing instructors five suggestions for responding to such entanglements, including two that I find particularly relevant to my TIWP: breathing before responding to an impulse to repair or otherwise address a safety dilemma; and asking students what they need in order to feel safer, then using their answers to inform follow-up communication or classroom decisions (pars. 56–57).

Additional strategies can also be used to support a TIWP's commitment to creating safer classroom spaces. One strategy is to turn a trauma-informed lens on syllabi, course documents, assignments, classroom routines, feedback and instructor comments, and conferencing strategies. For instance, writing instructors may notice authoritarian language and potential threats in their course materials. In this vein, I was dismayed when I found that my syllabi, routines, and conferencing strategies could have unintentionally retraumatized students affected by trauma. In previous versions of my syllabi, for example, I used authoritarian language such as "students will write three essays in this course," "students must take responsibility for their own learning," and "late work is not accepted in this course" to make my expectations clear to students. These statements were written in response to specific conflicts throughout the years, and my severe language was a direct attempt to avoid future conflicts. However, through a trauma-informed lens complemented by Alcoff's theory of positionality, as well as T. Passwater's definition of classroom spaces, I realized that the tone could remind some students of previous situations where authority figures had inflicted pain and distress on them. My authoritarian tone might have exacerbated feelings of helplessness or the frustrations of making already-impossible choices during the pandemic. In response to this new view of my course documents, I revised the language to include more inviting and nonthreatening phrasings that promote accessibility and inclusivity for all students.

THE FEMINIST CONCEPT OF POSITIONALITY BECOMES MOST USEFUL IN BUILDING SAFER CLASSROOM SPACES.

Guidance for reconsidering the language used in syllabi is also provided by Anne-Marie Womack in her article about implementing universal design in composition classrooms and syllabi. Womack points out the distinction between viewing the syllabus as a contract that delivers information and approaching it as a rhetorical situation that offers the opportunity to extend a tone of negotiation and flexibility. Based on this distinction, she offers strategies to guide writing instructors through a shift that employs universal design to create a tone of accommodation (501–20). Using her recommendations, I altered the language of my syllabi to extend a message of psychological safety that would potentially accommodate all students' identities, backgrounds, and experiences. Currently, my syllabi explicitly communicate my commitment to establishing a greater sense of safety in the time and space we will share during the term: "I aim to create an environment where you feel safer to take risks, share your challenges and victories, and express your ideas throughout the writing and learning processes we will be using this quarter." While I cannot ensure that every person of every identity will feel completely safe in my classroom, the act of explicitly stating my intention and communicating my commitment to safer spaces is one way I have chosen to address and promote greater psychological safety. The way I communicated my late-work policy also changed after reviewing my original language with a more nuanced awareness of trauma. This awareness helped me see the arbitrary and punitive tones that previously emerged in my course document. While I have revised the language to decrease the potentially triggering language, I have not altered my expectations for timely work:

> I completely understand how hectic life can become, so I encourage you to talk to me if you believe you will not be able to meet an upcoming due date. Email me at least 8 hours before the due date, and we will find a reasonable extension. A reasonable extension is defined as an electronic or hard copy submission within 48 hours of the original due date.

Other language has been altered throughout my syllabi, which now include statements such as the following: "You are invited to complete three formal essays." "When we are all in attendance and participating in the classroom, we are allies. The perceived risks of participating in and contributing to class will reward you and the classroom community." As a buffering role model, I cannot expect to eliminate all risks and threats to psychological safety for all identities in the classroom; moreover, I am not willing to sacrifice rigor and expectations. However, the minor adjustments noted here do allow me to communicate my intentions to foster psychologically safer environments and remain open to accommodations and flexibility. Since I now explain my policy rationales in a tone that is less authoritarian, in an attempt to decrease the risk of retraumatization, I am not exacerbating the chronic stress that my students experience due to adversities outside of the classroom. Furthermore, I am embracing the central concepts of UD by communicating my willingness to be flexible with all students and to work with them to discover acceptable accommodations.

Similarly, when I turned a trauma-informed lens on my conferencing practices, I noticed problematic routines that might unintentionally retraumatize students who are attempting to cope with traumatic experiences and responses by authority figures in their lives. For example, I used to ask the student to sit directly across from me while I engaged in frequent eye contact, both of which practices invoke social engagement cues that favor my cultural background and preferences. Students experiencing trauma responses or coming from other cultural backgrounds may have been triggered by this physical arrangement. After learning about Bruce Perry's neurosequential model, I immediately altered these practices and made accommodations that serve all of my students' cultural backgrounds and social engagement preferences.

Specifically, I adopted Perry's recommendations for being present, parallel, and patient. As with all writing instructors who carry a full load of basic writing and first-year composition courses, conference days are exhausting for me. I give students specialized attention, answer their questions, and offer encouragement as they embark on the next stage of the writing process. When I thought about my conference practices through a trauma-informed lens, however, I quickly realized that I was not present for each student and was probably dysregulated at times, given my own mobilized stress response. I was preoccupied with my own time limitations, grading obligations, personal responsibilities, and trauma history. Understanding Porges's polyvagal theory helped me realize that my students picked up on this dysregulation in my facial expressions and vocalizations. These unconscious signals were received by my students and registered as potential threats in their minds, bodies, and nervous systems. To follow Perry's recommendation for being present in one-on-one interactions with students, I now give myself more frequent breaks during my conference schedule and use mindfulness and movement during these breaks to stay present with each student. In an effort to adhere to Perry's recommendation for being parallel, I invite the student to place the draft in the middle of our space and to sit or stand parallel to me. Positioning the draft in the middle of

WHEN I TURNED A TRAUMA-INFORMED LENS ON MY CONFERENCING PRACTICES, I NOTICED PROBLEMATIC ROUTINES THAT MIGHT UNINTENTIONALLY RETRAUMATIZE STUDENTS.

the space, or sharing it on my screen during remote delivery, focuses our attention on the writing, not on interpersonal efforts such as eye contact. The parallel positioning is less threatening for all students and communicates that our reason for meeting is the writing. Finally, I have worked to implement Perry's recommendation for patience by avoiding the tendency to rush into a quiet moment. Instead, I offer students more silence and thus more time to process ideas or questions.

Perry's suggestions for accommodating students affected by trauma have allowed me to better carry out my work as a writing instructor while also serving more effectively and efficiently as a buffering role model. In each of these attempts to increase psychological safety in classroom spaces, I am cognizant of how my behaviors encourage either regulation or dysregulation and potentially serve as a model for how to self-regulate as well as inspire students to persevere despite the risks associated with writing. This focus on increasing psychological safety and serving as a buffering role model provides trauma-informed writing instructors with tangible pedagogical practices that we can implement confidently and immediately to support all students, not just those who disclose their traumatic experiences or their attempts at coping with adverse trauma responses.

Additionally, writing instructors may consider facilitating discussions and incorporating activities throughout the term that open conversations about safety and community to promote psychological safety. Such discussions and activities can be frequent but quick and can help support students affected by trauma since they promote regulation and emphasize psychological safety even as they cultivate the strong sense of community valued by writing instructors. One such activity I use is based on Sandra Bloom's work with the sanctuary model, the S.A.F.E. tool, and their applications in the classroom ("Trauma Informed School Climate"). Bloom describes how she asks her students to consider what kind of safe environment they will create and support during their time together. She explains to her students that they are responsible for managing their emotions as they work to sustain such an environment. I borrowed this practice, modified it to fit my writing students' needs, and designed an activity that introduces students to the importance of safer writing classroom spaces and community. To begin the activity, I ask students to watch Drew Dudley's TEDx Talk, which offers a humorous account of a student's first day of college and the everyday actions that should be celebrated as leadership. Students appreciate the humor to offset the tensions of the first day, and the video clip bridges the classroom community into a discussion about safety and confidence despite the challenges of transitioning into the first day of writing class. I emphasize how Dudley used his natural talents and had no awareness that his actions so profoundly affected another student's decision to stay in college; I also point out that the young woman in Dudley's anecdote needed a safe connection with a peer. From there, I ask students to record their definition of a classroom space that would help them feel comfortable enough to take the necessary risks involved in the writing process. They are also invited to record two concrete ways in which they might use their natural talents and strengths to help establish such an environment. The activity encourages students to carefully consider how safety and risk may converge, recognize themselves as key agents in creating safety in the classroom, and ultimately take ownership of their safer classroom spaces.

In this same spirit, I have attempted to integrate safety throughout my daily class routines so as not to lose the emphasis on psychological safety after the initial class sessions. Before I began considering how dysregulation can affect learning, my daily practice was to assume that students were following the schedule of assignments as closely as I was and to jump into the work planned for the session. When I viewed this practice through a trauma-informed lens, however, I realized how this assumption was unreasonable given the dysregulation that students may experience as they transition from their personal and professional lives into the classroom learning environment. Furthermore, when I applied Alcoff's theory of positionality, I recognized that I was privileging my position as a college-educated instructor who values and understands the schedule of assignments. After this careful analysis, I shifted my assumptions and made it a priority to step into the function of a buffering role model by beginning the class with a short mindfulness activity and a

THIS FOCUS ON INCREASING PSYCHOLOGICAL SAFETY AND SERVING AS A BUFFERING ROLE MODEL PROVIDES TRAUMA-INFORMED WRITING INSTRUCTORS WITH TANGIBLE PEDAGOGICAL PRACTICES.

TEACHING TIPS

Tayles discusses the limitations of composition theory (writing as healing) and incorporates clinical psychology to cultivate a trauma-informed writing pedagogy. She argues that instructors and students must feel some level of safety and security before they can engage in the risky and dauting work of learning and writing. This is an on-going and never-completed process, but educators must consistently look for potential environmental conditions that may threaten safety or increase the risk of retraumatization. Without altering high-quality writing instruction, disregarding course objectives, or compromising our respect for professional boundaries, writing instructors can buffer the impact of writing stress. For example, trauma-informed writing instructors can: have explicit and honest conversations about how stressors interrupt critical thinking involved at all stages of the writing process; normalize that pandemic stress creates threats to us and our writing processes; and share ways we manage writing stressors and self-care. Try the approaches offered by Tayles and turn a trauma-informed lens on your course syllabi, assignments, classroom routines, and student feedback. Implement opportunities to serve as a buffering adult and create a psychologically safer ELA classroom.

review of the class session's agenda. These voluntary guided mindfulness activities, which are designed to regulate the body and mind, last about three to five minutes and are prefaced as being rooted in the science of neuroplasticity and not tied to any religious affiliation. I walk students through two or three class objectives, which I label as follows: "By the end of today's class session, you should be able to . . ." This approach has been particularly helpful during remote learning, as the whole community experiences frequent distractions. In the final minutes of class, I invite students to review the agenda items and objectives and check for understanding. I remind students of the supports they might access if they have unanswered questions, such as using my virtual office hours, reviewing the recording of the class, or sending an email. These embedded routines consume about seven minutes of each class meeting, but they are productive moments designed to regulate the class, ground the writing community in a common goal for the class session, and fulfill the ideas central to UD.

We cannot change the uncertainties and disruptions associated with the collective traumas of the pandemic and systemic racism; nor can we expect to heal students who have trauma histories while they are in our writing classes. But we can make trauma-informed pedagogical choices that offer students the opportunity to observe and practice regulation, acquire flexible coping skills to mitigate the adversities of academic writing, and experience psychologically safer classroom spaces. Immediately altering our pedagogies is not a feasible response as we attempt to juggle the demands of teaching loads, committee work, and life in general. However, by using a trauma-informed lens to view course materials and embedding the two principles of my TIWP discussed here—instructor as buffering role model and psychologically safer classroom spaces—we can begin the movement toward a more robust and comprehensive TIWP that supports students affected by trauma without supplanting our commitment to high-quality writing instruction.

WORKS CITED

Alcoff, Linda Martin. "The Problem of Speaking for Others." *Cultural Critique*, vol. 20, Winter 1991–1992, pp. 5–32.

Anders, Samantha L., et al. "Prevalence and Effects of Life Event Exposure Among Undergraduate and Community College Students." *Journal of Counseling Psychology*, vol. 59, no. 3, 2010, pp. 449–57. APA, doi:10.1037/a0027753.

Batzer, Benjamin. "Healing Classrooms: Therapeutic Possibilities in Academic Writing." *Composition Forum*, vol. 34, Summer 2016. ERIC, https://eric.ed.gov/?id=EJ1113422.

Bishop, Wendy. "Writing Is/And Therapy?: Raising Questions about Writing Classrooms and Writing Program Administration." *Journal of Advanced Composition*, vol. 13, no. 2, Fall 1993, pp. 503–16. JSTOR, www.jstor.org/stable/20865930.

Bloom, Sandra L. *Creating Sanctuary: Toward the Evolution of Sane Societies*. 2nd ed., Routledge, 2013.

Burke Harris, Nadine. *The Deepest Well*. Mariner, 2018.

Carello, Janice, and Lisa D. Butler. "Practicing What We Teach: Trauma-Informed Educational Practice." *Journal of Teaching in Social Work*, vol. 35, no. 3, 2015, pp. 262–78. Research Gate, doi:10.1080/08841233.2015.1030059.

———. "Potentially Perilous Pedagogies: Teaching Trauma Is Not the Same as Trauma-Informed Teaching." *Journal of Trauma and Dissociation*, vol. 15, no. 2, 2014, pp. 153–68. Research Gate, doi:10.1080/15299732.2014.867571.

Day, Michelle. *Wounds and Writing: Building Trauma-Informed Approaches to Writing Pedagogy*. 2019. University of Louisville, PhD dissertation.

Dudley, Drew. "Everyday Leadership." *TED: Ideas Worth Spreading*, Sept. 2010, www.ted.com/talks/drew_dudley_everyday_leadership?language=en.

Duncan, Renae. "Childhood Maltreatment and College Drop-Out Rates: Implications for Child Abuse Researchers." *Journal of Interpersonal Violence*, vol. 15, no. 9, Sept. 2000, pp. 987–95, Sage, doi:10.1177/088626000015009005.

Graham, Linda. *Resilience: Powerful Practices for Bouncing Back from Disappointment, Difficulty, and Even Disaster*. New World Library, 2018.

Gross, Karen. *Breakaway Learners: Strategies for Post-Secondary Success with At-Risk Students*. Teachers College Press, 2017.

Gutierrez, Daniel, and Andrea Gutierrez. "Developing a Trauma-Informed Lens in the College Classroom and Empowering Students through Building Positive Relationships." *Contemporary Issues in Education Research*, vol. 12, no. 1, 2019, pp. 11–18. ERIC, doi:10.19030/ceir.v12i1.10258.

Harris, Maxine, and Roger D. Fallot. "Envisioning a Trauma-Informed Service System: A Vital Paradigm Shift." *Using Trauma Theory to Design Service Systems*, edited by Maxine Harris and Roger D. Fallot, Jossey-Bass, 2001, pp. 3–22.

Harris, Nadine Burke. *The Deepest Well: Healing the Long-Term Effects of Childhood Adversity*. Mariner Books, 2018.

Herman, Judith. *Trauma and Recovery*. Basic, 1992.

Jennings, Patricia. *The Trauma Sensitive Classroom: Building Resilience with Compassionate Teaching*. Norton, 2019.

Levine, Peter. *Waking the Tiger: Healing Trauma*. North Atlantic, 1997.

MacCurdy, Marian M. "From Trauma to Writing: A Theoretical Model for Practical Use." *Writing and Healing Toward an Informed Practice*, edited by Charles M. Anderson and Marian M. MacCurdy, National Council of Teachers of English, 2000, pp. 158–200.

MacCurdy, Marian Mesrobian. *The Mind's Eye: Image and Memory in Writing about Trauma*. University of Massachusetts Press, 2007.

Morgenroth, Thekla, et al. "The Motivational Theory of Role Modeling: How Role Models Influence Aspirants' Goals." *The Review of General Psychology*, vol. 19, no. 4, 2015, pp. 465–83, SAGE, doi:10.1037/gpr0000059.

Passwater, T. "Precarious Spaces, Institutional Places." *Composition Forum*, vol. 41, Spring 2019, http://compositionforum.com/issue/41/precarious-spaces.php.

Perry, Bruce. "The Impact of Trauma and Neglect on Young Children," The Clinic Technical Assistance Center, 2014, www.ctacny.org/sites/default/files/trainings-pdf/intro_devel_trauma_2014_bruce_perryfinal.pdf.

Porges, Stephen. *The Pocket Guide to The Polyvagal Theory: The Transformative Power of Feeling Safe*. Norton, 2017.

———. "The COVID-19 Pandemic is a Paradoxical Challenge to Our Nervous System: A Polyvagal Perspective." *Clinical Neuropsychiatry*, vol. 17, no. 2, 2020, pp. 131–34. doi:10.36131/CN20200219.

Ruzek, Erik A., et al. "How Teacher Emotional Support Motivates Students: The Mediating Roles of Perceived Peer Relatedness, Autonomy Support, and Competence." *Learning and Instruction*, vol. 42, 2016, pp. 95–103. doi:10.1016/j.learninstruc.2016.01.004.

Substance Abuse and Mental Health Services Administration. *Trauma-Informed Care in Behavioral Health Services*. Treatment Improvement Protocol (TIP) Series 57, Substance Abuse and Mental Health Services Administration, 2014. HHS Publication No. (SMA) 13-4801.

"Trauma Informed School Climate with Dr. Sandra Bloom." *Trauma Informed Education*, 26 March 2019, https://podcasts.apple.com/us/podcast/trauma-informed-education/id1202867697.

Van der Kolk, Bessel. *The Body Keeps the Score*. Penguin, 2014.

Womack, Anne-Marie. "Teaching Is Accommodation: Universally Designing Composition Classrooms and Syllabi." *College Composition and Communication*, vol. 68, no. 3, Feb. 2017, pp. 494–525. www.ncte.org/library/NCTEFiles/Resources/Journals/CCC/0683-feb2017/CCCC0683Teaching.pdf.

MELISSA TAYLES is a full-time English faculty member at Metropolitan Community College in Omaha, Nebraska, and a doctoral student in composition and rhetoric at the University of Nebraska–Lincoln.

This article originally appeared
in *English Journal* 109.5

LATINX MOTHERS AND DAUGHTERS DEFINING THEMSELVES THROUGH ART AND WRITING

A writing workshop designed specifically for Latinx mothers and daughters encouraged participants to share their collective wisdom through stories about their lives.

TRACEY T. FLORES

There is the ever present and often silent question "What are you?" I believe that is the wrong question that is being asked. The right and more accurate question is "Who are you?" It's a complicated and yet exciting question because I cannot answer it fully. I can only answer it partly because even I am not totally sure who I completely am. I may not know right at this instant but with each passing day I discover a new piece of myself like a penny you find the sidewalk.

—LALI, NINTH-GRADE WRITER

AT THE FIRST Somos Escritoras/We Are Writers workshop, Lali (all names pseudonyms), a ninth-grade self-identified Mexican American girl, read her writing aloud in response to the question, *¿Quién soy yo?* / Who am I? In her writing, she describes her evolving understanding of what this question means to her and how with each passing day, she is discovering a new piece of herself. Lali used this opportunity to write and begin to define herself in her own words.

Lali is one of seven Chicanx/Latinx/Mexican American girls (grades 7–12) who participated alongside their mothers in the workshop. Somos Escritoras is a creative space for Latinx mothers and daughters that invites them to excavate the stories from their lives using art and writing as tools for examination and critique of their worlds (Flores, "*Cultivando la voz mujer*"). The weeklong program took place at a local university and consisted of six, two-hour evening workshops (see Figure 1).

The central goal of Somos Escritoras is to open space for the intergenerational sharing of stories, experiences, and knowledges between Latinx mothers and their adolescent daughters. From my own experiences as a second-generation Chicana, I know firsthand of the deep wisdom and lessons that reside in the stories and *consejos* (advice) shared between mothers and daughters. Dolores Delgado Bernal refers to the wisdom, knowledge, and learning that take place in the home and community between Latinx mothers and daughters as "pedagogies of the home" ("Learning and Living" 624). This learning serves as a tool of resistance and courage, supporting Latinas and Chicanas in navigating their everyday realities. Similarly, Concha Delgado Gaitan documented the ways a group of Latinx mothers supported their daughters' participation in an academic and computer literacy program. Through participation in this program, these *mujeres* cultivated a network of *mamás* that allowed them to share "life narratives," learning from one another that their "life experience exemplified knowledge, intelligence, and courage" (268), which they then shared with their daughters. Within these spaces, from the kitchen table to community centers, Latinx mothers and daughters share their histories with each other to understand themselves, as tools of self-preservation and to relate *cosas de mujeres* to one another. Somos Escritoras continues in this tradition, centering the gendered and cultural ways of knowing and being of Latinx mothers and daughters by inviting the collective sharing of stories and histories through art and writing.

FIGURE 1
Somos Escritoras mothers and daughters participated in workshops.

In this article, I share my work writing and creating alongside Latinx mothers and daughters who participated in Somos Escritoras. First, I provide a brief overview of the workshops and the literacy activities that we engaged in to build community and learn about ourselves. Then, I share a description of an art and writing activity where mothers and daughters created self-portraits, in which they defined themselves and wrote artist statements that explained the symbolism in their art. Finally, I argue for the necessity of opening spaces in language arts classrooms that provide Latinx girls, and all youth, access to powerful literacy instruction that leverages their existing practices and amplifies their voices in the classroom and beyond (Gutiérrez et al.).

A Space for Latinx Mothers and Daughters

In designing Somos Escritoras as a creative space for Latinx mothers and daughters, my co-facilitators and I drew on the work of scholars who have written and created alongside Black and Latinx girls in creative spaces (García and Gaddes; Muhammad; Winn; Wissman, "Rise Up!"). Within these spaces, Black and Latinx girls have been invited to use art, writing, and theater as powerful literacies of self-expression and as tools to critique their worlds. In addition, learning from my work alongside former students and their families in family writing workshops was foundational to the design and practices of the space (Flores, "The Family Writing Workshop").

The iteration of Somos Escritoras described in this article took place in Arizona, a state with anti-immigrant and anti-Latinx policies and mandates (Abrego and Menjívar). This includes an ethnic studies ban (Cammarota and Aguilera) and mandated English-only policies (García et al.) that control and limit access to educational opportunities for youth from historically marginalized communities. Further, these policies replicate deficit perspectives of Latinx youth and families by framing them as lacking or in need of (re)mediation (Valencia). Somos Escritoras worked to disrupt these perspectives by framing Latinx mothers and daughters as "creators and holders of knowledge" (Delgado Bernal, "Critical" 106) and building a space that was rooted in their cultural and gendered ways of knowing and being.

Somos Escritoras sessions were loosely based on the workshop approach to writing, creating, and sharing (Atwell; Calkins; Graves). All workshops were facilitated and designed by a team of three self-identified Latinx/Chicanx women, including myself, with experiences in K–8 schools. We opened each meeting with a poem to introduce the daily theme. Then, we read and discussed a piece of text, relating it to our personal experiences and perspectives. Afterward, mothers and daughters used art (e.g., painting) and writing to respond to the text. Finally, we closed our meeting with author share time, in which the mothers and daughters were invited to share their art and writing with the entire group.

At the workshops, the mothers and daughters engaged in a variety of art and writing activities that served as a vehicle for expression and storytelling. An important aspect of Somos Escritoras was the selection of culturally sustaining (Paris) mentor texts (Dorfman and Cappelli), primarily written in English and Spanish, by self-identified Chicanx, Latinx, and Mexican American writers and artists. Examples of these mentor texts included "How to Tame a Wild Tongue" (Anzaldúa), "To Be a *Pocha* or Not to Be" (De Anda), and "*Mi Problema*" (Serros). These texts focused on themes related to *familia*, culture, language, and identity. Collectively, the intentional selection of texts, paired and group discussions, and the time and space to create, write, and share our stories extended our understandings of our experiences in relation to one another and the world (Flores, "*Cultivando la voz mujer*"; García and Gaddes).

Recruiting Latinx Mothers and Daughters

To recruit Latinx mothers and daughters to participate in the workshop, I created fliers with program and registration information. I delivered these fliers to teachers, literacy coaches, and principals serving middle school and high school students, shared them on social media (e.g., Facebook), and posted them at coffee shops and libraries. After a month of recruitment, five mothers registered to participate alongside their daughters and stepdaughters. The group included seven daughters and two pairs of sisters. Of the five mothers who participated, three were born in the United States, one was born in Mexico, and one was born in Honduras. All of the mothers defined themselves as bilingual and biliterate in Spanish and English. They all worked full- or part-time, and four worked within various K–12 educational spaces (e.g., dual language teacher).

All of the girls were born in the United States and self-identified as Latinx, Chicanx, and Mexican American. Two of the girls were recent high school graduates. Four attended high school and one was transitioning from elementary to middle school. Four of the girls defined themselves as bilingual, with varying self-perceptions of their abilities. Three girls described themselves as monolingual English speakers, stating that they could understand Spanish but had trouble speaking it.

Examining Self through Art and Writing

In the next sections, I provide a description of two connected activities that the mothers and daughters engaged in during the workshops: self-portraits and artist statements. These activities provided space for the mothers and daughters to first consider how they see and represent themselves through art and then link their portraits to writing a declaration of self.

SELF-PORTRAITS: HOW DO YOU REPRESENT YOURSELF?

On the first evening, we focused on building our community of *escritoras*. We planned activities—with the goal of introducing ourselves to each other, in our own words—that would encourage the writers to begin to construct their identities within the group. In addition, we invited the mothers and daughters to consider the ways they could use art and writing as powerful tools to share their stories, like the storytellers, poets, and artists that we explored. Our anchor activity at the opening workshop examined self-portraits painted by well-known Mexican artist Frida Kahlo. Born and raised in Mexico, Kahlo experienced and overcame many challenges in her personal and professional life. Her artwork opened a window into her life while providing the world with insight into her thoughts, feelings, and emotions (Fabiny). Together, we discussed Kahlo's artwork and then created our own portraits to represent who we are and who we are becoming.

To prepare for this workshop, I collected self-portraits painted by Frida Kahlo throughout different stages of her life (see Table 1). I selected pieces that showcased the complexity of her art. In addition, these examples illustrate the ways Kahlo used colors, objects, and symbols to express her feelings, emotions, beliefs, and reality.

As mothers and daughters arrived to the workshop, they entered the room surrounded by Kahlo's self-portraits. We began our activity with a quick-write in response to the question: "Who is Frida Kahlo? *¿Quién es Frida Kahlo?*" After we wrote, we briefly shared our responses. Dolores shared, "Frida Kahlo used her art to share her feelings. Her art pushed boundaries and showed us different ways of being a woman." Her daughter Cindy nodded and added, "Yea, she learned to paint while she was recovering from a bad bus accident . . . I feel like painting saved her and helped her to heal, not like from the injury, but in her feelings." Next, we watched a short video that provided background information about Frida Kahlo's life and her art. Then, I invited everyone to participate in a gallery walk to explore and discuss the feelings evoked and symbolism they noticed in Kahlo's self-portraits. Finally, we reconvened as a group and discussed our observations.

Seated at the table alongside the mothers and daughters, I held up a blank piece of white cardstock and asked, "How do you represent and define you?" (*¿Cómo se representa y se define a sí misma?*). I continued, "Now it is your turn. Here is your canvas. I am inviting you to think about yourself, how you represent yourself and how you define yourself. Like Frida Kahlo, create a self-portrait that represents who you are, in this present moment and who you are becoming." Everyone took the card stock from the middle of their tables, selected different oil pastels, colored pencils, and markers, and began creating their self-portraits. At various stages of completion, mothers and daughters chose to represent themselves in very different ways. When they finished the pieces, everyone placed their portraits on two empty tables in the front of the room. Some portraits consisted

TABLE 1

The workshop walls displayed paintings by the well-known Mexican artist Frida Kahlo.

Title of Painting	Year Created	Location of Painting
Self Portrait in a Velvet Dress	1926	Private Collection, Mexico City, Mexico
Self Portrait with Necklace	1933	Collection of Jacques and Natasha Gelman, Mexico City, Mexico
Self Portrait with Curly Hair	1935	Private Collection, California, United States
Self Portrait the Frame	1938	*Musée National d'Art Moderne*, Paris, France
The Two Fridas	1939	*Museo de Arte Moderno*, Mexico City, Mexico
Self Portrait with Cropped Hair	1940	Museum of Modern Art, New York City, United States
Self Portrait with Thorn Necklace and Hummingbird	1940	University of Texas at Austin, Texas, United States
Me and My Parrots	1941	Collection of Mr. and Mrs. Harold H. Stream, New Orleans, Louisiana, United States
Self Portrait as a Tehuana	1943	Collection of Jacques and Natasha Gelman, Mexico City, Mexico
The Broken Column	1944	*Museo Dolores Olmedo*, Mexico City, Mexico
*The Wounded Deer/*El Vendado Herido	1946	Collection of Carolyn Farb, Houston, Texas, United States
Self Portrait with Loose Hair	1947	Private Collection, Des Moines, Iowa, United States

FIGURE 2

Adriana's self-portrait embraced her waves and curls.

FIGURE 3

Cynthia represented herself as an animal in her self-portrait.

of full body views, others centered on the face and their features, and a few represented themselves as animals (see Figures 2 and 3). We had a gallery walk, silently observing each portrait and then coming together in a circle to discuss what we noticed about our own portraits and those created by others.

ARTIST STATEMENTS: HOW DO YOU DEFINE YOURSELF?

The next day we continued our exploration of self by writing an artist statement that described the self-portraits we had created on the previous day. In *Black Feminist Thought*, Patricia Hill Collins speaks of the importance of creating positive self-definitions as a tool of resistance and survival. We invited the mothers and daughters to critically reflect on and analyze the ways they represented themselves in their self-portraits, naming and defining themselves in their own words. As they settled in to write their artist statements, I asked them to consider the following prompts: Tell me the story behind your self-portrait. (*Describa la historia de su autorretrato*). How does it define or represent you? (*¿Cómo la define y la representa?*). Each mother and daughter shared what they had written with each other and then with the entire group.

Sara, a seventh-grade writer, volunteered to share her statement aloud. Holding up her self-portrait, she stood and read aloud.

> *Mi autorretrato representa que silenciosa y trabajadora, representa mi color favorito . . . verde. Representa que soy curiosa, con ojos que quieren saber más. Representa que aunque soy silenciosa no significa que no soy curiosa, soy silenciosa porque quiero escuchar y ver, quiero descubrir mi alrededor.* [My self-portrait represents how silent and hardworking I am . . . it represents my favorite color . . . green. It represents (green eyes) that I am curious, with eyes that want to learn. They represent that even though I am silent, it doesn't mean that I am not curious. I am silent because I want to hear and see and discover my surroundings.]

Following Sara, her mother, Magda, shared her artist statement aloud.

> *Mi autoretrato me representa como soy y como me siento, una mujer trabajadora, independiente y practica. La comodidad ante todo! Por eso mi ropa y mis zapatos son comodos, me gusta sentirme libre en mis pensamientos y movimientos. Me gusta sonreir. Me hace sentir bien y creo que la sonrisa es contagiosa!* (My self-portrait represents how I am and how I feel, a hard-working woman, practical and independent. Comfort above all! That's why my clothes and shoes are comfortable. I like to feel free in my movements and thoughts. I like to smile. Smiling makes me feel good and I believe smiling is contagious!)

Both Sara and Magda used their art and writing to create a positive self-definition while illuminating who they are and who they are becoming (Collins; Delgado Bernal, "Learning and Living").

Cultivating *Escritoras*

During the workshop, the Latinx mothers and their daughters worked alongside one another to create art and craft stories that spoke to their lived experiences as *mujeres y chicas*. At each meeting, they engaged in different art and writing activities designed to encourage them to examine their histories while considering their future lives. Through the intergenerational exchange of knowledges and histories, they used art and writing as a powerful literacy to define themselves, foster open dialogue, and build *comunidad entre chicas y mujeres*.

The mentor texts served a specific and intentional purpose in our exploration and examination of self and the world. Each workshop was organized around an exploratory question (e.g., *¿Qué significa ser* Latinx/Chicanx/Mexicana? What does it mean to be Latinx/Chicanx/Mexicana?) that threaded through our readings, discussions, art, and writing. These texts addressed themes related to culture, language, gender, and identity while centering the voices and perspectives of Chicanx/Latinx/Mexican American women and girls. This provided the mothers and daughters with a platform to name and contextualize their intergenerational experiences as Latinx women and girls as it inspired the personal sharing of histories and stories (Wissman, "Reading and Becoming").

Somos Escritoras is a family engagement space created with and for Latinx mothers and daughters that centers their voices and experiences as significant resources from which we literacy educators and scholars can learn important lessons for our work. Creating welcoming spaces for parents and families that recognize the importance of their perspectives and experiences can be fostered through the reciprocal sharing of stories and histories. The invitation to share histories reframes parents and families in important ways by amplifying their voices and perspectives while creating common ground through story. The activities described here are accessible and adaptable to K–12 family literacy programming efforts to build and learn within and alongside *comunidades*. However, it is important that

THE INVITATION TO SHARE HISTORIES REFRAMES PARENTS AND FAMILIES IN IMPORTANT WAYS BY AMPLIFYING THEIR VOICES AND PERSPECTIVES WHILE CREATING COMMON GROUND THROUGH STORY.

we also participate in these spaces alongside families, by entering as a learner, listening with our entire hearts, and sharing our own stories.

Amplifying Voices

Scholars have advocated for education that is culturally sustaining and rooted in the lived experiences and realities of youth (de los Ríos; Kirkland; Morrell; Paris). Somos Escritoras is a concrete example of Latinx girls engaging in literacy instruction in which their voices and experiences are repositioned from the margins to the center (hooks), framing them as "holders and creators of knowledge" (Delgado Bernal, "Critical" 106). The design and facilitation of the workshop, which includes the art and writing activities, themes we examined, mentor texts, and the use of both English and Spanish, highlights the kind of literacy instruction that is not only necessary, but also a right of the students and communities we serve.

My goal as a teacher of writers has always been to cultivate a community of lifelong writers who recognize the importance of their stories, the cultural and familial resources that reside in their histories (Yosso), and the power of their voices. In my work alongside the Latinx mothers and daughters in Somos Escritoras, this goal was further imagined by inviting the intergenerational telling and retelling of their stories and experiences. Through the reciprocal sharing of stories, mothers and daughters opened up to each other in new ways, realizing that they were not alone in their feelings or experiences. Art also served as an important prewriting strategy as well as a tool for self-reflection and self-examination. Providing multiple entry points for writing and sharing is vital, not only in cocurricular spaces like Somos Escritoras but also in our K–12 language arts classrooms, as we work with young writers to provide opportunities for engagement and growth.

At the Somos Escritoras workshops, Latinx girls were invited to enhance their craft and use art and writing as tools for thinking and critique, building from their interests and leveraging existing practices. They read and discussed texts that examined topics relevant to their lives, but often absent from the school curriculum (Jocson). It is critical to provide Latinx girls with access to texts and instruction that center their cultural and gendered ways of knowing and being. In addition, our girls deserve a literacy curriculum that connects them to the perspectives of Latinx youth, both contemporary (e.g., Edna Chávez, Emma González) and historically (e.g., Jovita Idár, Sor Juan Inés de la Cruz) who are using and have used their writing, stories, and voices as a platform to seek justice and promote change.

Historically, many social justice movements and revolutions have been fueled by the courage, fight, and hope of youth. The language arts classroom is a prime space to cultivate the leaders for today and tomorrow. If we believe in the potential and power of youth voices, our purpose as educators must be to provide powerful literacy instruction rooted in their lived realities and centered on their expertise to facilitate their growth as readers, writers, thinkers, and critically conscious human beings.

NOTE

I would like to thank the mothers and daughters who participated in Somos Escritoras for sharing their voices and stories. To honor their voices, I made the methodological decision to preserve their written and spoken words as shared at workshops. In addition, language variations, grammatical structures, and spelling used by students and families are shared in the original oral and written form.

WORKS CITED

Abrego, Leisy J., and Cecilia Menjívar. "Immigrant Latina Mothers as Targets of Legal Violence." *International Journal of Sociology of the Family*, vol. 37, no. 1, 2011, pp. 9–26.

Anzaldúa, Gloria. *Borderlands/*La Frontera*: The New* Mestiza. 3rd ed., Aunt Lute, 1987.

Atwell, Nancie. *In the Middle: New Understandings about Writing, Reading, and Learning*. Boynton/Cook, 1998.

Calkins, Lucy. *The Art of Teaching Writing*. Heinemann, 1994.

Cammarota, Julio, and Michelle Aguilera. "'By the Time I Get to Arizona': Race, Language, and Education in America's Racist State." *Race, Ethnicity, and Education*, vol. 15, no. 4, 2012, pp. 485–500.

Collins, Patricia Hill. *Black Feminist Thought: Knowledge, Consciousness, and the Politics of Empowerment*. Routledge, 2000.

De Anda, Iris. *Codeswitch: Fires from* Mi Corazón. Los Writers Underground Press, 2014.

de los Ríos, Cati V. "Writing from *La Panza*!: Exploring Monologue Literacies with Emergent Bilinguals." *English Journal*, vol. 105, no. 5, 2016, pp. 75–80.

Delgado Bernal, Dolores. "Critical Race Theory, Latino Critical Theory, and Critical Race-Gendered Epistemologies: Recognizing Students of Color as Holders and Creators of Knowledge." *Qualitative Inquiry*, vol. 8, no. 1, 2002, pp. 105–22.

———. "Learning and Living Pedagogies of the Home: The Mestiza Consciousness of Chicana Students." *International Journal of Qualitative Studies in Education*, vol. 14, no. 5, 2001, pp. 623–39.

Delgado Gaitan, Concha. "Family Narratives in Multiple Literacies." *Anthropology and Education Quarterly*, vol. 36, no. 3, 2005, pp. 265–72.

Dorfman, Lynne R., and Rose Cappelli. *Mentor Texts: Teaching Writing through Children's Literature, K–6*. 2nd ed., Stenhouse, 2017.

Fabiny, Sarah. *Who Was Frida Kahlo?* Penguin, 2013.

Flores, Tracey T. "*Cultivando la voz mujer*: Latina Adolescent Girls and their Mothers Rewriting Their Pasts and Imagining Their Futures." *Literacy Research: Theory, Method, and Practice*, vol. 67, no. 1, 2018, pp. 211–27

——. "The Family Writing Workshop: Latinx Families *Cultivando Comunidad* through Stories." *Language Arts*, vol. 97, no. 2, 2019, pp. 59–71.

García, Andrea, and Amy Gaddes. "Weaving Language and Culture: Latina Adolescent Writers in an After-School Writing Project." *Reading and Writing Quarterly*, vol. 28, no. 2, 2012, pp. 143–63.

García, Eugene E., et al. "The Education of English Language Learners in Arizona: A History of Underachievement." *Teachers College Record*, vol. 114, no. 9, 2012, pp. 1–18.

Graves, Donald. *Writing: Teachers and Children at Work*. Heinemann, 1983/2003.

Gutiérrez, Kris D., et al. "Re-mediating Literacy: Culture, Difference, and Learning for Students from Nondominant Communities." *Review of Research in Education*, vol. 33, no. 1, 2009, pp. 212–45.

hooks, bell. *Feminist Theory: From Margin to Center*. Pluto, 2000.

Jocson, Korina. "Unpacking Symbolic Creativities: Writing in School across Contexts." *Review of Education, Pedagogy, and Cultural Studies*, vol. 32, no. 2, 2010, pp. 206–36.

Kirkland, David E. "'The Rose That Grew from Concrete': Postmodern Blackness and New English Education." *English Journal*, vol. 97, no. 5, 2008, pp. 69–75.

Morrell, Ernest. "Critical English Education." *English Education*, vol. 37, no. 4, 2005, pp. 312–21.

Muhammad, Gholnecsar. "Creating Spaces for Black Adolescent Girls to 'Write It Out!'" *Journal of Adolescent and Adult Literacy*, vol. 56, no. 3, 2012, pp. 203–11.

Paris, Django. "Culturally Sustaining Pedagogy: A Needed Change in Stance, Terminology, and Practice." *Educational Researcher*, vol. 41, no. 3, 2012, pp. 93–97.

Serros, Michele. *Chicana Falsa and Other Stories of Death, Identity, and Oxnard*. Riverhead Books, 1998.

Valencia, Richard R. *Dismantling Contemporary Deficit Thinking: Educational Thought and Practice*. Routledge, 2010.

Winn, Maisha T. *Girl Time: Literacy, Justice, and School-to-Prison Pipeline*. Teachers College P, 2011.

Wissman, Kelly K. "Reading and Becoming Living Authors: Urban Girls Pursuing a Poetry of Self-Definition." *English Journal*, vol. 98, no. 3, 2009, pp. 39–45.

——. "'Rise Up!': Literacies, Lived Experiences, and Identities within an In-School 'Other-Space.'" *Research in the Teaching of English*, vol. 45, no. 4, 2011, pp. 405–38.

Yosso, Tara J. "Whose Culture Has Capital? A Critical Race Theory Discussion of Community Cultural Wealth." *Race, Ethnicity, and Education*, vol. 8, no. 1, 2005, pp. 69–91.

TRACEY T. FLORES is an assistant professor of language and literacy in the Department of Curriculum and Instruction at the University of Texas at Austin. She is a former English language development (ELD) and English language arts teacher, working for eight years in schools throughout Glendale and Phoenix, Arizona. She has been an NCTE member since 2009 and can be contacted at tflores@austin.utexas.edu and on Twitter @traceyhabla.

This article originally appeared in *Voices from the Middle 28.4*

HARM AND HEALING: Reading with an ABAR (Anti-Bias, Antiracist) Lens

ELIZA RAMIREZ & SARAH J. DONOVAN

Eliza: "Why do they hate us?" My students have asked me this question. My immigrant students, my Latinx students, my queer students have asked the same question posed by a Syrian immigrant child in *Other Words for Home* by Jasmine Warga. When reading through the incidents of prejudice, bias, and racism in verse novels for our teacher book club—like the one that prompted this question—I reflected on the way I, as a Mexican American, straight, cis-female introverted daughter of immigrants, present and discuss these moments with my students. I asked: How do I hold space for them to learn the vocabulary to name and discuss people in books, so they may name and discuss real-world incidents and find their path toward healing from the many incidents they witness and experience in their young lives? How do I ensure we discuss these incidents for what they are without perpetuating harm? How do I empower them to speak out against incidents of bias and injustice?

Sarah: I met Eliza through a summer online teacher book group. Across June and July, we read middle grade novels together and met online to talk about sharing these books with our middle school students. Eliza's questions about *Other Words from Home* prompted me, a white, straight, cis-female introverted granddaughter of immigrants, to reflect on how I present and discuss bias and racism with my students, mostly white pre- and inservice teachers preparing to teach grades 6–12. And I reflected on other reading I was doing that summer. Like many teachers, I read Ibram X. Kendi's *How to Be an Anti-Racist*, who wrote: "The opposite of racist isn't 'not racist.' It is 'anti-racist'" (p. 9). He explains there is no in-between safe space of "not racist" in that we either allow racial inequities to persevere as a racist or confront racial inequities as an anti-racist. So when I read with the teachers and when I now read with my students, I know that when I model reading in a way that does not confront racial or social inequalities, I model biased, racist reading. By not naming harm, I am not confronting bias and racism and therefore sustaining inequity. But I was not sure how to do this in a way that also nurtured healing.

As educators engage in the work to embrace anti-bias antiracist (ABAR) principles, disrupt texts (see Tricia Ebarvia, Julia Torres, Kimberly Parker, and Lorena Germán), and decolonize ELA curriculum, many are choosing to incorporate excellent texts by BIPOC and LGBTQ+ authors. With more texts presenting diverse experiences that include—but are not limited to—incidents of bias and/or racism, presented by #ownvoices (see Corinne Duyvis) and others, we are concerned that their use, without careful thought and planning from teachers, may

BY NOT NAMING HARM, I AM NOT CONFRONTING BIAS AND RACISM AND THEREFORE SUSTAINING INEQUITY. BUT I WAS NOT SURE HOW TO DO THIS IN A WAY THAT ALSO NURTURED HEALING.

cause harm to the very students to whom those texts can provide mirrors, windows, and sliding doors (see Rudine Sims Bishop). We met to plan for our next book discussion of *They Call Me Güero* by David Bowles to create a guided reading protocol with an ABAR lens that we share here.

ABAR Background

Anti-bias antiracist (ABAR) education—teaching against bias and racism—is not new. Through multicultural education programs of the 1970s (James, 1971; Ogbu, 1974; Garcia, 1974), educators worked to help students understand and celebrate diverse cultures. Recognizing the limitations of some multicultural education programs to solve social inequities, Paulo Freire (1970) advocated for critical pedagogy, a social justice approach of teachers and students engaging together with "critical information, awareness, and understanding of social inequities to take corrective action" (quoted in Bell, p. 31).

Gloria Ladson-Billings advocated culturally relevant teaching (CRT) in 1994, calling for teachers to consider culture to engage students excluded from the mainstream. Django Paris (2012) offered an alternative to CRT: culturally sustaining pedagogy (CSP). CSP seeks to foster and sustain linguistic, literate, and cultural pluralism as part of the democratic project of schooling. This resists assimilation and supports the value of our multiethnic and multilingual present and future. Geneva Gay (2018) also built on CRT to provide a framework for the practice of culturally *responsive* teaching. And Zaretta Hammond (2016) has both detailed the way the brain learns through CRT to develop students' cognitive abilities and advance their learning and clarified myths around CRT.

IF OUR GOAL IS TO CHANGE THAT AND NURTURE AUTONOMY AND AGENCY WITHIN OUR STUDENTS TO PRESENT THEMSELVES WHOLLY IN OUR CLASSROOMS, WE NEED AN ABAR LENS TO CHOOSE, SHARE, AND DISCUSS TEXTS WITH STUDENTS.

We read Dr. Bettina Love's work in *We Want to Do More Than Survive* (2019) while working on this protocol. Love's work calls for abolitionist teaching: "[T]he practice of working in solidarity with communities of color while drawing on the imagination, creativity, refusal, (re)membering, visionary thinking, healing, rebellious spirit, boldness, determination, and subversiveness of abolitionists to eradicate injustice in and outside of schools" (p. 2). So we see ABAR work as having a long tradition that is responsive and evolving.

Multicultural, social justice, culturally sustaining, culturally relevant, abolitionist—whichever framework(s) guide your curriculum and instruction—the need for ABAR work is clear. Bias and racism are contributing to deaths. If our goal is to change that and nurture autonomy and agency within our students to present themselves wholly in our classrooms, we need an ABAR lens to choose, share, and discuss texts with students.

Incident of Harm and Healing Analysis Using an ABAR Lens

Drawing on ABAR, we developed a guided reading approach we call Harm and Healing Analysis Protocol to nurture a capacity to notice harm and healing within a text. Before explaining the process, we offer the protocol in Table 1 to show how we named harm and noticed healing in *They Call Me Güero: A Border Kid's Poems* by David Bowles. This book is a collection of poems about growing up as a 12-year-old Mexican American boy. Readers never learn the boy's birth name, only that family and friends call him Güero. Güero, a nickname for boys with pale skin in Mexican culture, lives on both sides of the Rio Grande border, and he speaks both English and Spanish. He tells readers that he is "puro Mexicano," a reader, gamer, and a musician entering seventh grade.

After Eliza modeled her reading and thinking, our book group began to practice noticing harm and healing by selecting poems from the book and working through the protocol. Then, we shared out to name instances of bias/racism and discuss the systems in place that perpetuate harm. There was silence in this process, and that was welcome. We had to hold space, embrace discomfort, and support one another. This is necessary to transfer the professional development experience into a practice that offers us, as educators, and the students with whom we share our classrooms, a way of reading that interrupts the maintenance of bias and acknowledges what it takes to heal the harm done when we don't.

Reading with ABAR awareness means taking notice of incidents of harm and unfairness, "that an event has occurred that effects the maintenance or elimination of oppression" (Love, 2010, p. 600). ABAR awareness also means noticing healing in the characters' lives to see and celebrate individual and

TABLE 1

Harm and Healing Analysis Protocol

Process	Example from *They Call Me Güero*
Select a passage where a character was harmed; note ahead of time if there is harmful language and acknowledge it, but do not read it as to not perpetuate further harm.	On page 83, the main character and his town board a bus to the playoff basketball game against a neighboring town. As it becomes clear that his team might win, "The other fans now boo and scream / and then a sickening chant commences / horrible words that beat at our senses." The next lines contain racial and xenophobic slurs—intended to harm Latinx (immigrant) people—that we choose not to include here, nor did Eliza utter aloud during modeling. Continued: "A sea of white faces, twisting in rage / like all the brown bodies are there to invade."
Read the passage, pausing after the part depicting harm; summarize what you noticed and name the harm/unfairness	In this passage, I read that as the protagonist's team begins to win, the opposition's fans turn angry and chant a racial slur. I will name the harm racism and xenophobia. The harm is othering them, telling them they don't belong, implying that the Latina girls' basketball team is inferior not for how they play the game, but for their identity as fans perceive it.
Read on, search for healing: Reflect on any attempt to repair harm by an individual or a community/system; is it successful/enough?	"When all is over, the other team's coach / asks our forgiveness in front of the crowd. / Security clears us a path to our vehicles / and we march off together, proud and unbeatable." The coach attempts to repair harm through a public apology. An individual, not the community of fans who perpetrated the harm, merely apologized; no system/policy was altered. Will this change either community?
Search for healing from other sources! Perhaps the community or culture offers joy, celebratory representations of the character's identities to begin the healing.	It is not a coincidence that after the prejudice poem, follows "Spanish Birds": "Everyone I know / speaks a different Spanish: / The rural twang of border folk, / the big-city patter of immigrants, / the shifting mix of Tex-Mex" (p. 85). Then, descriptions of family members differing, via bird metaphors, communicates "we are not a monolith," we are individuals not to be judged by appearances and assumptions. He celebrates his culture, family, and language with "I hear the echo of their calls / when I speak. / My own tongue / is an aviary." But a harm as deep as what was portrayed required a dip into deep culture, so the author offers "Mis Otros Abuelos" where Güero visits his grandparents in Mexico until he declares, "[M]e siento recargado de cultura / more Mexican, I suppose, / with the gentle kisses / of my other abuelos / on my forehead / like lucky charms / against all / harms." (88) When he's recharged on culture, our students who see a mirror in him can feel that, too; our students who are walking through a sliding glass door can see beyond any limiting victim narrative.

group identities, and, in doing so, interrupt bias. (See Figure 1 for suggested middle grade titles.) Readers notice family and friends who comfort, hobbies and interests that bring joy and beauty, and places and experiences that restore confidence and liberate hearts, minds, and souls. When readers notice harm and healing in stories—literary and lived—they begin to identify and interrogate systems that harm and identify systems that heal.

A Closer Look at the Harm and Healing Protocol

BEGIN THE ANALYSIS OF HARM

Many of us need practice naming racism, classism, misgendering, sexism, colorism, homophobia, ableism, and patriarchy. For middle school students, we suggest beginning with the word "unfairness." When reading a passage where someone is

FIGURE 1

Middle grade novels to use with the Harm and Healing Analysis Protocol.

mistreated, ask *What is unfair here? What makes this unfair?* As students discuss the scene, the teacher can offer the language of -isms, co-constructing definitions that help students consider who has the power and why and what beliefs about humanity and belonging perpetuate the unfairness. Sometimes, unfairness will take the form of harmful sarcasm, insensitivity that demeans a person's identity, and/or comments or behaviors that exclude, negate, or dismiss a person or group's feelings or experiences. In most instances of unfairness, someone is not seen as an equal. Where do such beliefs originate? This is the beginning of delving deeper into systemic harm.

NOTICE AND ANALYZE HEALING

Once we name the harm, we look for evidence of healing or how the harm is repaired. Ask what needs to be done and then notice within the narrative what was done or not done to repair harm. Examine if our answers lie with individuals or systems and why. Can an individual repair systemic/institutionalized wrongs? Through this protocol, students begin to interrogate systems that enable the harm we notice in our reading: classroom or school rules, gender binaries, policies, laws, media coverage, and various institutions that allow for bystanders and inaction. Similarly, students can examine what systems are in place to repair and heal harm: From (chosen) family and friends to cultural, religious, and spiritual traditions, characters and people may turn to formal and informal structures, if they have access. This examination may reveal where systems for healing are not available or are inadequate in their ability to address the harm incurred, and in turn can lead students to an understanding of what society values and doesn't and where systems need change.

Dr. Barbara J. Love explains that noticing healing is about "locating the resources that empower another person to act with agency" (p. 603). If an apology was given, was there room for a choice in accepting it or turning it down? (Like in "Playoff Game," if they'd rejected the individual apology and demanded a community apology, would security allow them to leave?) Were amends made for the harm? What policies and systems need further dismantling to allow for amends and ensure agency? What we noticed in developing this protocol was that healing questions invite us to confront current systems, imagine new systems, and notice how individual characters (and our students) have had to find healing beyond public settings such as school.

Characters (and people) will seek out their own path toward healing; there is no one path. Understanding those paths means learning the language of joy, acceptance, expression, resistance, appreciation, pride, and love. How do the characters understand and seek out opportunities to repair harm or heal? Who or what brings the character comfort, safety, and connection? How are the pieces of their identity that were just attacked reaffirmed or celebrated? How does the author show the character experience joy? Characters may begin to heal through joy. Bettina Love said that joy is part of liberation. Thus, we want to be sure that the reading we do alongside our students names joy, affirms complex identities, and accepts many ways of being in the world.

We see the greatest potential of this protocol (see Table 2) in the hands of students when they choose the books, choose the passages, do the naming, and notice joy. Further, we imagine students will want to write their own experiences as personal or fictionalized accounts in prose, verse, comic, or digital spaces.

Adaptation and Limitations

Let's say you've done the inner work. You've used an ABAR lens to choose a particular text to read aloud to your students, and you arrive at a passage with an incident of prejudice. You cannot simply treat it as you would any other passage, having students make connections, infer a theme, or gather text evidence, without acknowledging the harm done.

TABLE 2

Additional Questions for Harm and Healing Analysis

1. What happened?
2. Name the unfairness (racism, sexism, colorism, homophobia, classism, ableism).
3. How did the incident cause harm/hurt?
4. What did the character think/feel during or right after the incident?
5. What did the bystanders do or not do?
6. Who caused the harm? *What systems are in place to enable the harm?*
7. What do you think needs to happen to make things right?
8. How did the author shift toward healing?
9. Where and with whom does the character find comfort, safety, love, and joy? Who or what accepts the character and who or what does the character celebrate?
10. *What systems are in place to help healing?*

To truly apply an ABAR lens, it's important to help students speak out against bias and injustice, meaning you've spent time creating a community with your students, you've developed a shared language, and you've listened to every student. You're preparing your interactive read aloud of a literary passage that provides an opportunity to engage in ABAR practices with your students. Your school context, classroom culture, students, and your relationships will vary, as will and should your use of this analysis.

What if there is no healing portrayed after bias or racist harm is portrayed in the book? What, then, is the impact on the students reading that portrayal of bias or racism? What will you as an educator do to offset the harm done to students who may see that character as a mirror? Is this one more message of racism they must internalize? Should and how will you provide opportunities for healing and joy?

Let us be clear: This is not just a protocol for teachers of Black and Brown students. This work is just as necessary, if not more necessary, for white students as they develop their racial consciousness and learn about white privilege and institutionalized racism enacted on individuals and racialized groups by long-standing systems designed to oppress through the maintenance of the status quo.

To be honest, the biggest limitation to ABAR work is you. Any educator engaged in this work will tell you that you have to do the inner work first. What you don't know can and will hurt you, your students, and our community.

Action: Next Steps as Co-conspirators

We appreciate Alicia Garza, cofounder of Black Lives Matter with Patrisse Cullors and Opal Tometi, and Dr. Bettina Love's definition of the concept of *co-conspirators* as people who are actively fighting against the system of white supremacy and in particular the benefits received from it. We see reading and naming literary harm as activism within the classroom, and hopefully, it may transfer beyond the classroom into what Freire says is reading the world. In the spirit of co-conspiring, we wonder how we can extend this protocol to engage students to create new systems of healing. We wonder how this protocol will evolve with our continued practice as Eliza reads with her students in Illinois and Sarah readers with her students in Oklahoma. We are looking for more examples in literature where we can name what happens when characters (and people) not only interrupt and name harm, but demand systemic healing; and, if the characters don't do this within the narrative, what would happen if they did; and, in life, when *we* do. What does a story with systemic healing look like? What does a story without harm look like? As Kendi reminds us in *Stamped*, "An anti-racist America is sure to come . . . and maybe that time is now"(quoted in Reynolds, p. xvi).

We are not experts on ABAR education; we are committed to learning and developing our ABAR lens, and we encourage you to seek out the many resources available from organizations and educators who have been doing this work for decades (see Table 3).

TABLE 3

Resources for Continued (Un)Learning

Instagram	Organizations and Other Resources
@teachandtransform, Liz Kleinrock	"Let's Talk: Facilitating Critical Conversations with Students" (Learning for Justice, https://www.learningforjustice.org/magazine/publications/lets-talk)
@britthawthorne, Britt Hawthorne	"Empowering Educators: A Guidebook on Race and Racism (First Book, https://www.fbmarketplace.org/free-resources/)
@tiffanymjewell, Tiffany M. Jewell	"Anti-Bias, Anti-Racist Education" (Crossroads Antiracism Organizing and Training, http://crossroadsantiracism.org/training/antibias_antiracism)
Podcasts	Institute for Racial Equity in Literacy, Dr. Sonja Cherry-Paul and Tricia Ebarvia
Nice White Parents	
ATN—Teaching to Thrive	
Third Space with Jen Cort	
Queer America	
Teaching While White	
The Anti-Racist Educator	

TEACHING TIPS

The authors explain that as educators work to include anti-bias and antiracist (ABAR) principles, disrupt texts (see Tricia Ebarvia, Julia Torres, Kimberly Parker, and Lorena Germán), and decolonize ELA classrooms, many are starting to choose and incorporate texts written by Black, Indigenous, and People of Color (BIPOC) and LGBTQ+ authors. Ramirez and Donovan argue educators can use #ownvoices texts and still cause harm to the communities they are supposed to be honoring if they do not carefully think through how to use such texts. Therefore, Ramirez and Donovan developed a "harm and healing analysis protocol." To use the protocol with integrity, educators must engage in inner work. Meet with co-conspirator colleagues to practice using the ABAR protocol. Then in your ELA classroom, choose #ownvoices texts. Start with one of the texts mentioned in the article, if you need suggestions. With guidance from the article, implement the protocol with your students. Ask your students how reading with an ABAR lens supports their learning and healing inside and outside of the classroom. Brainstorm ways to incorporate ABAR into your school's culture.

REFERENCES

Bell, L. A., & Adams, M. (2016). *Teaching for diversity and social justice*. Taylor & Francis.

Bishop, R. S. (1990). Mirrors, windows, and sliding glass doors. *Perspectives*, 6(3), ix–xi.

Bowles, D. (2018). *They call me Güero: A border kid's poems*. Cinco Puntos Press.

Craft, J. (2019). *New kid*. HarperCollins.

Garcia, E. (1974). Chicano cultural diversity: Implications for competency-based teacher education. In W.A. Hunter (Ed.), *Multicultural education through competency-based teacher education*. American Association of Colleges for Teacher Education.

Gay, G. (2018). *Culturally responsive teaching: Theory, research, and practice*. Teachers College Press.

Freire, P. (1970). *Pedagogy of the oppressed*. Herder & Herder.

Holt, K. A. (2019). *Redwood and Ponytail*. Chronicle Books.

Hammond, Z. (2014). *Culturally responsive teaching and the brain: Promoting authentic engagement and rigor among culturally and linguistically diverse students*. Corwin Press.

James, R. (1974). Multicultural education from a black educator's perspective. In W.A. Hunter (Ed.), *Multicultural education through competency-based teacher education*. American Association of Colleges for Teacher Education.

Jordan-Fenton, C., Pokiak-Fenton, M., & Amini-Holmes, L. (2010). *Fatty legs*. Annick Press.

Kendi, I. X. (2019). *How to be an antiracist*. One World.

Ladson-Billings, G. (1994). *The dreamkeepers: Successful teachers of black children*. Jossey Bass.

Love, B. J. (2010). Developing a liberatory consciousness. In M. Adams, W. J. Blumenfeld, C. R. Castañeda, H. W. Hackman, M. L. Peters, & X. Zúñiga, (Eds.), *Readings for diversity and social justice* (2nd ed., pp. 599–603). Routledge.

Love, B. L. (2019). *We want to do more than survive: Abolitionist teaching and the pursuit of educational freedom*. Beacon Press.

Nagai. M. (2019). *Under the broken sky*. Henry Holt and Company.

Ogbu, J. (1974). *The next generation*. Academic Press.

Paris, D. (2012). Culturally sustaining pedagogy: A needed change in stance, terminology, and practice. *Educational researcher*, 41(3), 93–97.

Reynolds, J. (2020). *Stamped: Racism, antiracism, and you: A remix of the national book award winning* Stamped from the beginning. Little, Brown.

Salazar, A. (2020). *The land of the cranes*. Scholastic.

Stone, N. (2020). *Clean getaway*. Random House.

Warga, J. (2019). *Other words for home*. Balzer + Bray.

ELIZA RAMIREZ, NBCT and Golden Apple Award recipient, teaches middle level students in Chicago, co-leads a writing group and a self-care book study for educator friends, and shares professional development experiences on Instagram @LearnHopeTeach.

SARAH J. DONOVAN is an assistant professor of secondary English education at Oklahoma State University, and her current research explores inclusive curriculum and pedagogy in teacher professional development.

This article originally appeared
in *English Journal* 110.2

#TEENPOETSMATTER: Writing Critical Micropoems as Urban Social Critiques

Two teacher educators share a creative way for youth to write short-verse, place-based poetry as social critiques.

JEVON DELEXANDER HUNTER
& GLISET COLÓN

AS TEACHER EDUCATORS in Buffalo, New York, we have the opportunity in the summer to step aside from our duties and responsibilities of preparing the next generation of classroom teachers and collaborating with current ones to be among our city teens dancing, eating, laughing, reading, singing, and writing in a literacy academy. This time allows us to combine the best features of our teaching experiences from high school (Jevon) and elementary school (Gliset) to create a unique poetry writing curriculum that focuses on the struggles and triumphs youth experience in schools and broader society. The young people in our learning space identify as African American and Hispanic/Latinx, and our conversations cover different injustices adolescents encounter in their day-to-day lives.

The discussions include (a) curricular misrepresentation or erasure of minoritized people; (b) many schools as sites of containment, control, punishment, and surveillance of Black and Brown bodies; (c) police-state sanctioned violence in their neighborhoods; and (d) white-based racial terrorism toward families and communities. We admit these topics are emotive and heavy, yet they are expressed by the adolescents with whom we work. As we navigate these terrifying moments together, we encourage the teens to seek solutions to the hostilities and realities they face outside their doors and in their schools.

Our young people often communicated their appreciation for this approach to poetry engagement, expressing they are unable to have these conversations and write about them in schools. Alicia, a sixteen-year-old, African American participant and self-identified poet, shared this sentiment with us as she explained her schooling experiences in English language arts (ELA) classrooms:

> We don't have the *platform* to say what we want to say. They'll [Teachers] never talk about how Black children in Buffalo or just the United States or the world in general are oppressed. They won't touch on the *subject* because maybe it's too *sensitive*, but we've never really touched on that in high school, ever! (emphasis added)

Unfortunately, Alicia's bold and revealing comments spoke directly to our combined experiences as observers, researchers, and teachers of ELA classrooms within the region. We have witnessed few opportunities within the curriculum for adolescents to study and write about the substantive oppressive forces affecting the living/lived social realities of African American and Hispanic/Latinx youth. As Alicia suggested, ELA classrooms need a platform (e.g., plans of action, ways of doing things, activities to be shared with an audience) to support students as they work through their sense-making of oppression, privilege, power, and other sensitive, but necessary, subjects. In response to the need for a platform to explore and convey sensitive subjects, we developed a place-based poetic form we call critical micropoetry.

In this article, we invite teachers to consider including as part of their poetry curriculum our version of critical micropoetry, a short-verse style using the local telephone number area code as a poetic organizational tool and structural format to articulate the localized challenges faced by teens, while also redressing these challenges with youth-initiated solutions. We present our instructional and curricular journey, providing insights and resources to complement delving into and learning about the lives of adolescents in our schools and communities. We believe teachers can adopt critical micropoetry as a rhetorical genre to (1) engage young people in poetry writing that speaks to their social realities, (2) foster discussions of localized injustices faced by adolescents, and (3) support explorations of youth-generated solutions to real-world problems.

Our Youth Summer Literacy Academy

During the summer of 2017, we co-created and co-taught a five-week multimodal and inquiry-based (Wilhelm) summer literacy academy for adolescents. We recruited high school students from across Buffalo to meet at our college campus, SUNY Buffalo State. To participate, teens only needed to complete an application and express an interest in attending. Forty-two youth participated, representing grades 9 through 12 from public, charter, and private schools. We taught the poetry curriculum Monday through Thursday for one and a half hours each day. Our academy focused on supporting youth experiences, and we knew that poetry was a productive medium for youth "to share their stories and develop their voices" (Williams 82) through writing.

We drew from our collective teaching experiences and knowledges of justice education (Kinloch; Nieto and Bode) to organize a respite and refuge for African American and Hispanic/Latinx city youth. The learning environment was cultivated as a place where educational fellowship and intellectual struggle would meet intergenerational hope, our version of an educational sanctuary (Espinoza) with radical healing (Ginwright). As part of our classroom practice, we referred to the young people as Brother and Sister Scholars, affirming their identities, histories, and expertise, while creating a fictive kinship.

Our academy's work was guided by an essential question: *What does it mean to be a teenager living, learning, and loving in Buffalo in 2017?* We communicated this question frequently to the youth to stimulate thought and capture the distinctive life experiences of racialized adolescents. Our teaching roles alternated between instructor and facilitator, providing explicit instruction around complicated material or misunderstood information, and then shifting to guide and help teens as they gained confidence with the concepts.

Reading and Writing the Wor(l)d

Our poetry work with youth centered on developing their literacy skills and supporting their sociopolitical awareness. The poetry writing journey began by anchoring ourselves in reading and discussing Chapter 2 from *Pedagogy of the Oppressed* by Paulo Freire. We chose this chapter because it afforded us a language of educational and social critique. As we read and discussed together, we covered key concepts with mini-lectures. Our conversations centered on Freire's discussions of critical consciousness, banking and problem-posing education models, and praxis and their application to the current conditions of schools and society. We regularly used the construct *The Way the World Is and The Way the World Could Be* to emphasize the problem/solution dichotomy and to encourage becoming agents of change.

To ground Freire's ideas in our youths' social realities, we led Scholars through multimodal activities with supporting prompts (see Table 1). We watched videos to examine school structures, curriculum design, and the feelings both generated in students. We also listened to select songs from rapper-activist Kendrick Lamar to discuss issues of identity, mental health, poverty, and complexion. Last, we facilitated performance pedagogy exercises (what we referred to as Teatro) to integrate physical movements with critical dialogue (Cahnmann-Taylor and Souto-Manning).

The performance pedagogy exercises were a crucial part of the academy's design. We encouraged Scholars to manipulate their bodies as a form of storytelling, using the body and its movements to illustrate, critique, and attend to injustices in school and society. Teatro helped us further emphasize *The Way the World Is and The Way the World Could Be* construct, as we asked youth to arrange their bodies

TABLE 1

Concepts, Activities, and Prompts

Freirean Concepts	Sample Activities and Prompts
Critical Consciousness Being aware of inequity and acting to resist oppressive norms and ways of being	**Exercise:** Take a Stand—Youth move their bodies to different parts of the room to indicate their answers to questions of escalating social significance. (Prompts: What season do you prefer? Does the local media represent teenagers fairly?) **Video:** "*Black-ish* Tackles Donald Trump Presidency" (Prompts: How do teens feel about the 2016 election? How do people with differing opinions about the nation work together?) **Music:** "King Kunta," "u," "Institutionalized," and "Complexion (A Zulu Love)" (Lamar) (Prompts: How is power discussed? Who has power and who does not?)
Banking Education and Problem-Posing Education Models Forms of education that either treat teachers and students as objects or afford opportunities to become subjects	**Exercise:** The Machine—Youth individually use their bodies to create unique motions and sounds. Then, one at a time, add the motions and sounds together as one large group to form a human machine. (Prompt: Create a motion and sound from school that makes you feel powerless, then one that makes you feel empowered.) **Videos:** "The People vs the School System" (Ea) (Prompts: How does school feel like an ancient activity? How can schools prepare students for the future?) "High School Training Ground" (London) (Prompts: How does school feel like it is breaking you down? What are examples of the ways teachers lift you up?)
Praxis Reflection and action on the world to transform it	**Exercise:** Change Your Seat—Youth switch their seating arrangements periodically during a lesson. (Prompts: How does your point of view change because of where you are sitting? What are the feelings you felt when you were asked to move?) **Video:** "The Danger of Silence" (Smith) (Prompts: What are the silences in your own life that need to be named? What is your truth that needs to be heard?)

These multimodal activities and prompts help to reinforce some Freirean concepts.

in ways to draft and write about challenges faced in school and their solutions. For instance, to indicate a challenge young people experience, Figure 1 shows a group of Sister Scholars arranging their bodies to demonstrate what happens when students fight each other in schools. As the three girls in the center of the image prepare to fight, the two girls squatting in the foreground reflected being in fear of their lives, while in the background another girl captured the unfolding events on her cell phone. In contrast, Figure 2 illustrates another group of Scholars bowing their heads with hands clasped to demonstrate respect for each other.

After an activity, the Scholars wrote their thoughts, reactions, and emotions in a journal to reference later when the poetry writing would take place. Collectively, the multimodal literacy activities helped to cement Freire's ideas and allowed us as co-instructors to communicate the importance

FIGURE 1

The Way the World Is: Sister Scholars pose their bodies to draft about peer violence in schools.

FIGURE 2
The Way the World Could Be: Scholars pose their bodies to draft about peer respect in schools.

of having a visceral impact when choosing words for a poem.

(716) Youth Critical Micropoetics

Critical micropoetry was the focal point of our poetic writing efforts. We treat critical micropoetry as a genre of short-verse poetry for the purpose of providing social, political, linguistic, historical, or personal critiques. Our working definition builds upon the blending of poetic brevity (Sebald; "What Is Micropoetry") and the social and political purpose for poetry, as described by poet-activists such as June Jordan (Quiroz 28). While existing poems may fall within our description, our version of critical micropoetry combined features of the Japanese haiku with the local three-digit telephone area code. For instance, our version used three lines, allowed for either syllables or words, juxtaposed the living and reimagined realities of youth, and encouraged inspiring and rhyming language.

The use of the local three-digit telephone area code, in our case (716), was done to be both symbolically meaningful and materially productive. Symbolically, an area code functions as a numerical identifier of a shared physical locale; in other instances, it serves as a geographical marker of identity where one's neighborhood, location, or group affinity is represented or reclaimed. Treating an area code in this manner can be found in popular culture practices familiar to youth. For example, rapper Dr. Dre highlights his Los Angeles heritage and identity by including 213, an area code for parts of southern and central Los Angeles, in his song "Still D.R.E.": "Still rock my khakis with a cuff and a crease / Still got love for the streets / Reppin' 213."

Materially, an area code offers a productive way to organize and structure our version of critical micropoetry. As we initially conceived it, the first number of the area code acted as the first line of the poem and represented the number of words or syllables a poet could use to articulate an experienced or witnessed struggle, challenge, or conflict in the writer's community. Next, the second number served as the second line of the poem and again indicated the number of words or syllables a poet can use to express change or action. Last, the third number operated as the final line of the poem and denoted the number of words or syllables a poet can use to communicate a solution or provide an inspirational response to the struggle identified in the first line (see Table 2).

Our usage of a local area code as a format for poetry writing unified Scholars under a shared,

TABLE 2
Critical Micropoetry

Critical Micropoetry	The Way the World Is and The Way the World Could Be
Using your life experiences, Scholars are invited to write a **(716)** critical micropoem that addresses teenage life in Buffalo, New York, and draws from our conversations about critical consciousness, problem-posing education, and praxis. Remember to title your critical micropoem.	
Line 1:	Write **7** syllables or words to describe a real-world struggle, challenge, or conflict Buffalo teenagers face. (This is the way the world is.)
Line 2:	Write **1** word that acts as critical change and action. (This line represents praxis.)
Line 3:	Write **6** syllables or words to propose a solution or recommendation to the problem stated in the first line. (This is the way the world could be.)
Rationale:	Complete a one-page rationale and/or explanation for your critical micropoem. Be detailed, explaining your choice of struggle, selection of words, and practicality of the solution.

Youth used this invitation to structure and frame their critical micropoems.

geographical identity (i.e., Buffalo teens) but also supported the "linguistic, literate, and cultural pluralism" (Paris 93) individuals experienced as they lived their lives out in the city. This structure, then, afforded writers the chance to represent their community, collectively and individually, by crafting short-verse poetry discussing their localized challenges, while also encouraging and supporting youth as solution seekers.

Our Culminating (716) Critical Micropoem: The Buffalo-ku

For the culminating writing activity, Scholars wrote a critical micropoem, affectionately referred to as a Buffalo-ku, that spoke to their lives as adolescents in Buffalo. Their Buffalo-kus addressed a range of topics affecting city teens (see Figure 3).

To illustrate the cognitive depth of the Buffalo-kus, we present two critical micropoems written by Alicia and Jayah, respectively. In each analysis, we draw from statements made in the rationale/explanation to contextualize the poems.

United States vs. Divided States: Alicia's Buffalo-ku

The immediate aftermath of the 2016 election profoundly affected Alicia. Her (716) word-based Buffalo-ku (see Figure 4) captured the angst and dis-ease she and others felt as her country processed the results of the election. We see this worry played out from the start of her poem, as the title served as a thought-provoking statement of contradiction between the espoused rhetoric of her nation (i.e., "United, We Proclaim") and its actions (i.e., "Divided, We Are"). The first line was a grammatical play on words as Alicia treated the United States not as a proper noun designating a country, but as a phrase in dispute. She wrote in her rationale that our country seemed to reject any notion of a common purpose or feeling and noted specifically, "A name that would actually fit is, the 'Divided' States."

Alicia's second line, the single word "Unite!" reflected a turn in the poem. The use of "Unite!," punctuation included, moved the word from being an adjective to a verb reflecting a transition from a country's questionable attribute or statement to its active engagement or call-to-action. According to Alicia, "I chose the 1 word, 'Unite!' with an exclamation point because it is important to emphasize and it is what we NEED to do. It is our duty as a society and as a nation. I notice a constant divide in the 'United' States. I now see the true colors of many Americans in the 'United' States."

Critical Micropoetry: A Buffalo-ku Enfleshed

"United, We Proclaim; Divided, We Are"

The keyword in United States is "United"
Unite!
We SHOULD be in this together

-Sister Scholar Alicia, 11th grade

Explanation / Rationale

I chose the 7 words, "The keyword in United States is "United", because as a nation that calls ourselves "United States", we seem to be everything but united. A name that would actually fit is the "Divided" States. I have realized that we cannot come together during hard times, we are always finding a reason to fight, argue and be divided.

I chose the 1 word, "Unite!" with an exclamation point because it is important to emphasize and it is what we NEED to do. It is our duty as a society and as a nation. I notice a constant divide in the "United" States. One event that brought the divide to light was when our new president was announced in November of 2016. That election was a major turning point in history. The nation was shocked! Having access to multiple media outlets allowed me to see the true colors of many Americans in the "United" States.

I chose the 6 words, "We SHOULD be in this together" with emphasis on "should" because you would think that as a country that proudly proclaims "United States" is actually united, but in fact, we are not. It is okay for everyone to have an opinion in which they are entitled to, but the controversy and blatant disrespect toward an opposing party is outright obnoxious, immature and humiliating to our nation. When people advocate and UNITE!, we get the attention of authorities and we can make change in our democracy. After all, the "United" States is of the people, by the people and for the people.

FIGURE 4

Alicia writes about the United States after the 2016 election.

Sample of Buffalo-ku Topics

- Educational violence
- Gun violence
- Police terrorism
- Poverty
- Political disenfranchisement
- Racial discrimination/ terrorism
- Religious persecution
- Sexual violence
- Substance abuse
- Teen pregnancy

FIGURE 3

Youth communicated a variety of topics within their critical micropoems.

The final line invoked a sense of responsibility, duty, and obligation as Alicia offered her vision for gathering around a common cause. She explained that a country proclaiming its unity must have actions that align with its rhetoric. Her final poetic statement reminded us of our interconnective lives as voting members in this nation. It was no surprise that she ended her rationale by reciting a portion of Abraham Lincoln's "Gettysburg Address" (i.e., "of the people, by the people and for the people") to reinforce principles of unity within a democracy.

Escaping Unworthiness: Jayah's Buffalo-ku

Jayah had a wise old soul and regularly drew from his life as a young Latinx male growing up in Buffalo. He was transparent and honest with his feelings and perspectives. That is why it came as no surprise when he chose to write his (716) word-based Buffalo-ku about his personal experiences with mental health disorders (see Figure 5). In the first line, Jayah expressed a personal vulnerability, calling himself out with a provocative self-reflective statement and describing his identity struggling with depression as a "nameless shadow." In his rationale, he elaborated on describing how his days were "slow and painful . . . everything I did felt like it wasn't good enough," using language like being in a "dark void" and "a prisoner in my own skin."

For his second line, Jayah chose "crisis" to reflect Freire's idea of praxis. Jayah wrote that he was heading toward a downward spiral, unable to climb back up. According to him, "everything I did couldn't and didn't want to work." There was a sense of defeat in his words. And yet, Jayah's reflection and action represented a turning point in his poem, a transition in his struggle with depression as he acknowledged in one word that he is in crisis. This critical moment was more than just a word; it was an act of self-awareness serving as an entry into his last line.

The final line represented his willingness to seek assistance. He recognized he was "ready to escape darkness for light" and accessed the people in his life who could assist him. The move from darkness to light is a classic trope in poetry, one with biblical undertones. For Jayah, this motion was about being able to lean on others, a reach for a community of supporters. He knew this was a difficult step but probably the most crucial one, as he saw in his ability to be "making a comeback."

Both Alicia and Jayah used their critical micropoems as tools to explore and communicate topics (i.e., the presidential election and mental health) each felt represented some aspect affecting Buffalo youth, thereby allowing us to gain insights into how they were thinking about their social worlds.

Critical Micropoetry: A Buffalo-ku Enfleshed

"Trapped in the Darkness"

You're not worthy; an unwanted nameless shadow
crisis
Ready to escape darkness for light

-Brother Scholar Jayah, 12th grade

Explanation / Rationale

The reason why I describe myself within this Buffalo-ku was because this is what I had to go through in my life. I felt unwanted and felt like I wasn't anyone in life. People reminded me that I would fail and wouldn't get anywhere. I struggled to keep up and wanted to hide inside myself and not let anyone in. My days was slow and painful. Everything I did felt like it wasn't good enough. This was when I fell into a greater depression than I was in before. I started to keep more to myself and didn't reach out for help and lost myself in the progress of trying to remember and realize who I am. I become the "nameless shadow" because when I looked behind myself against the sun and I couldn't see my shadow. I looked into the mirror couldn't see myself just a dark void that I fear the most in my life. I was in the middle of a crisis that I couldn't escape from. I had no light to shine my way and was wondering an empty abyss. A prisoner within my own skin and just accepted how things was. Leading me down a downward spiral and unable to climb myself back. Everything I did couldn't and didn't want to work. So I gave up.

But later on after years of going through this, something shined in my void a darkness. I couldn't see it at first but over time I began to realize that. Someone did care someone wanted to help me escape the darkness. I decided to make the effort to reach into that light. That was the hardest and greatest step that I had to take in my life. There was a lot of things that made me want to say no but I decided that I should give it a try. It's better to try. Even if you fail you make the effort to do what's important. If I didn't take that step I don't know what I would be now. I know that I do go back into that state once in awhile, but I always go back into the light because I have an anchor that holds me in and doesn't let go. I rather be trapped in the light and sometimes slip into darkness once in awhile than be trapped in the darkness and afraid to walk into the light. So I'm glad that the people that showed me a helping hand was full of life and light my way., than people who are full of darkness and corruption holding me back from achieving what I was made to do.

FIGURE 5

Jayah writes about teen mental health.

Learning from Their Wor(l)ds

Through our journey, we learned about the various ways youth use poetry to see, re-envision, and articulate their social worlds by calling attention to immediate concerns and exploring how to redress them. We were encouraged by the comments our Scholars shared with us in support of our efforts (see Figure 6).

Our area code-based critical micropoetry becomes an additional tool for teachers to consider using in the classroom when the attention is centered on supporting the creative poetry writing goals of students. For teachers who want to extend these poetry writing activities, we offer the resources and recommendations in Figure 7.

Youth Feedback

- "Exercises like take a stand, teatro, image theater, and buffalo-ku helped me become more aware through identifying and comprehending injustices in everyday life."
- "Buffalo-Ku—This exercise really motivated me to express how I really feel about everyday situations in life and to come up with a solution to help fix the situation without violence where we can all be free to express ourselves."
- "I felt like after reading I knew these concepts, but after making the machine and writing our poems these concepts were reinforced."

FIGURE 6

Youth offered their opinions about the critical micropoetry activity.

Resources and Recommendations

- Integrate short-verse poetry from activist-poets such as "S.O.S." by Amiri Baraka, "We Real Cool" by Gwendolyn Brooks, or "For the Consideration of Poets" by Haki R. Madhubuti.
- Partner with a teacher and classroom within the same area code or from a different one and have students exchange and discuss their critical micropoems with each other.
- Invite students to get involved with local human rights organizations that align with the students' articulated interests.
- For area codes with a zero, consider replacing the number by using four syllables or words (i.e., the number of letters in the word) or have zero represent silence or a dramatic pause.

FIGURE 7

These resources and recommendations extend the work of critical micropoetry.

There is significant potential for our version of critical micropoetry to occupy a purposeful place in the ELA curriculum. Our unique contribution supports a type of deliberate, precision writing, focusing young people's attention in a recognizable way on their localized conditions and experiences by virtue of a shared geographical identifier: a local area code. This form of poetry writing also affords discussing the social, political, and personal dimensions of youth lives, while supporting an increasing awareness of the conditions in which their lives are intertwined. As activist poet Tony Medina reminds us, "Any poet worth his or her weight in syllables and words uses poetry for certain reasons, be it to define one's self, to defend one's self, or to describe one's environment with accuracy, communicating a clear understanding of what is going on in the world" (xx).

By providing a poetry writing space that reflects and represents how adolescents see themselves and how they see the world, teens can reimagine what the world could be and think about ways to influence change. We believe this is a platform students, like Alicia, are seeking, enabling them to provide social critique and work toward social transformation. As ELA teachers and teacher educators, let us continue to encourage and support our youth by using critical micropoetry to write and speak about those sensitive subjects as a way of asserting and claiming their dignity and humanity in their lives and our own as we work with young people in poetic solidarity.

TEACHING TIPS

Consider the ways Hunter and Colón invite students to create critical micropoetry using their local telephone number area code as an organizational and structural tool. Invite students to participate in multimodal (movement, songs, written texts, etc.) social critiques about their homes, communities, and/or the issues in the broader world. With guidance from the article, engage in critical pedagogy and develop a unit on critical micropoetry. Invite students to consider what it means to be a student in the middle of a pandemic. Ask students how developing critical micropoetry attends to harm and healing. Facilitate opportunities for students to share their critical micropoems in the school, district, on college campuses, and/or in the community.

WORKS CITED

Baraka, Amiri. "S.O.S." *The LeRoi Jones/Amiri Baraka Reader*, edited by William J. Harris, Basic Books, 2009, p. 218.

"*Black-ish* Tackles Donald Trump Presidency." *YouTube*, uploaded by ABC News, 11 Jan. 2017, www.youtube.com/watch?v=vAryxfCxNnA.

Brooks, Gwendolyn. "We Real Cool." *The Essential Gwendolyn Brooks*, edited by Elizabeth Alexander, Literary Classics of the United States, 2005, p. 60.

Cahnmann-Taylor, Melisa, and Marianna Souto-Manning. *Teachers Act Up!: Creating Multicultural Learning Communities through Theatre*. Teachers College P, 2010.

Dr. Dre. "Still D.R.E." 2001, Aftermath-Interscope, 1991.

Ea, Prince. "The People vs the School System." *YouTube*, uploaded by Prince Ea, 26 Sep. 2016, www.youtube.com/watch?v=dqTTojTija8.

Espinoza, Manuel. "A Case Study of the Production of Educational Sanctuary in One Migrant Classroom." *Pedagogies: An International Journal*, vol. 4, 2009, pp. 44–62.

Freire, Paulo. *Pedagogy of the Oppressed*. 30th anniversary ed. Translated by Myra Ramos, Continuum, 2000.

Ginwright, Shawn. *Hope and Healing in Urban Education: How Urban Activists and Teachers Are Reclaiming Matters of the Heart*. Routledge, 2016.

Kinloch, Valerie, editor. *Urban Literacies: Critical Perspectives on Language, Learning, and Community*. Teachers College P, 2011.

Lamar, Kendrick. *To Pimp a Butterfly*, Top Dawg Entertainment, 2015.

London, Malcolm. "High School Training Ground." *TED Talks Education*, May 2013, www.ted.com/talks/malcolm_london_high_school_training_ground.

Madhubuti, Haki. "For the Consideration of Poets." *Poetry Foundation*, poetryfoundation.org/poems/51275/for-the-consideration-of-poets.

Medina, Tony. Introduction. *Bum Rush the Page: A Def Poetry Jam*, edited by Tony Medina and Louis Reyes Rivera, Three Rivers Press, 2001, pp. xix–xxii.

Nieto, Sonia, and Patty Bode. *Affirming Diversity: The Sociopolitical Context of Multicultural Education*. 8th ed., Pearson, 2018.

Paris, Django. "Culturally Sustaining Pedagogy: A Needed Change in Stance, Terminology, and Practice." *Educational Researcher*, vol. 41, no. 3, 2012, pp. 93–97.

Quiroz, Julie. "'Poetry Is a Political Act': An Interview with June Jordan." *Colorlines*, vol. 1, no. 3, 1999, p. 28.

Sebald, Winfried Georg. *Unrecounted*. New Directions, 2007.

Smith, Clint. "The Danger of Silence." TED@NYC, July 2014, www.ted.com/talks/clint_smith_the_danger_of_silence?language=en.

"What Is Micropoetry?" *Micropoetry*, Micropoetry Society, micropoetry.com/.

Wilhelm, Jeffrey D. *Engaging Readers and Writers with Inquiry: Promoting Deep Understandings in Language Arts and the Content Areas with Guiding Questions*. Scholastic, 2007.

Williams, Wendy R. "Every Voice Matters: Spoken Word Poetry in and outside of School." *English Journal*, vol. 104, no. 4, 2015, pp. 77–82.

JEVON DELEXANDER HUNTER is the Woods-Beals Endowed Chair for Urban Education at SUNY Buffalo State where his teaching and research explore the ways literacy dis/mis/empower youth, their teachers, and families in urban communities. He has been a member of NCTE since 2006 and can be reached at hunterjd@buffalostate.edu.

GLISET COLÓN is an assistant professor with the Exceptional Education Department at SUNY Buffalo State. Her teaching and research focus on literacy and language outcomes for multilingual students with and without disabilities, multi-tiered systems of support, disproportionality, culturally relevant and sustaining pedagogies, and intersectionality. She can be reached at colong@buffalostate.edu.

This article originally appeared
in *English Leadership Quarterly* 42.4

SHINING LIGHT IN DARK CORNERS: Choosing Heavy Books for the Classroom

Today's students are struggling with stress and trauma every day. How can curriculum be a force in supporting these learners?

JESSICA GALLO & BAILEY HERRMANN

MANY STUDENTS in our classrooms are dealing with considerable stress in their lives outside of school. Nearly half of youth in the United States have experienced one or more adverse childhood events, or ACEs, and one in ten youth have experienced three or more ACEs (Sacks & Murphey, 2018). ACEs are "potentially traumatic experiences and events, ranging from abuse and neglect to living with an adult with a mental illness.

They can have negative, **lasting effects** on health and well-being in childhood or later in life" (Sacks & Murphey, 2018, para. 1). Often, we don't know about the stressful situations our students are dealing with, nor are we equipped to provide the kinds of interventions that counselors or social workers provide. However, as English leaders, we believe that the books we choose to offer in our classrooms can provide powerful support for students, allowing them to see themselves in literature, examine difficult situations through a new lens, and engage in conversations with peers about life's challenges.

How Do ACES Affect the Classroom?

Education Brief: ACES for Educators and Stakeholders, *The Illinois ACEs Response Collaborative*

Addressing Adverse Childhood Experiences in School, Supporting Mental Health in Schools, *ASCD*

ACEs and Resilience: What Can We Do? *Public Schools First NC*

Many English teachers have made progress in choosing books and curriculum materials that more accurately reflect the racial and gender demographics of our schools. We have begun to think more carefully about representation of demographic diversity in our curriculum and have worked to broaden our literature selections. Bishop (1992) has written about the value of books in helping students see themselves and others in literature. When we choose books that act as windows, mirrors, and sliding glass doors for our students (Bishop, 1990), we provide them with opportunities to think about their lives through the lens of a character in a book. This act of providing opportunities for students to see their own realities and others' realities benefits all students. As Bishop (1990) says, "Children from dominant social groups

Trauma-Informed Classrooms

Trauma-Informed Curriculum Helps Prepare Teachers to Support Troubled Students, *Insight into Diversity*

Trauma-Informed Teaching Strategies, *ASCD*

Where Can You Find Books about ACES?

Book Lists, *American Library Association*

The Classroom Bookshelf, *School Library Journal*

Books for Middle and High School Age, *Cooperative Children's Book Center* have always found their mirrors in books, but they, too, have suffered from the lack of availability of books about others. They need books as windows into reality, not just on imaginary worlds" (para. 5). Yet the progress we have made with racial and gender representation hasn't always extended to books that represent adverse childhood experiences.

As we learn more about ACEs, and in the spirit of continuing our work to use books as mirrors, windows, and sliding glass doors, it might be a good time to ask ourselves whether we are choosing curriculum that reflects the **lived experiences of our students**, including difficult or challenging life experiences.

Books that focus on events or situations that depict ACEs, such as drug use, physical and emotional abuse, suicide, or mental health problems, can feel especially heavy when we discuss them with students because we, as teachers, feel uncertain about how to talk about these difficult topics sensitively and accurately. Adolescents often are drawn to books about these heavy topics "that make many adults uncomfortable" (Ivey & Johnston, 2018, p. 143). These books are engaging for many of our students, sometimes because their lives have been impacted by these issues and sometimes because they are curious about what it would be like to face such difficult circumstances (Ivey & Johnston, 2018). Allowing students space to think about difficult topics through literature is another way of providing windows, mirrors, and sliding glass doors.

It is understandable that some teachers, at first, may be hesitant to teach these books and provide them in their classrooms. Some teachers express concern about exposing their students to topics like violence, sexual assault, and drug use. For example, Kate Messner's middle-grade book *The Seventh Wish* explores the experiences of a girl whose college-age sister is addicted to heroin. Soon after the book's publication, Messner's long-planned visit to a school was canceled with very short notice. In this case, some of the administrators and librarians felt that the students weren't equipped to handle the controversial topic of drug abuse (Messner, 2016).

However, Messner wrote the book to address a very real problem in families today and to spark **conversations about addiction**. Given the current opioid crisis in the United States, it seems likely that this is a situation that has touched the lives of some of our students. Reading a book about a family member's addiction, written from the point of view of a middle school girl, can provide teachers and students with an opportunity to talk about drugs in an empathetic and constructive way. Students who may feel alone and ashamed of their family's experiences with drug addiction might find solace in seeing their story represented in a novel, while students who have not experienced addiction might be better prepared to understand peers who have. This was Messner's hope in writing the book. She says:

> I understand that school administrators are afraid to talk about tough issues sometimes. Authors are, too. But we're not protecting kids when we keep them from stories that shine a light in the darker corners of their lives. We're just leaving them alone in the dark. (Messner, 2016, para. 13)

We can't let our own fear of talking about these stories prevent us from sharing them with students who might need to hear them.

Sometimes the books that tackle difficult topics shed light on situations that are **considered taboo or are rarely discussed** in other parts of teenagers' lives. For students who are struggling with these issues, books like these could help them feel less alone. For example, Jay Asher's *Thirteen Reasons Why* has been challenged in schools and libraries all over the country for its depictions of depression, suicide, and sexual assault. In the book, Hannah leaves an audio diary of the 13 reasons she died by suicide, including the bullying and sexual harassment she experienced in school. The book is a testament to the negative impacts of peer violence. Told from the perspective of a teenage boy who has lost his crush to suicide, *Thirteen Reasons Why* depicts the grief and confusion that he feels and his struggle to

Additional Books about Addiction

8 YA Reads to Spark Authentic Discussions about Drugs and Alcohol, *We Are Teachers*

Books for Kids and Teens about Alcohol and Drug Abuse, *Common Sense Media*

Additional Books about Mental Health

12 Kid-Approved Middle Grade Books That Tackle Mental Health, *Brightly*

50 Must-Read YA Books about Mental Illness (Plus a Few More), *Book Riot*

understand why and how this could have happened to Hannah. Since its publication, the book has been made into a television series that has caused concern over its graphic depictions of the book's content. In spite of all the controversy surrounding both the book and the TV series, *Thirteen Reasons Why* remains a popular choice for young adults because "adolescents, like all readers, become engaged with books they find personally relevant" (Ivey & Johnston, 2018, p.143). Suicide is the second leading cause of death for adolescents ages 15–19 (Heron, 2019), so it is possible that many of our students are thinking about the impact that suicide has had on their own lives. Like Messner, Asher wrote his book to shed light on a topic that hasn't been discussed openly. He says that after a teenage relative attempted suicide, he felt he had to write this story so that other teenagers don't feel as alone as his relative did. He says, "So it made me feel like, yeah, you're writing about very sensitive issues, but that's why we need to talk about it: because it's hard to" (Hamblin, 2017, para. 6). When we avoid books that deal with difficult situations, we might assume that we are protecting our students from reading about scary topics that they are not yet ready to face. However, we may be missing the fact that some of our students have already experienced situations like these, and a book that provides a mirror for these students might offer them an opportunity to feel seen.

In our conversations with other English teachers about the idea of teaching books with heavy content, we have often turned to the essay "Why We Shouldn't Shield Children from Darkness" by children's and young adult book author Matt de la Peña (2018). In it, he describes how during the publishing process for his book Love, he was encouraged not to include an illustration of "a despondent young boy [who] hides beneath a piano with his dog, while his parents argue across the living room" (de la Peña, 2018, para. 9). Some people involved in the publication process believed that this illustration, which included an empty old-fashioned glass sitting on top of the piano, was too heavy for children. De la Peña and the book's illustrator, Loren Long, fought to keep the illustration.

Independent and Choice Reading in the Classroom

NCTE's Statement on Independent Reading

5 Teaching Strategies to Facilitate Independent Reading, *TeachHub*

Literature Circles: Getting Started, *ReadWriteThink*

> In the book world, we often talk about the power of racial inclusion—and in this respect we're beginning to see a real shift in the field—but many other facets of diversity remain in the shadows. For instance, an uncomfortable number of children out there right now are crouched beneath a metaphorical piano. There's a power to seeing this largely unspoken part of our interior lives represented, too. And for those who've yet to experience that kind of sadness, I can't think of a safer place to explore complex emotions for the first time than inside the pages of a book, while sitting in the lap of a loved one. (de la Peña, 2018, para. 14)

When we have shared this article with teachers, many of them have had visceral responses. They remember times when they had felt that their own challenges from childhood were not represented in books and how comforting it would have been to have a book that showed their real lives. The beauty of de la Peña's article encourages these teachers to rethink their positions about using heavy books in their classrooms so that they are able to provide that comfort to their students.

Being willing to include heavy books in our curriculum means being willing to employ other good reading practices too. **Rather than thinking of these books only as potential whole-class novels, offer books that include depictions of difficult situations as independent choices or book club books.** Sharing short daily book talks with your students can pique their interest in the variety of books you offer in your classroom (Miller, 2009). When you book talk a heavy book, think about how you will represent any potentially difficult content in it; your book talk should guide students to use their own discretion in choosing books that are right for them. Students should be allowed and encouraged to abandon books that are not a good fit for them (Kittle, 2013). In thinking about our approaches to including heavy books in our curriculum, consider these guidelines and talk with your team about how to incorporate them in your teaching:

- Be brave in your willingness to allow students to read about situations that are challenging for us as teachers.
- Be willing to trust students' ability to choose a book that is relevant and valuable, even if it makes us uncomfortable.
- Be ready to talk about these topics when students bring them up in the context of sharing their reading.
- Be sensitive and thoughtful in how you represent the content of books that you include in your curriculum and classroom.
- Be honest with your students about the potential challenges of reading books that depict difficult situations.

As English leaders, it is important to engage in conversations with one another about how to include books that have challenging topics in our classrooms and curriculum. We can support one another as teachers by thinking together about how to address heavy topics in books with our students. We can share approaches that will help us sensitively and thoughtfully support students in reading the books that represent their lives, no matter how challenging or difficult those lives are. When we have conversations about how to approach potentially sensitive content in books with students, we need to recognize our own discomfort that comes with reading those books as well as consider the benefits that can come from teaching them. As teachers, we want to choose books and curriculum that are in the best interests of our students. Just as we have worked to more accurately represent the racial and gender characteristics of our students in the books we choose, so too must we consider how to represent the challenging, difficult, complicated lives of our students in ways that help them see themselves in the books they read.

TEACHING TIPS

The authors argue that educators must "consider how to represent the challenging, difficult, complicated lives of our students in ways that help them see themselves in the books they read." Building from Rudine Sims Bishop's work on texts as "windows, mirrors, and sliding doors" the authors invite educators to include texts on heavy topics. Do you teach texts that deal with "heavy topics," such as drug use, physical and emotional abuse, suicide, or mental health issues? If not, then what micro- and macro-level supports would you need to be better equipped to do so? Connect with a professional learning community to brainstorm trauma-informed and healing-centered ways to choose and use "heavy texts" in your teaching context.

REFERENCES

Bishop, R. S. (1990). Mirrors, windows, and sliding glass doors. *Perspectives: Choosing and Using Books for the Classroom*, 6(3), ix–xi.

Bishop, R. S. (1992). Multicultural literature for children: Making informed choices. In V. J. Harris (Ed.), *Teaching Multicultural Literature in Grades K–8* (pp. 27–53). Christopher-Gordon.

de la Peña, M. (2018, January 9). Why we shouldn't shield children from darkness. *Time*. https://time.com/5093669/why-we-shouldnt-shield-children-from-darkness/

Hamblin, B. (2017, June 19) "Thirteen reasons why" author says: We had to show it. *The Charlotte Observer*. https://www.charlotteobserver.com/entertainment/arts-culture/article157019099.html

Heron, M. (2019). Deaths: Leading causes for 2017. *National Vital Statistics Reports*, 68(6). Hyattsville, MD: National Center for Health Statistics. https://www.cdc.gov/nchs/data/nvsr/nvsr68/nvsr68_06-508.pdf

Ivey, G., & Johnston, P. (2018). Engaging disturbing books. *Journal of Adolescent & Adult Literacy*, 62(2), 143–150.

Kittle, P. (2013). *Book love: Developing depth, stamina, and passion in adolescent readers*. Heinemann.

Messner, K. (2016, June 16). A blog post I never thought I'd be writing on book release day... [Blog post]. http://www.katemessner.com/a-blog-post-i-never-thought-id-be-writing-on-book-release-day/

Miller, D. (2009). *The book whisperer: Awakening the inner reader in every child*. Jossey-Bass.

Sacks, V., & Murphey, D. (2018, February 12). *The prevalence of adverse childhood experiences, nationally, by state, and by race or ethnicity*. Child trends. https://www.childtrends.org/publications/prevalence-adverse-childhood-experiences-nationally-state-race-ethnicity

JESSICA GALLO is an assistant professor of English education at the University of Nevada, Reno. Her research focuses on English teacher preparation, middle and secondary writing pedagogy, and rural education. Before becoming a teacher educator, Dr. Gallo taught high school English in rural schools in Wisconsin. She has been a National Writing Project Teacher Leader since 2008 and is a former co-director for the Rural Wisconsin Writing Institute, a site of the Fox Valley Writing Project.

BAILEY HERRMANN is an associate professor of leadership, literacy, and social foundations at the University of Wisconsin Oshkosh. She teaches courses in adolescent literacy, literacy engagement, and literacy leadership. Her areas of research include educator professional development, middle and secondary literacy, and teacher preparation.

This article originally appeared in *Voices from the Middle 28.2*

ENHANCING STUDENTS' MENTAL HEALTH LITERACY THROUGH THE PARATEXT OF TWO MIDDLE-LEVEL NOVELS

BROOKE B. EISENBACH & PAULA GREATHOUSE

EARLY ADOLESCENCE represents a time of significant biological, physical, social, and emotional change. As these changes occur, adolescents become susceptible to mental health challenges. According to the National Institute of Mental Health (2017), approximately 20% of young adolescents experience a mental illness, with depression being the most common disorder. This equates to "more than 17 million young people who meet criteria for disorders that affect their ability to learn, establish relationships and navigate a turbulent social and cognitive landscape" (Blakemore, 2019, p. 2030).

Despite the fact that many of our students are impacted by mental illness, directly or indirectly, educators often avoid the topic of mental health in the classroom. Perhaps this is because middle level educators feel they are not equipped to provide the psychological support or counseling students need. But educators can take steps towards destigmatizing mental illness and promoting mental health support within the classroom. As middle level teachers, we can utilize mental health-themed adolescent literature and its paratext to enhance our students' mental health literacy.

AS MIDDLE LEVEL TEACHERS, WE CAN UTILIZE MENTAL HEALTH-THEMED ADOLESCENT LITERATURE AND ITS PARATEXT TO ENHANCE OUR STUDENTS' MENTAL HEALTH LITERACY.

Navigating Depression in Two Middle Level Novels

Two middle level novels that engage paratext, or material surrounding the main text, as a means of enhancing readers' mental health literacy are *The Science of Breakable Things* (Keller, 2018) and *The Year We Fell from Space* (King, 2019). Both titles feature protagonists navigating significant changes in their lives and relationships as the result of experiences with a loved one's depression.

In *The Science of Breakable Things*, seventh-grade Natalie seeks a way of "saving" her mother from her current bout with depression. She recalls the mother she always knew—the one fascinated with botany. Now, Natalie keeps her feelings of frustration and disillusionment to herself as her mother withdraws from daily activities. When she learns of an egg-drop competition that will secure prize money for the winner, Natalie believes it is just the ticket to "rescuing" her mother. If she can win, she can use the money to purchase an elusive Cobalt Blue Orchid, the very flower that once represented the love between her and her mother. Perhaps this flower will be the key to unlocking the mother Natalie remembers and misses so very much.

King's *The Year We Fell from Space* chronicles a year of significant change for Liberty Johnson. As her sixth-grade year draws to a close, she learns that her parents are separating and filing for a divorce. Until now, Liberty's life centered on the stars. Her star maps, each drawn in intricate and accurate detail, allow her to see the unique constellations that form her personal experience. But now, she simply can't see where to connect the dots. One night, an asteroid lands in her yard as if it were sent from space just for her. The asteroid becomes her only friend, the only one with whom she can share her secrets. As she grieves the life she once knew, and copes with navigating her father's depression, she fears that she, too, might be spiraling into her own depressive state.

Peritext as Opportunity for Analysis and Support

Peritext refers to images and textual elements that accompany the primary text of a published work. For instance, a book's cover, introduction, footnotes, title page, chapter titles, and illustrations are just a few examples of peritext. Mental health-themed adolescent literature often features peritext that extends the story, offering a layer of support in guiding readers through the prominent mental health themes featured within the narrative.

AUTHOR'S NOTES

Both *The Year We Fell from Space* and *The Science of Breakable Things* feature author's notes for adolescent readers. Keller begins her author's note with the single statement, "*Depression* is not a dirty word" (p. 295). She then continues, sharing the number and website for the National Alliance on Mental Illness. King notes, "If you want to learn more about mental health, finding resources online for young readers is difficult" (p. 261). Here she offers readers website addresses and phone numbers for those seeking mental health support. Teachers can take time to read the author's note with students, reference the resources, and unpack the author's intention in sharing these resources. Researching and learning more about these resources can support young adolescent learners in their mental health literacy development while also offering access to mental health support.

GRAPHICS AND IMAGES

Graphics and images can provide a layer of textual support that encourages connection and empathy with characters and experiences beyond the narrative. King utilizes illustration to accompany Liberty's references to her star maps throughout *The Year We Fell from Space*. In one star map, Liberty sees a broom, an explosion, and a frying pan (p. 92). She then ponders, "I am the broom. I am the explosion. I am the frying pan." (p. 93). In this scene, readers learn more about Liberty's perceptions of self as well as how the images represent a metaphor of her experience and emotional state of being. Later in the novel, Liberty shares the image of a diamond ring (p. 133). This personal constellation represents not only her growing sense of guilt but also that she has reached the bargaining stage in her grief over the loss of her family unit.

In *The Science of Breakable Things*, Keller introduces images that guide readers through the process of growth as illustrated by the science of botany. She begins with empty flowerpots that transition to fully bloomed orchids by the final page of the book. Such illustrations, though minimal, serve as a platform for discussions surrounding the characters' experiences with depression and their emotional growth over the course of the story, as these experiences metaphorically mirror the scientific process of growing orchids.

Epitext as Opportunity for Analysis and Support

Epitext is another element of paratext that offers a valuable resource for destigmatizing mental illness. Epitext, or textual supports found outside of the main text, takes many forms: author websites, book reviews, author interviews, and social media posts. In seeking to aid our learners in the dismantling of stigmas surrounding mental illness, we can utilize epitext as an essential aspect of engaging with literature.

AUTHOR'S WEBSITES

Often, authors who write novels focused on aspects of mental health will utilize such epitext as a source of hope, mental health education, and support for those who encounter their work. Upon visiting Amy Sarig King's website, readers can find information on King's school visits and presentations, such as "On Being a Superhero: An Exploration of Your Personal Suitcase." This presentation aims to help students unpack personal trauma and offers ways they can move forward in developing their unique identities and sense of self. In a Kirkus-sponsored interview (Heimbach, 2019), King shared information on anxiety and

MENTAL HEALTH-THEMED ADOLESCENT LITERATURE OFTEN FEATURES PERITEXT THAT EXTENDS THE STORY, OFFERING A LAYER OF SUPPORT IN GUIDING READERS THROUGH THE PROMINENT MENTAL HEALTH THEMES FEATURED WITHIN THE NARRATIVE.

depression, drawing attention to a need for conversation around and dismantling of mental health stigma for today's youth.

When visiting Tae Keller's website, readers can click on her "Love Letters" to sign up for communications from the author centered on a variety of topics. One such letter features her own experiences with "perfectionism" and the dangers that stress and pressure can place on one's mental health. In sharing the realities of her own experiences, and providing a sense of vulnerability throughout her letters, Keller demonstrates how everyone experiences lows and highs in life and can benefit from speaking the truth regarding their mental health and wellness.

MENTAL HEALTH RESOURCES

We can utilize epitext to identify and disseminate mental health resources that enhance our readers' mental health literacy and break down misconceptions surrounding mental illness. Aid students in researching and learning more about mental health conditions they encounter within the story to not only understand the context of the novel but to guide them toward an understanding that a single story about the experience of mental illness does not exist. While the novels our students read depict an individual experience with mental health, it is important they understand this is just that—one single story. Epitext share additional insights, statistics, experiences and stories surrounding mental health that offer students opportunities to see the many ways mental health plays a role in our daily lives, and how one person's story is unique and independent of another's.

Conclusion

Through the inclusion of contemporary mental health-themed middle level texts, we can promote awareness and empathy while combating the stigmas so often associated with mental illness and mental health. In our efforts to destigmatize mental illness and seeking mental health support, it is not enough to introduce students to texts that explore mental health issues and themes. We must also provide students opportunities to work through these themes and topics. And while many teachers have already begun using adolescent literature as a medium through which to begin these explorations and conversations, they must also make a commitment to utilizing paratext that complement these stories in order to move students forward in their understanding, empathy, and mental health development. Through the knowledge gained from paratext, teachers and students can begin to dismantle the stigma of mental illness and promote the development of mental health literacy.

REFERENCES

Blakemore, S. (2019). Adolescence and mental health. *The Lancet*, 393(10185), 2030–31.

Keller, T. (2018). *The science of breakable things*. Yearling.

King, A. S. (2019, September 24). *Sponsored interview: Amy Sarig King discusses her new middle grade novel,* The year we fell *from space* (A. Heimbach, Interviewer). *Kirkus Reviews*. https://www.kirkusreviews.com/news-and-features/articles/sponsored-interview-amy-sarig-king-discusses-her-n/

King, A. S. (2019). *The year we fell from space*. Arthur A. Levine Books.

National Institute of Mental Health. (2017). *Mental illness*. United States Department of Health and Human Services. https://www.nimh.nih.gov/health/statistics/mental-illness.shtml

BROOKE B. EISENBACH is a former ELA teacher and current associate professor of middle and secondary education at Lesley University. She is coeditor of *Fostering Mental Health Literacy through Adolescent Literature* and has published in *Voices from the Middle* and *English Journal*. She is a past recipient of NCTE's Outstanding Middle Level Educator Award.

PAULA GREATHOUSE is an associate professor of secondary English education at Tennessee Tech. Prior to becoming faculty, she taught middle and high school English and Reading for sixteen years. She has won several awards for teaching and scholarship, including NCTE's Teacher of Excellence Award (2012) and the 2021 Divergent Book Award for Excellence in 21st Century Literacies Research.

This article originally appeared
in *Language Arts* 98.5

USING PICTUREBOOKS TO TEACH WITH AND AGAINST SOCIAL AND EMOTIONAL LEARNING

Using critical literacy, this study examines how teachers can use quality picturebooks to read both with and against social emotional learning competencies.

CAROLINE T. CLARK, ALYSSA CHRISMAN & SUZANNE G. LEWIS

SOCIAL AND EMOTIONAL LEARNING (SEL) is a hot topic in K–12 schools. According to the Collaborative for Academic, Social, and Emotional Learning (CASEL), as of 2018, more than half of all US states had established SEL standards, with fourteen states adopting SEL standards for PreK through 12th grade (Dusenbury et al., 2018). One of CASEL's most influential and pervasive moves was identifying and naming what have come to be the core SEL "competencies." Grounded in emotional intelligence (EI; Goleman, 1995), CASEL has codified the SEL competencies to include self-awareness, self-management, social awareness, relationship skills, and responsible decision-making (CASEL, 2017). Despite critiques of EI, grit, and related concepts as race- and class-based "victim-blaming" (Ris, 2015), more and more states see SEL competencies as foundational for academic and future success (Weissberg & Cascarino, 2013) while giving little attention to the harmful assumptions and social ideologies they reflect and reproduce (Hoffman, 2009; Staub, 2016) or the time they take away from the broader curriculum (Poiner, 2018).

We share these concerns. As states forge ahead with SEL standards, our home state of Ohio has plans to monitor SEL competencies and include these data in its statewide accountability system (Poiner, 2018). In this context, we worry about how these standards will manifest themselves in classroom practice and the impact this will have on curriculum and pedagogy. Already, we have seen evidence of elementary schools in Ohio using pre-packaged SEL materials at the expense of quality literature, and displacing art, music, and other "specials" with time set aside for SEL teaching. More worrying still is the uncritical uptake of another set of standards and materials and the unforeseen and potentially damaging consequences for students. SEL competencies and standards focus on the behaviors of individual children and target the management of emotions, such as anger. Stereotypes relating race to anger are common and have particularly affected minoritized students. Tropes related to "loud" and "angry" Black girls with "an attitude" as well as teachers' (mis)perceptions of Black male students continually position Black children as outside the "norms" of school behavior (Koonce, 2012; Sealey-Ruiz & Greene, 2015). With their lack of attention to culture (Mahfouz & Anthony-Stevens, 2020), SEL standards threaten to create an "attitude gap" that Black and Brown students must carry on top of the so-called "achievement gap" they have borne for decades (Ford, 2020).

Against this backdrop, we considered the potential impacts of these standards on communities outside the social-emotional "norm." What will they mean for gender diverse students, students with disabilities, and communities of color? What new "failure narratives" might emerge (Johnson, 2015)? And what might be done, preemptively, to disrupt these stories? These questions grow out of a larger study using critical discourse analysis (CDA; Fairclough, 1992) to 1) examine the truth claims, social aims, and social effects of Ohio's K–12 Social and Emotional Learning Standards (Ohio Department of Education, 2019) in terms of race and dis/ability (Clark, Chrisman, & Lewis, 2020a); and 2) examine anger and related social ideologies in texts designed to teach SEL competencies in contrast to quality children's and young adult literature (Clark & Chrisman, 2020b). This paper reflects a third strand of this larger study.

Recognizing that complex topics and difficult histories are always already present in classrooms (Mahfouz & Anthony-Stevens, 2020) and that children can be guided to engage critically in these discussions (Campano, Ghiso, & Sánchez, 2013), we wondered what insights reading quality picturebooks alongside SEL competencies through a critical literacy lens (Vasquez, 2017) might afford. If teachers in Ohio and other states *must* teach SEL, how might using picturebooks as part of SEL and the language arts curriculum allow them to do this without reproducing social injustice? These wonderings led us to the focal research question for this paper: *How might teachers choose and use quality picturebooks to teach both **with** and **against** the SEL competencies?* We first engage this focal question by describing the critical literacy framework that informs our analysis. Then, we discuss the foundational core competencies promulgated in SEL and how these, among other factors, shaped our selection of focal texts for analysis. Next, we offer critical readings of five quality picturebooks and related SEL competencies, and provide anchor questions to guide others in choosing and using picturebooks to do similar critical literacy work in their own research and teaching. Finally, we discuss the implications of our project for the field, including the need to prepare and support teachers in critically choosing materials in order to more ethically engage in teaching for SEL.

IF TEACHERS IN OHIO AND OTHER STATES *MUST* TEACH SEL, HOW MIGHT USING PICTUREBOOKS AS PART OF SEL AND THE LANGUAGE ARTS CURRICULUM ALLOW THEM TO DO THIS WITHOUT REPRODUCING SOCIAL INJUSTICE?

Critical Literacy and Reading *with* and *against* SEL

Recognizing SEL standards and competencies as an externally imposed mandate that educators nationwide must address, but wishing to avoid and help others avoid becoming "unconscious agents of their distribution" (Janks, 2012, p. 150), we sought an approach that would both accommodate and trouble this expectation. Our histories as white, cisgender, female teacher-researcher-activists predisposed us to a critical literacy perspective (Vasquez, 2017). We understand critical literacy as both a way of doing and of being (Vasquez, Janks, & Comber, 2019), a constant in our lives both in and outside of schools that shapes how we read and engage in work with words and work in the world (Freire, 1970). Following from this, we understand that texts—including the SEL standards and competencies themselves—are "socially constructed or designed from particular perspectives . . . [and] work to have us think about and believe certain things in specific ways" (Vasquez, 2017, p. 8). This critical literacy perspective is the theoretical framework that informs our reading of both the SEL competencies and our focal picturebooks. We first describe *how* one might read with and against SEL through a brief description of a classroom where pre-packaged SEL materials are in use, demonstrating the affordances of a critical literacy lens. Then we turn to the heart of this article: choosing and using quality picturebooks to do this kind of teaching. Both are important. Since many teachers will be required to teach to the SEL standards, having the knowledge and skills to choose materials that support this critical work in classrooms is vital.

READING WITH AND AGAINST SEL: AN EXAMPLE

As Short (2019) and her colleagues point out, "[w]hat makes a study 'critical' is the theoretical framework used to think within, through, and beyond the text" with a focus on "locating power in social practices by understanding, uncovering, and transforming conditions of inequity embedded in society" (p. 5). In a similar vein, Lewis (2020) notes that a critical literary response must attend to "(1) how texts . . . position readers . . . ; (2) how readers position texts . . . ; and (3) how texts . . . and readers are positioned within social, political, and spatial contexts" (p. 274). Implicit in these criteria is what Janks (2019) terms "reading with and against." As she notes, "to read with texts, we have to understand the positions on offer, follow and engage with the writers' arguments, and be willing to consider their standpoints and ideas" (p. 561). But, the capacity to read against texts is equally important. Janks argues that texts "hail readers" into subject positions. In doing so, they invite us to be certain kinds of people, sometimes explicitly but often implicitly. A brief vignette based in our larger corpus of data provides an example of reading *with* and *against* the "text" of SEL competencies:

> Rural Ohio second graders line up to attend their daily specials period. Due to state budget cuts and an increased belief that students need more work on behavior and SEL skills, the district has eliminated art as a weekly special for kindergarten, first and second grades in favor of this SEL-focused class. Today, the class focuses on identifying and managing anger. Students join in with videos of children dancing and singing upbeat songs such as the "Anger Song" with lyrics like "Name your feeling: mad! I feel mad!"
>
> After showing a large picture of two children fighting over a basketball, the teacher asks how the students can use visual clues to identify the feelings of the children, then shows a video segment where one child kicks another child's ball away. Pausing the video, the teacher asks the students how they might resolve the problem, and one child offers, "I would go kick him back." "You'd need to think about what the child would do back if you did," responds the teacher before pressing play on the video to see how the curriculum presents the appropriate way to solve the problem. After class, the students line up, and as the students and classroom teacher leave, the SEL teacher says to the classroom teacher, "Today we learned about anger and strategies for dealing with it."

Looking closely at this vignette allows us to consider how texts, including SEL competencies, "hail readers," both teachers and children, into being "certain kinds of people." Moving to a different room for SEL creates a different spatial positioning of students. The SEL teacher uses specific curricular materials, which carry the authority of the SEL standards and reinforce their coverage. The playground video "hails" the students as children who might steal someone's playground ball—or who might have their own stolen. In taking up the latter position, the student who responds "I would go kick him back" is positioned as someone who gets angry and who perhaps doesn't appropriately manage their emotions. Of course, this assumes that the teacher, in turn, is reading *with* the SEL competency of self-awareness, which indicates that K–2 students should be able to "identify and begin to use strategies to regulate emotions and manage behaviors" (Ohio Department of Education, 2019, p. 12), another position on offer in this classroom and through this text. How a student is positioned by this SEL competency, however, and how the teacher "reads" both the student and the competency, may be different if the student is a boy or a girl, Black or white, feminine or masculine, and so on. Being aware of these biases is challenging, because they are often occurring unconsciously. As Janks (2019) notes, "Texts are never neutral; they hail us by inviting us to take up the positions they offer. We often do so without recognizing their power to shape our identities" (p. 561). This challenge is compounded because it is hard to engage critically with texts that offend us and easy to read with texts that support our views—and vice versa. Nonetheless, doing so is essential:

> Only when readers (in this case, students and teachers) have read with and against a text are they ready to make ethical (not literacy) decisions about whether to take up the positions on offer or to oppose them–to decide which, if any, positions can be defended because they contribute to weaving a social fabric that is just and equitable. (Janks, 2019, pp. 563–64)

SEL CORE COMPETENCIES AND QUALITY PICTUREBOOKS

As noted above, demands for SEL are on the rise, with myriad stakeholders investing time and money into making SEL a centerpiece of 21st-century education (Stringer, 2019). Here in Ohio, despite assurances that "these standards are meant to be integrated into the regular daily activities in school, and they do not mean more classes for students or more work for teachers" (Ohio Department of Education, 2019, p. 1), adoption of SEL standards has led to a proliferation of pedagogical materials aimed at filling this SEL curricular "gap." Videos and songs, like those in our vignette above, and titles such as *Zach Gets Frustrated* (Mulcahy, 2012) and *How to Take the GRRRR Out of Anger* (Verdick & Lisovskis, 2015) have flooded the market with the aim of enabling educators to easily meet and address the SEL standards but often through texts that lack "artfulness" (Cart & Jenkins, 2006), are more didactic (O'Sullivan, 2004), and are presented as if such lessons are ideologically neutral and context independent, which they are not (Smagorinsky & Taxel, 2004).

Although specific state SEL standards vary, thanks to the "Collaborating States Initiative," all of them are rooted in the work of CASEL and its core competencies (Dusenbury, et al., 2020), with some publishers "leveling" and tagging books relative to the SEL core competencies and grade bands (see, e.g., Lerner Books). Therefore, we focus our subsequent analysis on these five CASEL core competencies: self-awareness, self-management, social awareness, relationship skills, and responsible decision-making (see Table 1). The ordering of these is significant and is the same across all CASEL materials and in all of the state standards we've reviewed, including Ohio's. This ordering reflects an implied developmental trajectory of these competencies, all of which foreground observable behaviors. Moreover, none of these SEL competencies or the standards emerging from them attend to race, ethnicity, gender, social class, sexuality or other aspects of "culture" (Ford, 2020) or the implications of this absence for the interpretation and application of the standards in classrooms (Mahfouz & Anthony-Stevens, 2020).

To counter the proliferation of pre-packaged SEL materials that often skirt both culture and complexity, we intentionally set out to find quality picturebooks to pair with the five CASEL core competencies. First, we sought award-winning or star-reviewed picturebooks, because awards and positive reviews are generally accepted as indicators of "quality" and these books are more apt to be widely read and available in libraries, schools, and classrooms. Second, we chose books that would be considered "literary fiction"—that is, books that contained figurative language; narratives told from shifting perspectives; dynamic characters; and images that are emotionally charged and open to a wide range of interpretation and subsequent response (Kozak & Recchia, 2019; Nikolajeva, 2013). This choice was based, in part, on recent research suggesting that literary fiction has the power to develop social understanding, emotional literacy, and empathy in readers, making it an excellent potential context for exploring SEL content in classrooms beyond didactic, pre-packaged materials. Finally, we selected texts with people as characters, rather than animals, because we are attuned to the severe lack of diversity in picturebooks, the misrepresentations that are all too frequent, and the fact that there are more children's books with animals as characters in them (27%) than there are books with American Indian (1%), Latinx (5%), Asian (7%), or African American (10%) characters *combined* (Dahlen, 2019). This fact, coupled with the lack of

TABLE 1

Core Social and Emotional Competencies (CASEL, 2017)

Core SEL Competency	Definition
Self-Awareness	The ability to accurately recognize one's own emotions and thoughts, including how they relate to one's identity and culture and own emotions and thoughts and how they influence behavior. Self-awareness is the ability to accurately assess one's strengths and limitations with a sense of integrity, confidence, and optimism.
Self-Management	The ability to navigate one's emotions, thoughts, and behaviors across different situations while managing stress, controlling impulses, and motivating oneself. Self-management includes the ability to set and work toward personal and academic goals.
Social Awareness	The ability to consider diverse perspectives of and empathize with others, including those from diverse backgrounds and cultures. It also reflects the ability to understand social and ethical norms for behavior across settings and to be able to identify and use family, school, and community resources and supports.
Relationship Skills	The ability to establish and maintain healthy relationships with diverse individuals and groups. Developing relationship skills promotes the ability to communicate clearly, listen well, cooperate with others, resist social and peer pressure, negotiate conflict, and seek help or offer it to others.
Responsible Decision-Making	The ability to make constructive choices about personal behavior and social interactions within the context of ethical standards, safety concerns, and social norms. It involves making realistic evaluations of the consequences of one's actions and a consideration of the well-being of oneself and others.

attention to culture in SEL, led us to prioritize picturebooks with diverse human characters in our analysis.

With these qualities in mind, we sought five contemporary picturebooks (published between 2010 and 2020) that reflected our criteria for "quality" and which, in our judgment, aligned with at least one of the SEL core competencies. Because we were attentive to the qualities of literary fiction as well as human diversity, our list was quickly narrowed to a handful of books. In finalizing our corpus, we each read a range of picturebooks and summarized them relative to the SEL competencies, paying close attention to images (Kozak & Recchia, 2019), to select the best exemplars, in our estimation, of each SEL competency.

We recognize that our list is not exhaustive and may not align with selections that others might make; however, our primary purpose is to demonstrate a *process* of using critical literacy and choosing quality picturebooks to read with and against SEL, along with the affordances of this approach, not to identify the ideal texts for engaging in this work. Finally, drawing from our prior work reading with and against the SEL competencies (Clark, Chrisman, & Lewis, 2020a), we read each picturebook as a potential vehicle for teaching that competency, and attending to the positions on offer in each, the potential social effects on various readers, the kinds of values and norms included in each, and issues of inclusion/exclusion (Janks, 2019).

Teaching *with* and *against* SEL Using Quality Picturebooks

To illustrate using picturebooks to teach with and against SEL, we provide an overview of each core SEL competency alongside an exemplar text, describing key questions that teachers might use in order to interweave SEL competencies and equity into their teaching of quality literature using critical literacy.

SELF-AWARENESS IN *WHY DO WE CRY?*

Self-awareness is oriented around an individual's ability to identify their emotions and thoughts and understand how these emotions and thoughts relate to identity, culture, and behavior (CASEL, 2017). This competency also requires students to determine and manage their strengths and limitations by thinking positively and confidently (Ohio Department of Education, 2019). Written by Fran Pintadera and illustrated by Ana Sender, *Why Do We Cry?* (2020) provides a compelling text for exploring this competency.

Centering around a conversation between a mother and her young son after he asks the question "Why do we cry?", the story examines her response, with each page turn revealing another reason for our tears. For example, one explanation the mother gives is ". . . we cry because we're full of anger / and we need to let it out, like a storm cloud releases rain. / After that we become lighter, just like the cloud." The sans-serif font draws subtle attention to the bolded, focal emotion without directly defining it. Instead, the double-page spreads are rendered in muted, matte colors and extraordinary imagery that supports the figurative language of the text (see Figure 1).

Teachers and students reading this picturebook with the SEL standards might center their discussion around the naturalness of emotions and how many different emotions can be expressed through tears. As the book points out, people cry for a variety of reasons, all of which are valid and important. The book could also be used to identify and name the emotions depicted by the mother throughout, as each illustration of her reasons for crying differs in terms of tone, color, and visual elements. For instance, the accompanying images for anger (see Figure 1) are portrayed in dark neutral grey, beige, and black. The mother is shown as part of a dark grey rain cloud, tears of rain falling down on the page, with dark black birds flying below. Her expression is fierce, looking forward past the edge of the page,

FIGURE 1
Illustration from *Why Do We Cry?*

as if toward the future. The image could cultivate a discussion about identifying and naming feelings, as well as discussing the illustrator's choices in terms of color and imagery, since the self-awareness competency and related standards emphasize identifying emotions themselves, recognizing places to process emotions, and understanding how emotions can be related to current events.

Why Do We Cry? could also be used to read against the self-awareness competency, inviting readers to reject what is labeled natural, rational, or neutral. Despite the SEL claim that there are natural emotions and appropriate times and places to safely process emotions, the definition for appropriate is never given. *Why Do We Cry?* illustrates a range of ways of feeling and being without considering the appropriateness of the feelings shown or who can feel them—adults or children, boys or women. Instead, the text emphasizes, "we cry because we feel like crying" without stopping to identify or manage the emotional responses. Sometimes, there are systems that actively do hold people back (or walls "that seem impossible to climb," as the text pictorially and discursively refers to them), there are challenges that feel too big, and the result is that we cry. The self-awareness competency seems to lay out a clear course to dealing with challenges: identify and name the emotion that is felt or the challenge that confronts us; reframe the negative emotion or challenge in a positive light using self-talk; seek help from a trusted adult; and try again. However, in life, the way through a challenge or certain emotions isn't always so clear cut, and sometimes we cry because it's the right thing to do in that moment.

SELF-MANAGEMENT IN *THE JOURNEY*

Self-management builds upon the core competency of self-awareness. While self-awareness stresses the recognition of one's thoughts and emotions, self-management requires "the ability to navigate one's emotions, thoughts, and behaviors across different situations while managing stress, controlling impulses and motivating oneself" (Ohio Department of Education, 2019, p. 4). *The Journey* (2016), written and illustrated by Francesca Sanna, offers a timely and important story with which to explore this competency. This Amnesty/CILIP Honour book, inspired by two girls the author met at a refugee center in Italy, does not specify a particular immigrant or refugee group, but instead depicts a child narrator and their family as they leave their unidentified country amidst a dangerous war and their father's related death.

Taken together, the text and images offer opportunities to teach both with and against this SEL competency. Midway through their journey, for instance, the family must sleep without shelter in a forest (see Figure 2 and Figure 3). In facing pages, rendered in muted tones against a black background, we get nearly identical images of the mother and her children. On the left-hand page, the child's narration is presented in white letters: "In the darkness the noises / of the forest scare me." Wrapped in their mother's arms and cocooned in her long, dark hair, the forest hues are bright, with whimsical

FIGURE 2
Illustration from *The Journey* (1 of 2)

FIGURE 3
Illustration from *The Journey* (2 of 2)

creatures peeking through the dense foliage. Only the eyes are shown on each of the characters—the children with black ovals looking fearfully up at their mother, the mother with black half circles gazing down at her children. On the right-hand page, we see the children, eyes closed, mouths soft, and read "But mother is with us / and she is never scared. / We close our eyes / and finally fall asleep." The image, however, tells a different story. Now the page is nearly all black, and the forest hues are darker and more saturated. Instead of friendly creatures, we see red eyes and darkly silhouetted human hands reaching toward the family. Although the mother still holds the children close, we now see her full face, where her eyes are red-rimmed black circles with tears spilling down her cheeks and into her long black hair.

As teachers and students read this scene, they might explore competency-aligned questions: How does the mother help her children to navigate their emotions? What does she do, and what do they do, to manage their stress? This scene, while not explicit, shows readers how the children are able to manage their emotions during this difficult time. Emotions like fear can be managed with the support of a trusted adult.

Importantly, there is also space to read against this SEL competency. Although the standards suggest that people *advance through* SEL competencies, picturebooks like *The Journey* and *Why Do We Cry?* show that adults also feel fear and express these feelings through tears. More critical questions might be asked as well, like "Why does the family have to sleep in the forest?" and "Why do some families have to leave their homes?" Implicit in the self-management competency is the idea that students must understand and obey school rules—and, by extension, the law. Just before hiding in the forest, the family explicitly breaks the law, "illegally" crossing borders. When the family reaches the border, after days of traveling via various means, they reach a guard: "'You are not allowed to / cross the border. Go back!' / shouts an angry guard. / We have nowhere to go / and we are very tired." The guard is pictured as a giant, colored in shades of red, looming over the border wall while the tiny family stares up at him. This scene can be used to question rules and what happens when we decide that it is actually in our best interest to not comply with them. Self-management as a construct becomes a Catch-22 here: the family's goals include escaping the danger of their home, but in order to persevere they must break the law.

SOCIAL AWARENESS IN *LET THE CHILDREN MARCH*

With its focus on empathy, diversity, and norms, social awareness is ripe for critical interrogation. The Coretta Scott King Award-winning picturebook *Let the Children March* (2018), written by Monica Clark-Robinson and illustrated by Frank Morrison, provides an excellent text for reading with and against this SEL competency. Social awareness entails consideration of diverse perspectives and the capacity to empathize with others, "including those from diverse backgrounds and cultures," as well as the ability to "understand ethical norms for behavior across settings" (Ohio Department of Education, 2019, p. 4).

In its child-centered retelling of the Birmingham Children's Crusade of 1963, *Let the Children March* invites teachers and students to consider the tensions in these SEL expectations. The illustrations are bold, and the entire book is made up of double-page spreads, including images of Dr. Martin Luther King Jr. and quotes from his speeches. Families and communities, rendered in myriad shades of black and brown, fill church pews and sidewalks, showing the diversity within communities of color.

The diversity of Black and Brown people in this book, along with the representations of white people, does subtle but important work in terms of social awareness. Initially, it is quite easy to read with the SEL competencies and empathize with the child narrator. The opening spread shows an empty, fenced-off playground featuring a placard that reads "WHITE ONLY." Readers are clearly positioned on the outside, looking in, and the printed text, on the facing page, firmly establishes this perspective: "I couldn't play on the same playground as the white kids. / I couldn't go to their schools. / I couldn't drink from their water fountains. / There were so many things I couldn't do." At this point, a teacher might ask questions such as "Who is allowed to play on this playground?" "Why isn't the narrator allowed to play there?" or "How would you feel if you were not allowed to play on the playground?" All of these questions align with this SEL competency and reinforce one of the specific K–2 standards, "Discuss the concept of, and practice, treating others the way you would want to be treated" (Ohio Department of Education, 2019, p. 18).

This picturebook, however, invites deeper questions about who "you" and "others" might be, providing an opening to read against this SEL competency. On the one hand, child readers might relate to the narrator by age and affinity for playgrounds, and share in the feelings of not being allowed to play because of rules imposed by adults. The signage, however, and the story that unfolds, make it clear that Black people, adults and children alike, are the ones being excluded. Here, readers who aren't Black children might feel sad for the Black children who are excluded in this story, but as children, they may not see themselves as implicated in or able to change these kinds of racist exclusions. The historical events depicted, however, along with the powerful illustrations, invite deeper questioning of not only individual empathy but systemic racism and the role that even very young people can play in social change. In a spread showing the children marching because their parents cannot for fear of losing their livelihoods if not their lives, a crowd of angry white adults look on (see Figure 4), their eyes bulging, their faces twisted in rage. The children march on, heroically, despite the sadness and fear they must have felt, shown in the tears running down the face of one of the young girls

FIGURE 4
Illustration from *Let the Children March*

and echoed in the archival photographs of the actual Children's Crusade at the end of the book.

Reading against the competency of social awareness highlights the collective nature of the children's march, which contradicts the individual emphasis in the standards. Teachers might ask critical questions such as "How do different communities work together to contribute to the well-being of the community and the world?' and "What happens when we think of ourselves as parts of diverse communities instead of as individuals?" White readers, teachers and students alike, can also take heed of the need to listen to and learn from Black and Brown people who are the experts in knowing the ways their communities might want help (as opposed to the ways that more powerful and privileged people might want to offer it)—an important social awareness skill not forwarded by SEL.

RELATIONSHIP SKILLS IN *EACH KINDNESS*

Like all of the SEL competencies, relationship skills are positioned to focus on individuals rather than groups or systems. Individual students must be able to manage their emotions in order to establish and maintain healthy social relationships with diverse individuals and groups if they are to succeed in the world. This entails clear communication, listening, cooperating, resisting peer pressure, and negotiating conflict (CASEL, 2017).

The Coretta Scott King Award-winning picturebook *Each Kindness* (2012), written by Jacqueline Woodson and illustrated by E.B. Lewis, beautifully supports teaching with this SEL competency as well as against it. The realistic, watercolor illustrations portray school-based friendships in ways that are both familiar and complex. When a new girl, Maya, joins their class, most of the children reject her. Maya is poor and white, and her hand-me-down clothes and ragged toys mark her as strange. Nonetheless, she persists in trying to make friends with her new peers, including with the narrator, a Black girl named Chloe whose "best friends that year were Kendra and Sophie." That friendships are marked in school-years points to the impermanence of relationships that are often circumscribed by institutional arrangements like shared lunch time, recess, and the proximity of desks in classrooms. Over and over, Maya attempts to befriend her peers, including Chloe. One day, rejecting yet another invitation to play at recess, Chloe recounts: "That afternoon, when we got back

/ into the classroom, Maya whispered to me, / *Bet you can't guess who the new Jacks Champion of the World is.* / Behind me, Andrew whispered, / *Chloe's got a new friend. Chloe's got a new friend.* / *She's not my friend,* I whispered back."

Teaching with this SEL competency, teachers and students might discuss the peer pressure that Andrew exerts on Chloe and her inability to resist it. It would also be appropriate to discuss multiple perspectives and how different characters like Andrew, Chloe, and Maya show different perspectives and feelings in this situation. But the expression on Chloe's face in the illustration is difficult to reconcile with the text and invites reading against this SEL competency. One of the components of the relationship skills competency revolves around the prevention, management, and resolution of interpersonal conflict. The reality is, though, that remaining neutral can be harmful in the face of racism, sexism, classism, and so on. Chloe does not overtly engage in conflict in this story; in fact, she avoids conflict by choosing not to play with Maya but never speaking directly against her. In the eyes of the SEL competency, Chloe has been successful in her conflict management. However, the damage that is done to both Chloe and to Maya as a result of avoiding conflict is clear by the expressions on both girls' faces as the story progresses. Additionally, to read against the competency, teachers and students might discuss in-school and out-of-school friend groups, what it means to "communicate clearly," and how communication is not only individual but collective and is shaped by class and race.

Later in the story, the teacher, Ms. Albert, conducts a lesson on kindness with a rock and a pail of water. She explains that dropping in the rock is like a single act of kindness, but that the ripples on the surface show how much a single act can impact the world. In the final, double-page spread, Chloe appears small and alone against a dappled green background of grass, trees, and water, having foregone the opportunity to build a relationship with Maya: "I watched the water ripple / as the sun set through the maples /and the chance of a kindness with Maya /became more and more /forever gone" (n.p.). As with the earlier scene, the story ends in complexity and nuance. Recognizing that some relationships are ephemeral and cannot always be repaired and that relationships are layered and affected by others are positionings offered by this text that go beyond this SEL competency in important ways.

RESPONSIBLE DECISION-MAKING IN *SAY SOMETHING*

This final core competency refers to "the ability to make constructive choices about personal behavior and social interactions within the context of ethical standards, safety concerns, and social norms. It involves making realistic evaluations of the consequences of one's actions and a consideration of the well-being for self and others" (CASEL, 2017).

The inclusive picturebook *Say Something* (2019) by Peter H. Reynolds can be used to read both *with* and *against* this competency. The text uses the second person, "you," to inspire the reader to "say something"—be that through their voice, artistic expression, or even actions. This picturebook is not plot-driven, but rather aligns with the genre of self-development. Unlike similar texts specifically developed for SEL curricula, however, this picturebook provides inclusive images and nuance. Each vividly colored, two-page spread features an "if/then" scenario. The left-hand page of one such spread, for example, depicts a child looking back over their shoulder as a second child, with a sneering face, holds a third child down on the ground. A white text bubble appears that says "If you see someone being hurt . . . "—and on the facing page, the ellipsis is completed by another text bubble that says, "SAY SOMETHING by being brave." These speech bubbles emerge from the gutter, between the two pages, as if the author is speaking directly to the reader. On the right-hand page, the first child is shown alone, now with his arms outstretched, yelling "HEY! STOP!"—the implication being that the child is intervening in the bullying on the prior page.

Reading with this SEL competency, teachers and students might think about the decisions being made by the three children depicted: What choices do these characters have? Who do their decisions affect? From the images, we can see that the first child uses his words—literally, saying something—and makes the "responsible" decision to intercede without putting himself in more danger by reacting physically.

But *Say Something* can also be used to read against this competency, allowing for a critical interpretation. For example, in contrast to the one-on-one bullying scene described above, a later spread takes up systemic problems. Here, the initial page shows a person holding a sign that says, "No more hurting people" and the word "PEACE" written in bright, primary colors. The figure stands under a white speech bubble that says "If you see an injustice, SAY SOMETHING peacefully. INSPIRE others to do the same." On the opposite page, children hold up various signs related to peace: the word "peace" spelled in American Sign Language, "I (heart) the ocean," the "om" symbol, and a drawing of a dove holding an olive branch. This spread suggests that responsible decision-making is not always an individual act and can come to fruition through community. Juxtaposing this spread with the cover art furthers this critique: the children on the cover wear t-shirts that point to different movements—"Be the Change," "I Have a Dream," and "I Persist"—inviting teachers and students to think about "ethical standards, safety considerations, and social norms" (CASEL, 2017) and questions such as "Whose safety is considered important in society?" and "What happens when we need to act against the social norm in opposition to injustice?" Readers can even think beyond the possibilities provided in the book by asking what additional opportunities for "saying something" may exist and what our options are in response to injustice.

The endpapers of the book reiterate this potential. While the inner front cover depicts speech bubbles with provocative phrases such as "Turn energy into action," "Listen and learn," "Hate has no home here," and "Let's make history," the final spread evokes reader response (see Figure 5).

FIGURE 5
Illustration from *Say Something*

One last completed speech bubble comes directly from the author's name: "Your voice can / inspire, heal, and transform. / Your voice can change the world. / Are you ready / to say something?" Young readers are then left with eight blank speech bubbles, insinuating space for them to think of their own ways to "say something" (see Figure 6 and Figure 7). Readers are thus invited to mobilize their emotions (Lewis, 2020), which students and teachers can use to critically think through how they can not only engage in responsible decision-making but also the many facets of SEL.

FIGURE 6
Illustration from *Say Something* (1 of 2)

FIGURE 7
Illustration from *Say Something* (2 of 2)

Toward a More Ethical Teaching of SEL

As Pyscher and Crampton (2020) remind us, SEL and related programs are now "deemed 'essential' in almost every corner of the social services sector" including schools, but in its "commodified and packaged" form, "SEL appears mainly concerned with pro-social emotional expression" that emphasizes "conformity and compliance" with no expectation that teachers "reflect upon their interactions with children and youth" (p. 3). Our analysis bears this out. Two key facets that run throughout the SEL competencies are a focus on individuals and an emphasis on social skills rather than emotional learning. Little attention is given to the broader context or to how individuals are always acting and reacting to people in socially, culturally, and ideologically situated ways. As for emotions, the goal of SEL seems to be for students to recognize these in themselves and others and to "manage" them through appropriate social skills so that they don't interfere with their academic success in school or their later success in life. That norms for interacting or ways of expressing emotions might vary across cultures is never acknowledged, nor is the fact that "success" in life isn't always equitably achievable for all.

Lewis (2020) reminds us that "understanding what emotion *does* to signs is central to teachers and researchers of critical literacy and literary response" (p. 275). Drawing from scholarship on affect, race, and emotions, she demonstrates how texts can mobilize emotions by offering coded, affective signs that "reproduce White supremacy and racial injustice" (p. 275). She offers as examples both the tweets of President Trump that attach "totally broken and crime infested places" to immigrants, as well as a more well-intentioned book discussion, among teachers, of *The Watsons Go to Birmingham–1963* (Curtis, 1995), in which a joyful point of connection around a reference to Buster Brown shoes was also a reification of whiteness, and a resistance to racism, by the readers. As she notes, "These signs need not be explicitly attached to an object; rather, any coded message that even remotely suggests these affective signs foments hatred and supports the sick logic of White supremacy" (Lewis, 2020, p. 275).

We see our work as drawing on and extending from that of Lewis (2020). One outcome we see in using picturebooks to read with and against SEL is the opportunity to mobilize rather than simply manage emotions. Inviting teachers to critically choose and use picturebooks to teach with and against SEL is not simply asking them to take on a critical literacy stance. Rather, paraphrasing Janks (2019), it's inviting them to make an ethical decision about whether to take up the positions on offer in the SEL competencies or to oppose them in order to better weave "a social fabric that is just and equitable" (p. 564). While we believe that the picturebooks described here and linked to specific SEL competencies afford particularly strong opportunities for doing this work, we offer core, anchor questions aimed at uncovering the underlying social effects of the positions on offer and the ideologies they support relative to the SEL competencies to guide teachers in critically and ethically evaluating other picturebooks and literary texts that might be used when teaching with and against SEL competencies (see Table 2).

Embracing this work will fall not only on teachers but also on teacher educators. As SEL becomes yet another K–12 mandate, we must give preservice teachers the critical literacy tools they need to make ethical decisions about SEL. We also need to turn a critical eye to our own practices and be proactive in using any power and leverage we have to inform and push back on state legislatures and departments of education that would forward SEL standards devoid of culture and context. Instead of teaching to the SEL standards or using pre-packaged SEL curriculum, we encourage teachers and teacher educators to take up SEL through a critical lens, using quality picturebooks, as a means to open space for critique, hope, and ethical action, using SEL not only to improve student behavior and social skills but to forward social justice and positive social change.

REFERENCES

Campano, G., Ghiso, M. P., & Sánchez, L. (2013). "Nobody knows the . . . amount of a person": Elementary students critiquing dehumanization through organic critical literacies. *Research in the Teaching of English*, 48(1), 97–124.

Cart, M., & Jenkins, C. A. (2006). *The heart has its reasons. Young adult literature with gay/lesbian/queer content, 1969–2004*. Scarecrow Press.

CASEL. (2017). *What is SEL?* casel.org/what-is-sel.

Clark, C. T., Chrisman, A., & Lewis, S. (2020a). (Un)standardizing emotions: Using DisCrit to surface ideologies and critique damaging discourses in SEL. Paper presented at the annual meeting of the National Council of Teachers of English Assembly for Research, Nashville, Tennessee.

Clark, C. T., & Chrisman, A. (2020b). Self-control, social change, and literacy learning: Representations of anger in SEL materials and children's and young adult literature. Paper presented at the annual meeting of the National Council of Teachers of English Assembly for Research, Nashville, Tennessee.

Dahlen, S. P. (2019, June 19). *Diversity in children's books 2018 infographic*. readingspark.wordpress.com/2019/06/19/picture-this-diversity-in-childrens-books-2018- infographic

Dusenbury, L., Yoder, N., Dermody, C., & Weissberg, R. (2020). *Collaborating states initiative: An examination of K–12 SEL learning competencies/standards in 18 states*. casel.org/wp-content/uploads/2020/03/CSI- Frameworks.pdf

Dusenbury, L., Dermody, C., & Weissberg, R. P. (2018). *State scorecard scan*. casel.org/wp-content/uploads/2018/09/csi-scorecard-sept2018.pdf

Fairclough, N. (1992). *Discourse and social change*. Polity Press.

Ford, D. (2020, February 6). Social-emotional learning for Black students is ineffective when it is culture-blind. *Diverse: Issues in Higher Education*. diverseeducation.com/article/166341

Freire, P. (1970). *Pedagogy of the oppressed*. Seabury Press.

Goleman, D. (1995). *Emotional intelligence: Why it can matter more than IQ*. Bantam Books.

Hoffman, D. M. (2009). Reflecting on social emotional learning: A critical perspective on trends in the United States. *Review of Educational Research*, 79(2), 533–56.

Janks, H. (2019). Critical literacy and the importance of reading with and against a text. *Journal of Adolescent & Adult Literacy*, 62(5), 561–64.

Janks, H. (2012). The importance of critical literacy. *English Teaching: Practice and Critique*, 11(1), 150–163.

Koonce, J. B. (2012). "Oh, those loud black girls!": A phenomenological study of black girls talking with an attitude. *Journal of Language and Literacy Education* [Online], 8(2), 26–46.

Kozak, S. & Recchia, H. (2019). Reading and the development of social understanding: Implications for the literacy classroom. *The Reading Teacher*, 72(5), 569–77.

Lewis, C. (2020). Emotion, critical response, and the transformation of signs: The fundamentals of language arts. *Language Arts*, 97(4), 274–78.

Mahfouz, J. & Anthony-Stevens, V. (2020). Why trouble SEL? The need for cultural relevance in SEL. *Bank Street Occasional Paper Series*, 2020(43), 58–70. educate.bankstree.edu/occassional-paper-series/vol 2020/iss43/6.

Nikolajeva, M. (2013). Picturebooks and emotional literacy. *The Reading Teacher*, 67(4), 249–54.

Ohio Department of Education (2019). *Ohio's K–12 social and emotional learning standards*. education.ohio.gov/getattachment/Topics/Learning-in-Ohio/Social-and-Emotional-Learning/Social-and-Emotional-Learning-Standards/K-12-SEL-Standards-Full-Final.pdf.aspx?lang=en-US

O'Sullivan, S. (2004). Books to live by: Using children's literature for character education. *The Reading Teacher*, 57(7), 640–45.

Poiner, J. (2018, September 10). Social-emotional learning matters, but Ohio's new strategic plan goes too far. *Thomas B. Fordham Institute*. fordhaminstitute.org/ohio/commentary/social-emotional-learning-matters-ohios-new-strategic-plan-goes-too-far

Pyscher, T., & Crampton, A. (2020). Issue 43: Possibilities and problems in trauma-based and social emotional learning programs. *Occasional Paper Series*, 2020(43), 3–9. educate.bankstreet.edu/occasional-paper-series/vol2020/iss43/1

Ris, E. W. (2015). Grit: A short history of a useful concept. *Journal of Educational Controversy*, 10(1), 1–18.

Sealey-Ruiz, Y. & Greene, P. (2015). Popular visual images and the (mis)reading of black male youth: A case for racial literacy in urban preservice teacher education. *Teaching Education*, 26(1), 55–76.

Short, K. G. with the Worlds of Words Community (2019). Critical content analysis of visual images. In H. Johnson, J. Mathis, & K. G. Short (Eds.), *Critical content analysis of visual images in books for young people* (pp. 3–22). Routledge.

Smagorinsky, P. & Taxel, J. (2004). The discourse of character education: Ideology and politics in the proposal and award of federal grants. *Journal of Research in Character Education*, 2(2), 113–40.

Staub, M. E. (2016). Controlling ourselves: Emotional intelligence, the marshmallow test, and the inheritance of race. *American Studies*, 55(1), 59–80.

Stringer, K. (July 9, 2019). SEL in the house: Democrats approve millions in landmark federal funding for social-emotional learning in bill that now faces test in senate. *The 74*. https://www.the74million.org/sel-in-the-house-democrats-approve-millions-in-landmark-federal-funding-for-social-emotional-learning-in-bill-that-now-faces-test-in-senate

Vasquez, V. M. (2017). Critical literacy. *Oxford Research Encyclopedia*. doi:10.1093/acrefore/9780190264093.013.20

Vasquez, V. M., Janks, H., & Comber, B. (2019). Critical literacy as a way of being and doing. *Language Arts*, 96(5), 300–311.

Weissberg, R. P., & Cascarino, J. (2013). Academic learning + social-emotional learning = national priority. *The Phi Delta Kappan*, 95(2), 8–13.

CHILDREN'S LITERATURE CITED

Clark-Robinson, M. (2018). *Let the children march* (F. Morrison, Illus.). Houghton Mifflin Harcourt.

Curtis, C. P. (1995). *The Watsons go to Birmingham—1963*. Delacorte.

Mulcahy, W. (2012). *Zach gets frustrated* (D. McKee, Illus.). Free Spirit Publishing.

Pintadera, F. (2020). *Why do we cry?* (A. Sender, Illus.). Kids Can Press.

Reynolds, P. H. (2019). *Say something!* Orchard.

Sanna, F. (2016). *The journey*. Flying Eye Books.

Verdick, E., & Lisovskis, M. (2015). *How to take the grrrr out of anger*. Free Spirit Publishing.

Woodson, J. (2012). *Each kindness* (E. B. Lewis, Illus.). Nancy Paulsen.

CAROLINE T. CLARK is a professor in the Department of Teaching and Learning and has been a faculty member of Ohio State University since 1996. She specializes in English education, young adult literature, adolescent literacies, and supporting diverse people in schools. She is the faculty lead for the English Language Arts AYA licensure program, and her research focuses on language and literacy practices and collaborative research with teachers, young people, and families in service of advocacy for social justice.

ALYSSA CHRISMAN is a PhD candidate in teaching and learning at the Ohio State University and a full-time visiting instructor in the educational studies department at Denison University. She has previously taught middle and high school ELA, and her research interests include mental health in young adult literature, social emotional learning, and critical literacies and pedagogy.

SUZANNE G. LEWIS is a PhD candidate in teaching and learning at the Ohio State University. Previously, she was an ELA teacher at a career-technical high school and a program manager for an after-school program in elementary schools. Her research interests focus on the pursuit of social justice within adolescent literacies, English education, and career-technical education.

This article originally appeared in *Voices from the Middle* 29.1

DESIGN THINKING IN READING WORKSHOP: Flexible Strategies for Sparking Empathy in Middle School Readers in the Time of COVID-19

KATIE DURKIN

Introduction

In the wake of the COVID-19 pandemic, many students and teachers were living in a world of unknowns. Yet through the uncertainty of 2020, new opportunities were born. Teachers began to innovate solutions for the new school year: I was one of those teachers. Over the summer, groups of educators worked together to create reentry units for the fall of 2020 to learn about students' strengths and areas of growth. I used this opportunity to draw from a primary resource, *Designed to Learn* by Lindsay Portnoy, to create a design-thinking unit that explored my students' reading identities to support empathy development. Reading is an activity with the potential to spark empathy if readers have voice and choice in the texts they read. When we read about other perspectives, we are able to both see ourselves in the stories we read as well as "imagine ourselves into other people's experiences" (Patrick, 2016). In this article, I argue that using design thinking in a reading workshop benefits middle school students in developing empathy by examining personal reading identities; this approach elevates student voice and choice in their learning and guides students to acknowledge reading as a social process.

Identity before Design Thinking

Freire and Macedo (1987) suggest empathy development requires students and teachers to examine how their own identities affect how they "read the word and the world" (p. 35). Muhammad (2020) defines identity as "who we are, who others say we are (in positive and negative ways), and whom we desire to be" (p. 67). Further, Muhammad (2020) highlights the importance of identity in her Historically Responsive Literacy framework in which students look for themselves in the curriculum, instructional practices, and books they read; she posits that students seek to understand how their multilayered identities shape the way they approach and understand themselves and texts.

Design thinking is a pedagogical approach that can be used to design units or lessons based upon students' experiences; it explores "creating learning environments that foster students' ability to design solutions to today's pressing problems" (Portnoy, 2020, p. 2). This framework helps students engage in collaborative, social work around solving a problem. Design thinking begins with "understanding through empathy," where students assume the perspectives of others to create solutions to problems they have identified (Portnoy, 2020, p. 15–17). Students communicate with one another about this problem and how they are working toward finding and creating solutions. Grounded in empathy, design thinking aligns with the reading workshop model as it pushes students to develop skills associated with being empathetic.

Students' identities are often reflected in their reading identities. By examining students' reading identities first, students are anchored in their own personal reading history, which in turn sets the foundation for design thinking (Durkin, 2020). Reading identities are uncovered by having students examine their past experiences with reading to inform their choices for the future. As motivation to voluntarily read diminishes for many middle school students (Troyer, 2017), engagement in the social aspect of reading is more important than ever. Ivey (2014) argues engagement is necessary to ensure students can develop empathy collaboratively and independently; if we want students to be engaged in what they are reading, they must look for, choose, and discuss texts that relate to aspects of their identities.

Cultivating Empathy as a Teacher: HEARTS before Heads

Drawing on a strategy called "HEARTS before Heads," I launched this unit with my own empathy development for my new students through one-on-one conferences (Portnoy, 2020) (see Figure 1). This strategy enabled me to design lessons that take into account my students' identities and model my own empathy development while incorporating design thinking into my classroom. I completed these conferences individually while students were working on assignments or independently reading. The reading workshop model prioritizes making time for conferences with students, as each day begins with a mini-lesson. This allowed the class to spend time working on the assignment from the mini-lesson while I conferenced with students.

"HEARTS before Heads" asks specific questions about students' home, educational experiences, activities, reasons for learning, transformative life experiences, and special attributes (Portnoy, 2020). The questions invited students to share experiences and enabled me to learn about my students' reading identities. This strategy was the perfect introductory activity to build empathy with my students and understand them as people and learners. These conferences were an opportunity for students to share their voices and identities before developing their reading skills (Muhammad, 2020). In addition to developing my empathy as the teacher, elements of the reading workshop were conducive to designing this unit with a focus on building empathy, including the creation of

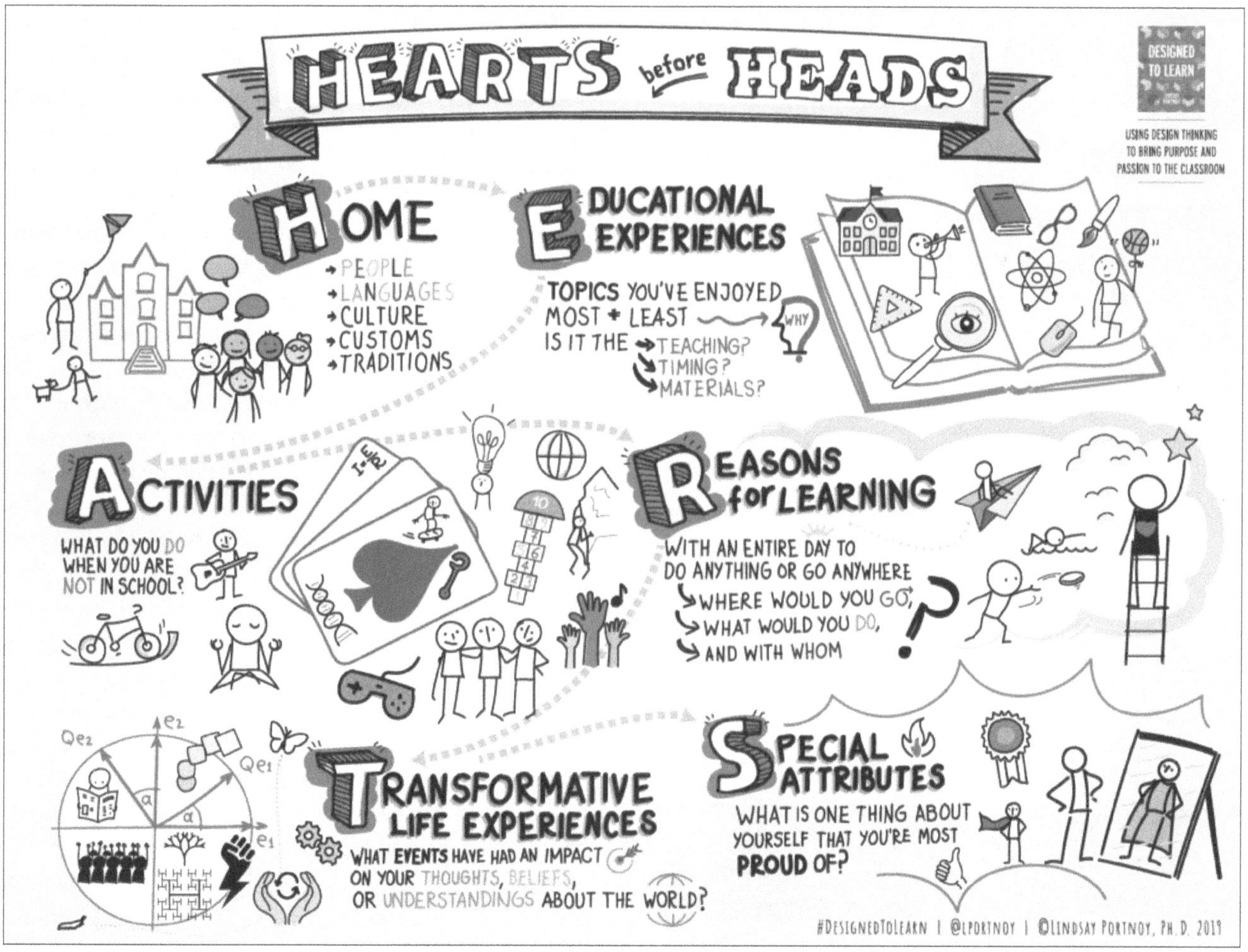

FIGURE 1
The "Hearts Before Heads" infographic highlights questions to ask students during reading workshop conferences.

FIGURE 2
Mission Monday's student work examples.

mini-lessons, the structure of independent time for free reading, and opportunities for reflection.

Igniting Empathy: Strategies for Remote and In-Person Learning

Following the "HEARTS before Heads" conferences, the majority of work in this unit was focused on students' empathy development. Three strategies I used to help me accomplish this goal were: (1) Mission Mondays (Roberts, 2018), (2) Free Read Wednesdays, and (3) Reflection Fridays (see Figure 2). These strategies were enacted in both virtual and physical classroom experiences through the hybrid model of COVID-19 teaching.

MISSION MONDAYS

Each week began with Mission Monday, a 10-minute mini-lesson during which learners were given their "mission," or assignment for the week (Roberts, 2018). Building upon what I learned from their "HEARTS before Heads" conferences, I recommended books to students and allowed them to choose texts that connected to some aspect of their identities. Each mission then focused on students using these books of choice to think deeply about how their identity impacted how they were comprehending texts. Students used identity shields and charts they created in social studies to find connections between themselves and their characters. James (all names are pseudonyms) used his favorite quote from Babe Ruth to relate to his main character's internal and external struggles in *Drums, Girls, and Dangerous Pie* (see Figure 3). Students employed Rudine Sims Bishop's (1990) metaphor of "windows and mirrors" to determine if the book they were reading was teaching them something new or offered a reflection of their own lives (p. ix). Lily reflected on her book, *Counting by 7s*, explaining how this book was both a window and mirror for her as a reader. Finally, students looked at the ways we "work" while we read to understand what thinking we do with our minds and hearts (Cherry-Paul & Cruz, 2019). Kate was able to use her book, *Mockingbird*, to identify literary elements and think about her empathy for Holly, the main character in the story.

Each of these missions allowed me to assess students' skills and learn about their preferences for books. All of this work was done digitally through the use of Google Slides. Through Mission Mondays (Roberts, 2018), students used their books of choice to develop empathy, and these missions were natural

Questions Posed to Students	Student Responses

Mission Monday #1

How does the book you are currently reading relate to one aspect of your identity?

Mission Monday #1

DRUMS, GIRLS + DANGEROUS PIE

JORDAN SONNENBLICK

Personal Motto: "Every Strike Brings Me Closer to My Next Homerun." -Babe Ruth

Relates to My Personal Motto: In *Drums, Girls and Dangerous Pie*, Steven Alper is left angry and unstable. His younger brother has been diagnosed with leukemia, and his parents are struggling with finances, Steven is struggling in school. But, with hard work and determination through tough times, Steven is able to prevail through tough times.

Example: Just when the world around Steven Alper is crumbling, he kept on persevering and working hard, until he finally had a breakthrough.

Written by: James

Image Citation:

Scholastic, Inc. (2014). Drums, girls, and dangerous pie. [Paperback book]. Amazon. https://www.amazon.com/Drums-Girls-Dangerous-Jordan-Sonnenblick/dp/0545722861

Mission Monday #2

Is the book you are currently reading a window or a mirror? How does one part of your identity relate to this book being a window or a mirror? (Bishop, 1990)

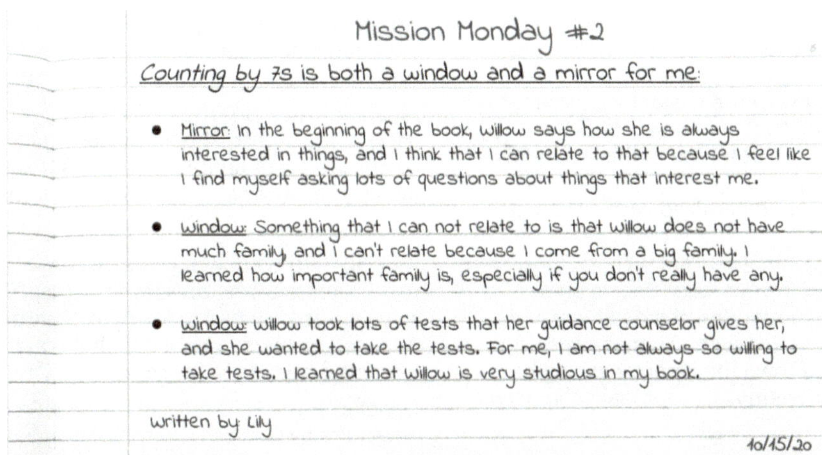
Mission Monday #2

Counting by 7s is both a window and a mirror for me:

- Mirror: In the beginning of the book, Willow says how she is always interested in things, and I think that I can relate to that because I feel like I find myself asking lots of questions about things that interest me.
- Window: Something that I can not relate to is that Willow does not have much family, and I can't relate because I come from a big family. I learned how important family is, especially if you don't really have any.
- Window: Willow took lots of tests that her guidance counselor gives her, and she wanted to take the tests. For me, I am not always so willing to take tests. I learned that Willow is very studious in my book.

written by Lily

10/15/20

Mission Monday #3

Mind Work

Identify the setting, conflict, characters, and theme. Think about how two of these literary elements interact/affect one another.

Heart Work

How does your identity affect the way you read the book? Do you feel empathy for your characters in the story?

(Cherry-Paul & Cruz, 2019)

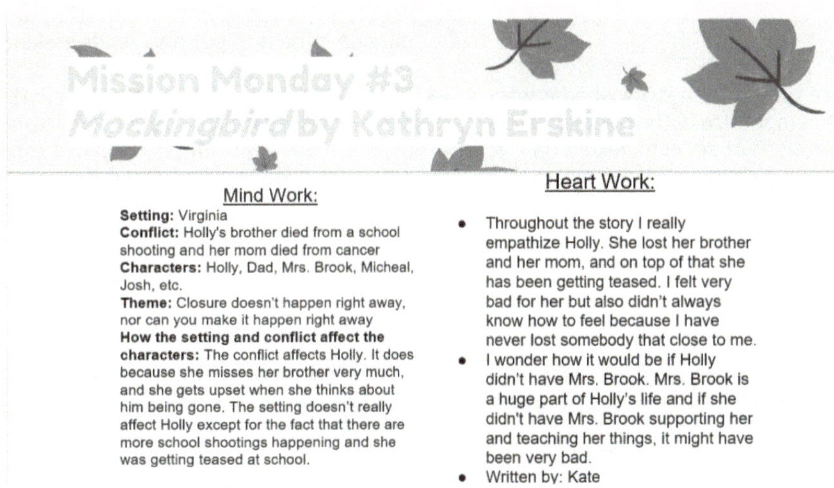
Mission Monday #3

Mockingbird by Kathryn Erskine

Mind Work:

Setting: Virginia
Conflict: Holly's brother died from a school shooting and her mom died from cancer
Characters: Holly, Dad, Mrs. Brook, Micheal, Josh, etc.
Theme: Closure doesn't happen right away, nor can you make it happen right away
How the setting and conflict affect the characters: The conflict affects Holly. It does because she misses her brother very much, and she gets upset when she thinks about him being gone. The setting doesn't really affect Holly except for the fact that there are more school shootings happening and she was getting teased at school.

Heart Work:

- Throughout the story I really empathize Holly. She lost her brother and her mom, and on top of that she has been getting teased. I felt very bad for her but also didn't always know how to feel because I have never lost somebody that close to me.
- I wonder how it would be if Holly didn't have Mrs. Brook. Mrs. Brook is a huge part of Holly's life and if she didn't have Mrs. Brook supporting her and teaching her things, it might have been very bad.
- Written by: Kate

FIGURE 3

Mission Monday's student work examples (all names are pseudonyms).

segues into Free Read Wednesdays and Reflection Fridays.

FREE READ WEDNESDAYS

Making time for students to read in school is essential, not just for reading success but also for engagement in reading (Ivey & Broaddus, 2000). Free Read Wednesdays enabled students to enjoy reading their chosen books while answering questions targeted toward developing students' skills with empathy. These questions moved from sharing with others how their current choice books related to their identities into more in-depth questions about empathy. Students were asked to think about the impacts books can have on us as readers, if they were to have the same feelings as a character, if they experienced a similar situation or conflict, and to identify a character with whom it may be hard to empathize. Student responses reflected their developing empathy. While thinking about *The Prince and the Dressmaker*, Kendall identified with a character struggling with being judged and voiced that everyone should accept themselves for who they are. Claire, whose mother had surgery when she was younger, connected her own experience with Digory's in *The Magician's Nephew*, recognizing the character was dealing with his mother's grave illness. Brielle demonstrated empathy when she connected to Hannake, a character from *Girl in the Blue Coat*, appreciating the freedoms she had but her character had lost (see Table 1).

TABLE 1

Questions and Student Answers to Develop Empathy on Free Read Wednesdays

Questions Posed to Students	Student Responses
Because of our identity, we comprehend and interpret stories differently. This means that when we read stories we can make connections with the characters, share feelings with them or empathize with them. Think about a time in the story you are currently reading when you made a connection or empathized with a character.	• Brittany: I am reading *The Hunger Games* and, right now, Katniss is in a very scary situation where a lot of people can kill her, so she has to get away. I think I would also feel very scared if I were in her situation. • Amanda: When Bri (the main character) in *On the Come Up* can't get into the Ring (a rapping contest) she fights her way through and becomes very aggressive and decides to try to fight her way in. But she ends up getting banned. I would have just walked away and not try to get in trouble.
Think about a major event a character experienced in your story. Decide on a feeling or emotion the character is having during this major event. Then, describe an event in your own life where you may have had similar feelings as your main character.	• Kendall: In the book that I read, *The Prince and The Dressmaker*, the prince had really liked wearing dresses and the problem was that he felt that he was going to be judged. He had to keep his identity a secret when going out and dressing up. And this problem I could definitely relate to because we all sometimes feel like we would be judged for something when in reality you should be yourself! • Ophelia: *In The Fellowship of the Ring*, Frodo had to make a big decision to go on the adventure by himself or with his friends. He probably felt very torn and confused on what to do. I would feel torn and confused as well because that is a very hard decision to make: going on a mission by yourself. He may not be able to finish the mission or he may put his friends in danger or he may not be able to destroy the ring.
Were there times in the story when it was difficult to empathize with your characters? Did their actions or speech make it hard to empathize with them?	• Claire: Sorta. I'm reading *The Magician's Nephew* and Digory's mom is very sick. In some ways, it's difficult to emphasize, other ways, it's not. When I was in 3rd grade, my mom got a hip surgery because she had this disease in her hip since she was 3 or 4. So I was worried about her when I was little but it wasn't like she was in a life and death situation like Digory's mom. Digory's mom is very ill, and it's possible that she could die, so Digory would do anything to cure her. He's looking for a cure while a bunch of crazy, adventurous stuff happens. • Warren: I found it difficult to empathize with my character because I don't have parents who are divorced, so I don't know what it's like.
Does the author help you think about how you can incorporate empathy into your own life? If so, how? Think about what you are meant to learn from the story's themes.	• Brielle: I'm reading *Girl in the Blue Coat*, and it takes place during World War II. The main character is Hannake, and she has a lot of Jewish friends. Many of her friends have died or disappeared. A lot of her freedom and abilities are taken away (such as having food). It really makes you feel empathy because you appreciate that you have these freedoms and your family. and things that we usually over think. • Lily: In *Counting by 7s*, the author makes me think about empathy in my own life because one way she does is she explains a lot about what Willow is feeling some of those feelings I have had before.

Students shared their answers virtually via Zoom, which gave them the opportunity to voice how they understood their books. Students were reading different genres but were able to share how their empathy developed while reading their stories. Free Read Wednesdays offered the students a chance to independently read personally selected books or those recommended by me based upon their "HEARTS before Heads" conferences. It also gave them time to work toward the reading goals they set at the beginning of the unit before reflecting upon and adjusting the goals each Friday.

REFLECTION FRIDAYS

Reflection Friday was time for students to reflect on their reading goals, sharing them with each other to ideate solutions to challenging goals. Reflection is an essential part of design thinking; it helps students continue building empathy as they share their reading goals with their peers. Each Friday, students looked back at the goals they had set at the beginning of the unit and reflected upon the peaks and pitfalls of their plan. They had to communicate with their peers three bullet-points that would help them adjust their reading goals over the course of the next week. In their reflections, students focused on understanding their personal reading while also expanding their reading identities, seeking out solutions to the problems they identified within their reading lives.

Through peer review, students empathized with their classmates as they concocted solutions to setting and achieving goals. This integral part of the design thinking process enabled students to adjust their reading goals week after week, sharing and recommending their books while collaborating with classmates. One student, Sara, decided to focus her work on picking specific titles she was interested in reading while thinking about identifying themes. Over the course of the four-week unit, she was able to reflect and revise her goals as needed and set goals for the upcoming unit (see Figure 4).

These weekly and final reflections on goals helped students to ideate solutions individually and collaboratively in relation to their reading identities. They were able to share their voices in the final reflection with their peers in order to think about how they would like to grow as readers during the year. All three of these strategies build upon the foundation of empathy. Students developed empathy when thinking about their books of choice, while also

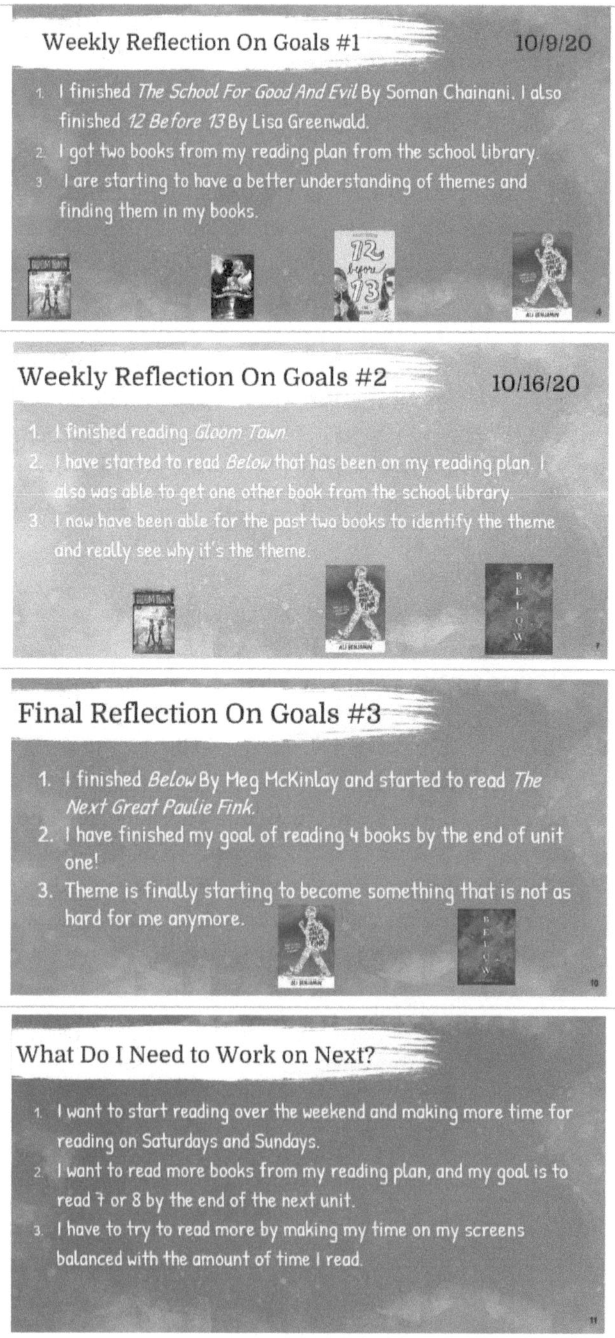

References

Candlewick Press. (2013). Below. Amazon. https://www.amazon.com/Below-Meg-McKinlay/dp/0763661260/

Clarion Books. (2020). Gloom town. Amazon. https://www.amazon.com/Gloom-Town-Ronald-L-Smith/dp/1328841618/

HarperCollins. (2013). School for good and evil. Amazon. https://www.amazon.com/School-Good-Evil-Soman-Chainani/dp/0062104896/

Katherine Tegen Books. (2019). 12 before 13. Amazon. https://www.amazon.com/Friendship-List-12-Before-13/dp/0062411780/

Little, Brown Books for Young Readers (2019). The next great Paulie Fink. Amazon. https://www.amazon.com/Next-Great-Paulie-Fink/dp/0316380881

FIGURE 4

Reflection Friday's student work example from Sara (all names are pseudonyms).

practicing empathy as they reflected on and shared their reading goals with each other.

Designing for the Future

This unit on design thinking to foster empathy was created in response to the global pandemic, resulting in transformative outcomes for my learners. Using design thinking next year will help me to build deeper relationships with my students as learners and readers. I will begin the year by "stepping back before stepping in," creating a strong foundation grounded in understanding reading identities while fostering empathy (Portnoy, 2020, p. 63). Getting to know our students as readers does not require us to "recreate the wheel"; rather, we are making space to learn alongside our students using design thinking (Portnoy, 2020, p. 41).

Using elements of design thinking to expand their reading identities, goals, and empathy skills, my students were prepared to enact change in the subsequent nonfiction unit. Using the "HEARTS before Heads" conferences as a guide, each student identified problems they wished to solve in their lifetimes. From climate change to world peace to equality, students are prepared to take on the hard work of seeking solutions and not simply identifying problems. While many people may say middle school students cannot solve such mighty problems, I, for one, am looking forward to seeing them show us all otherwise.

REFERENCES

Bishop, R. S. (1990). Mirrors, windows, and sliding glass doors. *Perspectives: Choosing and Using Books for the Classroom*, 6(3), ix–xi. https://scenicregional.org/wp content/uploads/2017/08/Mirrors-Windows-and-Sliding-Glass-Doors.pdf

Cherry-Paul, S., & Cruz, C. (2019, Nov. 18–20). *Equity institute: Facilitating conversations about race: Grades k–8* [Conference presentation]. The Reading and Writing Project: Teachers College, Columbia University.

Durkin, K. (2020). Anchoring readers in the times of change: 3 strategies to elevate student identity in reading workshop. *MiddleWeb*. https://www.middleweb.com/43584/anchoring-students-in-the-tides-of-change/

Freire, P., & Macedo, D. (1987). *Literacy: Reading the word and the world*. Bergin and Garvey.

Ivey, G. (2014). The social side of engaged reading for young adolescents. *Reading Teacher*, 68(3), 165–71. https://doi.org/10.1002/trtr.1268

Ivey, G., & Broaddus, K. (2000). Tailoring the fit: Reading instruction and middle school readers. *Reading Teacher*, 54(1), 68. http://search.ebscohost.com.ezproxy.neu.edu/login.aspx

Muhammad, G. (2020). *Cultivating genius: An equity framework for culturally and historically responsive literacy*. Scholastic.

Patrick, B. (2016, Jan. 27). Sunil Yapa: "Empathy is a radical act": In conversation with Bethanne Patrick about race, writing, and love. *Literary Hub*. https://lithub.com/sunil-yapa-empathy-is-a-radical-act/

Portnoy, L. (2020). *Designed to learn: Using design thinking to bring purpose and passion to the classroom*. ASCD.

Roberts, K. (2018). *A novel approach: Whole-class novels, student-centered teaching, and choice*. Heinemann.

Troyer, M. (2017). A mixed-methods study of adolescents' motivation to read. *Teachers College Record*, 119(5), 1–48. http://search.ebscohost.com.ezproxy.neu.edu/login.aspx

YOUNG ADULT LITERATURE MENTIONED

Collins, S. (2008). *The hunger games*. Scholastic Press.

Erskine, K. (2011). *Mockingbird*. Puffin Books.

Hesse, M. (2017). *Girl in the blue coat*. Little, Brown Books for Young Readers.

Lewis, C. S. (1955). *A magician's nephew*. The Bodley Head.

Sloan, H. G. (2014). *Counting by 7s*. Puffin Books.

Sonnenblick, J. (2004). *Drums, girls, and dangerous pie*. Scholastic.

Thomas, A. (2019). *On the come up*. Balzar and Bray.

Tolkien, J. R. R. (1954). *The fellowship of the ring*. Allen and Unwin.

Wang, J. (2018). *The prince and the dressmaker*. First Second.

KATIE DURKIN is a seventh-grade reading workshop teacher in Wilton, Connecticut, and a doctoral student at Northeastern University, studying the impact of classroom libraries on students' reading engagement. She was the 2020 recipient of the Edwyna Wheadon Postgraduate Training Scholarship from the National Council of Teachers of English.

This poem originally appeared in *English Journal 110.4*

I DON'T WANT TO WRITE A POEM FOR MY DEAD STUDENTS

for Diana and Chris

Just last June
I watched them both walk across the stage,
my dead students.
And once,
I taught them ninth-grade English
while they were still alive,
breathing, walking, talking.

Someone drove a car
the wrong way down I-94
and killed them.
That's what happened.
My students killed.
My students? No—

When I remember Diana
memorizing
I Have a Dream
by Martin Luther King Jr.,
when I see her standing in front
of her classmates, saying those words,
and her classmates hearing them—
that is not mine.
It is not mine
when she said *she*
wanted to work for that kind of justice TODAY.
It is not mine when Chris
was cutting up in class,
making his stupid jokes,
asking what it would take,
you know,
for me to "forget"
that he hadn't done his homework today?

And I don't want to understand
the cosmic calculus of this.
And I don't want to think of forgiveness.
I just want to cry
big salty tears.
I want long sucking sobs.
I want this day to last a long, long time,
the first day Diana and Chris
weren't walking and talking
in the world,
but I was,
writing this poem.
September 27, 2017

—Zach Czaia

ZACH CZAIA is a high school English teacher living and working in Minneapolis, Minnesota. His first poetry collection, *Saint Paul Lives Here (In Minnesota),* was published at Wipf & Stock Press in 2015. Zach can be reached at zczaia@hotmail.com.

This article originally appeared in *Language Arts* 96.6

"DEATH DIDN'T COME UP AT CENTER TIME": Sharing Books about Grief in Elementary Literacy Classrooms

Four educators reflect upon sharing children's picturebooks about grief with students and colleagues, encouraging others to take up similar brave and difficult conversations.

NICHOLAS E. HUSBYE,
BETH A. BUCHHOLZ,
CHRISTY WESSEL POWELL
& SARAH VANDER ZANDEN

> **I was kind of embarrassed. I wasn't looking forward to reading it, because I read about everything.... There's literally nothing off limits, so I was like, "Oh my gosh. How, as a critical literacy educator, am I refusing to read this book?"**
>
> —MEREDITH

MANY CHILDREN ENCOUNTER challenging life experiences that they carry—sometimes overtly, sometimes discreetly—into classrooms daily (Child and Adolescent Health Measurement Initiative, 2013). Childhood trauma takes many forms but includes abuse or neglect, witnessing violence, and, of particular interest in this work, the death of a parent or loved one. Despite the overwhelming frequency with which bereaved students are present in classrooms—one survey found 70% of participating teachers taught students who recently experienced the loss of a loved one (American Federation of Teachers and New York Life Foundation, 2012)—teachers continue to feel unprepared, reluctant, and even resistant to engaging students in talk about grief in the classroom (Mahon, Goldberg, & Washington, 1999).

We draw upon experiences of four educators sharing picturebooks about grief with elementary and adult audiences to illuminate insights, tensions, and strategies these educators utilized to engage their respective audiences in open-ended discussions. We begin by situating grief within a multidisciplinary perspective before delineating the reasons we must tackle these hard conversations in classroom spaces, shifting toward acknowledging, rather than policing, emotions. We then turn our attention to the experiences of the educators as they shared these books with their audiences, paying particular attention to why they engaged in this daunting task, when they engaged in this activity, and how these read-alouds and ensuing discussions were enacted. Our aim with this work is to move beyond book recommendations (e.g., Corr, 2004) to the complex *use* of books in classrooms to create opportunities for all students to collectively talk about death and grief as part of regularly occurring literacy routines. Our exploration can be positioned as a response to Wollman-Bonilla's (1998) call in the pages of *Language Arts*: "How are these texts *actually used* and *discussed* in classrooms?" (p. 294, emphasis added).

Literature Review and Theoretical Framing

SITUATING DEATH AND GRIEF

Death is often conflated with grief and is mostly addressed with reactive intervention—that is, support to help a child maintain an even-keel emotional state. By considering a more complex view of grief informed by work in the fields of psychology, sociology, philosophy, education, and medicine, educators are invited to critically (re)consider the role of classrooms in providing space, time, and resources to engage children in talk about both death and grief as part of the regular curriculum.

We use the terms death and grief conjointly, though we recognize their discrete characteristics. Death is a biological imperative (Poling & Evans, 2004): living things are born and, subsequently, die. Grief, conversely, is a social phenomenon. People learn how to grieve through their participation in/across meaningful social communities. Within a social constructionist frame, grieving is a "situated interpretive and communicative activity . . . [whereby] the narrative processes by which meanings are found, appropriated, or assembled occur at least as fully between people as within them" (Neimeyer, Klass, & Dennis, 2014, p. 485). Consequently, children experiencing grief seek to make meaning through interactions with families, religious institutions, and the broader communities and cultural spheres—such as schools—in which they participate.

Previous scholarly work exploring death- and grief-related literature for children can be sorted into two strands. The first strand includes book lists, book reviews, and analyses of picturebooks addressing themes of death and grief (Bargiel, Beck, Koblitz, O'Connor, Pierce, & Wolf, 1997; Corr, 2004; Johnson, 2004; Poling & Hupp, 2008; Wiseman, 2013). The second strand involves *theorizing about potential* uses, benefits, and issues of bringing these books into classrooms (e.g., Klingman, 1980; Wiseman, 2013; Wollman-Bonilla, 1998). Johnson (2004) noted the significant increase in the diversity, number, and specialization of these books for children over the last hundred years; however, the paucity of scholarly work examining *actual* classroom interactions around these books suggests continued cultural/social reluctance to bringing these texts into classrooms.

TACKLING HARD CONVERSATIONS

The literacy field has been active in theorizing and examining questions around the inclusion of "risky" (Lewison, Leland, & Harste, 2015), "traumatic" (Dutro, 2008), and "controversial" (Kimmel & Hartsfield, 2018) books and topics in the classroom. Critical literacy advocates have long advocated a sociopolitical focus within the literacy curriculum, illuminating "the *risky topics* that surround children's lives" (Lewison, Leland, & Harste, 2015, p. 170, emphasis added) and working to help children consider multiple perspectives. The "risky topics" are commonly connected to questions around race, gender, class, language, religion, politics, and power. Death and grief are rarely presented as possible topics, raising the question of whether some social issues are simply too risky for elementary classroom spaces.

Elizabeth Dutro (2008, 2009, 2017) has written extensively about the "perilous potential of trauma" (2017, p. 326) in literacy classrooms, leveraging ideas from trauma studies to better understand "how challenging life experiences . . . are carried into and lived within classrooms" (Dutro & Bien, 2014, p. 11). Though trauma has a range of causes—poverty, food insecurity, abuse, family separation, etc.—many of Dutro's examples of students sharing trauma in classrooms are connected to the death or illness of a loved one. She theorizes children's stories of trauma are a powerful, often overlooked, and discounted form of *response* to literature, whereby a child's "testimony" invites others to engage in "critical witnessing" (Dutro, 2008, 2009, 2017).

GRIEF, CONVERSELY, IS A SOCIAL PHENOMENON. PEOPLE LEARN HOW TO GRIEVE THROUGH THEIR PARTICIPATION IN/ACROSS MEANINGFUL SOCIAL COMMUNITIES.

Notably, the literature prompting a child's testimony does not fall into neatly defined labels/categories. One of Dutro's (2008) most searing stories involves two fourth-grade girls intimately discussing their respective parent's death during a small-group meeting about an American Girl book. Because teachers cannot always predict when a child might feel compelled to provide "testimony" in response to a shared book, Dutro focuses less on identifying specific texts and more on developing "pedagogies of reciprocal testimony and critical witness" (Dutro, 2013; Dutro & Bien, 2014). The aim is to create literacy instruction and classroom spaces where these stories/testimonies are welcomed in response to literature rather than dismissed or pathologized as something more appropriate for a private session with the school counselor. Rather than an either/or scenario, we advocate, through the use of read-alouds, that the classroom teacher can support a grieving student in tandem with the school counselor.

ACKNOWLEDGING RATHER THAN POLICING EMOTIONS

Certainly death- and grief-related literature is not the only way to invite children into sharing and collectively processing traumatic experiences in the classroom, but inclusion of these books sends a clear and explicit message to children that this is a classroom where these topics, experiences, and testimonies are welcome. The reality is often quite the opposite: providing "testimony" about a personal experience with death and expressing typical grief-related emotions (e.g., anger, guilt, despair, anxiety) are not welcome in many public settings, including classrooms. One of the reasons death doesn't usually come up in classroom literacy instruction is the implicit and explicit policing children, teachers, and families engage in: "society polices bereavement . . . control[ing] and instruct[ing] the bereaved [in] how to think, feel, and behave" (Neimeyer, Klass, & Dennis, 2014, p. 493). Teachers "self-censor" (Kimmel & Hartsfield, 2018) the books they choose to share with students, their own grief in the classroom (Rowling, 1995), and which parts of the grieving process children are invited to make public (Dutro, 2008; Boler & Zembylas, 2003). One of our teachers shared a powerful, yet familiar, example: while trying to help a young child struggling to process the recent death of his mother, the child reported, "I'm not supposed to talk about [my mother's death] here at school." As educators, we can be complicit in policing when we censor the personal stories we decide to share or not share, the texts we select or reject, and the ways we move toward or away from glimpses of grief in classroom spaces.

Boler and Zembylas (2003) recommend educators examine their "emotional habits" to interrogate the ways they—unconsciously and without malice—"enact and embody dominant values and assumptions in [their] daily habits and routines" (p. 111). By examining what is censored from classroom life, educators can identify "unconscious privileges as well as invisible ways in which one complies with dominant ideology" (p. 111). In some ways, resistance or reluctance to centering death and grief as topics/books for classroom discussion can be understood as part of an "inscribed habit of inattention" (Boler, 1999, p. 16), whereby teachers (like all humans) choose/learn/teach which emotions to notice and attend to. All of us are caught up in/by this emotional phenomena, but for educators the implications are significant: "[T]hese inscribed habits of inattention [become] embedded in discourses and in educational practices and philosophies" (Boler, 1999, p. 16) that influence how and what teachers choose to see, or conversely, not to see, all of which have long-lasting, life-altering impacts on children's health and well-being. We expand on this idea to explore how educators' inscribed inattention influences "how and what is chosen to be read, or conversely, not read" in school about death and grief, and what happens when inscribed inattention is disrupted through sharing and discussing a single picturebook.

Unexamined patterns of inscribed inattention can lead to avoidance of emotions associated with bereavement, creating potential for both students and teachers to experience disenfranchised grief, "grief that persons experience when they incur a loss that is not or cannot be openly acknowledged, publicly mourned, or socially supported" (Doka, 1989, p. 4). In classrooms, some emotions are seen/taught/encouraged as acceptable parts of the official literacy curriculum (empathy, enthusiasm, confidence), whereas other emotions are seen as deterrents to learning (anger, frustration, fear, despair, sadness) (Lewis & Tierney, 2013).

There are significant opportunities to consider how schools might become places where grieving and processing grief *with others* is not only allowed but expected and encouraged. When framed as a social issue, critically minded educators are challenged to invite riskier texts and discussions into their classrooms—texts that allow for sharing multiple perspectives, diverse narratives, and a range of experiences with death and grief that can be developed as part of an interpretive community.

Teachers Review Books and Share Stories

The impetus for this project emerged from a themed issue of the children's literature journal *First Opinions, Second Reactions*. Nicholas (first author) edited this volume centered around five children's literature titles grappling with issues of death and grief, with invited scholars providing a first opinion on the books and educators offering a second reaction on the books' use in classrooms. When inviting contributors, Nicholas sought a wide range of perspectives, recruiting Beth (second author), Christy (third author), and Sarah (fourth author) to contribute as first opinion writers and, drawing from his professional networks, recruiting novice and veteran educators ranging from early childhood teachers to districtwide administrators. Each contributor received a copy of a text chosen by Nicholas (see Table 1). As these books were considered by scholars and shared in classrooms, educators expressed feelings of tension and uncertainty beyond what was

TABLE 1

Selected books from text set exploring perspectives on death and grief

Book Title	Author / Illustrator	Synopsis	Read By
Duck, Death, and the Tulip	Wolf Erlbuch	When Death appears to Duck on a summer's day, she is surprised he has not come to fetch her. The two spend time together over the season, with Death bearing witness as Duck dies at the onset of autumn.	Meredith
The Heart and the Bottle	Oliver Jeffers	When she loses someone important to her, an unnamed little girl places her heart in a bottle so she may not be hurt again. It is not until she is older and meets a young girl not unlike her younger self that she works to free her heart from captivity.	Clara
The Scar	Charlotte Moundlic / Olivier Tallec	Awaking to find his mother has died, the unnamed boy in the story becomes sad, angry, and fearful. Afraid to forget her, he hypothesizes ways to keep her near him. His grandmother, visiting, provides another channel through which he can remember her.	John
Cry, Heart, but Never Break	Glenn Ringtved / Charlotte Pardi	With their grandmother ill upstairs, four siblings attempt to distract Death from claiming her. Death tells them a story, helping them say their final goodbyes.	Allyson

TABLE 2

Biographical sketches of each educator interviewed

Teacher	Biographical Information	Book Audience
Clara	In her 28th year of teaching, Clara currently teaches kindergarten in a southeast Michigan public school. She views her work as a challenging and joyful privilege with the core goal of teaching to ensure making the world a better, more equitable place for all.	Kindergarten Students
Meredith	Currently a kindergarten teacher in St. Louis, MO, Meredith also teaches literacy courses at the University of Missouri–St. Louis. Her work focuses on early childhood literacy and critical literacy, and much of her research is conducted in her own kindergarten classroom, where she enjoys learning from an amazing group of five- and six-year-olds.	Kindergarten Students
Allyson	An educator with the Farmington R-7 school district in southeast Missouri, Allyson is a former librarian and reading teacher. She currently serves as a curriculum and instructional practice coordinator, supporting students and teachers throughout the district.	K–8 Teachers
John	A graduate of the elementary education program at the University of Missouri-St. Louis, John engaged in this work during his second semester of student teaching in a St. Louis metropolitan area elementary school.	5th-Grade Students

communicated in their reviews. Wanting to understand the experience of sharing these books in classrooms, and buoyed by our own experiences with the books, we invited the educators to participate in a semi-structured interview (Kvale, 2007). Four educators, Clara, Allyson, Meredith, and John, agreed to be interviewed. A brief biographical sketch of each participating educator can be found in Table 2.

An interview protocol (Carspecken, 1996) initiated the conversation. Questions invited personal responses to their book and an opportunity to elaborate on challenges related to sharing the book

TABLE 3
Examples of interview prompts

Domain	Interview Prompts
Personal Response to the Book	Death and grief are particularly tricky concepts to address in the classroom, one of the reasons the issue of *First Opinions, Second Reactions* was brought together. We are interested in your personal take on the book. In other words, what are your thoughts on the book? What did you enjoy or not enjoy about the book and why?
Challenges to Sharing the Book	We are interested in the tensions you may have experienced while sharing this book with the children you teach and/or your colleagues. If you shared the book with an audience, tell me about that experience.

(see Table 3). All four interviews, ranging from 33 to 48 minutes, were transcribed as part of the analysis process. We reviewed transcripts independently to explore potential codes to explain the mechanisms undergirding the experiences of sharing these books with classrooms; then we collaboratively debriefed before confirming themes in several face-to-face analysis meetings. The conversation continually moved between and across interview transcripts and the books in our analytic process.

The four educators provided rich descriptions of the strategies they enacted to share these titles and reflected on how death and grief might be recognized at school in healthy and supportive ways for students. Interviews further illuminated the difficulty and grace in addressing heavy topics like these in schools, particularly when addressed outside of an immediate need, like the death of a student's loved one. As Meredith commented, "Death [doesn't] come up at center time."

Teachers' Key Insights

These educators' experiences do not weave together into a morality tale, where good and bad are clearly delineated. Rather, they form an imperative tale, urging all educators to take up this work and to move forward with best intentions, understanding it will rarely be wholly good or bad, but will impact students and teachers alike. In this section, we share insights from across the interview data in relation to three key questions, exploring the *why*, *when*, and *how* of bringing these books and conversations into classroom spaces.

WHY EDUCATORS SHARED BOOKS WITH THEMES OF DEATH AND GRIEF IN THE CLASSROOM

Addressing death and grief in the classroom is not simply a matter of having the courage to use a book about these topics with children, it is also a larger commitment to work with children in a classroom environment where they are made comfortable to speak to their experiences as human beings. For Clara, reading books that reflect this range of human experience, regardless of her own comfort, is an aspect of keeping a diverse classroom library and is, therefore, a social justice issue:

> I want my kids to see themselves in the books. I think there needs to be inclusion of experience as well. That's what I think some of these books will provide. This happens, and though not everyone's life is like this . . . at least you can learn some empathy for the people who have [experienced it]. And if this has happened to you, then you get to hear you're not alone.

Clara's insights reflect the National Institute of Health's (NIH, 2015) claim that "death is lonelier" than ever before. Whereas adults and children once "mourned together, and comforted each other" (NIH, 2015, p. 2), some children are now left to experience grief alone, following cultural norms about where, when, and how death can be processed and discussed. In light of these cultural and historical changes, access to the space and time to experience/examine/explore death and grief within a supportive interpretive community are not add-ons to an already packed curriculum, but an issue of social justice and equity related to the healthy development of all children.

Given the social nature of grief, teachers seeking to bring this topic into their classrooms may experience discomfort, a sensation each of the participating educators needed to work through. This discomfort manifested in different ways for each educator. To understand *why* educators might bring these books into their classroom conversations, attention also needs to be paid to why educators may not. Meredith, for example, felt uneasy after providing space in her kindergarten classroom for discussion in response to *Death, Duck, and the Tulip* (Erlbuch, 2011). She had concerns that the topic had been too risky, or, more specifically, the topic would be viewed as too risky by *other* adults, especially for the parent(s) of one of her kindergartners whose brother had died recently.

> I immediately talked to her mom: "I just want to let you know what happened today in kindergarten," and the mom said, "Oh, I'm so happy that happened. She's not been wanting to talk about it at home. . . . I'm glad she felt like she could tell her classmates."

Rather than policing expressions of grief, this caregiver was relieved at her child's ability to convey her loss, illuminating that potential caregivers may welcome, rather than reject, these opportunities.

Meredith's dilemma over *why* relates to the more global concern that young students aren't "ready" for the themes, images, and storylines in these kinds of books. Allyson experienced this pushback firsthand when she shared *Cry, Heart, but Never Break* (Ringtved, 2016) with fellow educators enrolled in a course on childhood trauma. As the course's assistant instructor, Allyson felt this group was the "perfect audience" for considering how this book might be used in a preK–12 classroom. Surprisingly, when she read the book to her class, "They just pretty much said, we hate this. . . . They didn't feel it was appropriate for children to have this book in their hands, parents would object. They thought we could let middle school and higher look at this." Their responses surprised Allyson because the course had spent weeks exploring support for children experiencing trauma, and she felt the educators shared her concern for students' need for safe school spaces to process grief.

SHE HAD CONCERNS THAT THE TOPIC HAD BEEN TOO RISKY, OR, MORE SPECIFICALLY, THE TOPIC WOULD BE VIEWED AS TOO RISKY BY *OTHER* ADULTS.

This section began with an explicit claim about *why* these books should be brought into classroom conversations; when translating this belief into action, the educators interviewed found themselves confronted with the various reasons why death- and grief-related books should be excluded, resulting in reluctance and resistance. In examining their own initial reluctance/resistance to reading these books aloud, these educators acknowledge how grief, both in students and within ourselves as educators, works against several characteristics of the identity kit that comprises teaching. Put another way, teachers often view themselves as needing to "be 'all knowing,' that is, having all the answers; and of being 'in control' of their reactions and the situation" (Rowling, 1995, p. 323).

Death and grief can neither be known nor controlled, creating a nearly impossible situation for any teacher who feels they must be "all-knowing." The claim children are not ready may have as much or more to do with teachers'/adults' own patterns of inscribed inattention (Boler 1999), leading to feelings of being unready, underprepared, and/or ill-equipped to engage with these issues themselves.

HOW EDUCATORS DECIDED *WHEN* TO SHARE THESE BOOKS IN THE CLASSROOM

For all four educators, finding the "right" time to share the books was less pressing than finding and making time to read the book at all. Prior to reading these titles to their classes, all teachers experienced varying degrees of trepidation. Clara wrote:

> I wanted to, I really did. I wanted to read this book, *The Heart and the Bottle* by Oliver Jeffers, multiple times to my twenty-three kindergarten students and share it with my empathetic, intelligent, caring colleagues. But I didn't. Instead, I carried it in my bag to and from school for weeks. I read it to myself. I promised myself, "I'll start tomorrow." Why the hemming and hawing, the reluctance? (Thiry, 2018, p.27).

Meredith hesitated similarly, recalling, "Actually, I waited until the last minute to read it to the class. . . . I just kept the book on my desk and I just really didn't want to read it." Despite this hesitation, both Meredith and Clara moved forward in reading the books with their kindergarten students.

While "the inhibitions and the protective tendencies of adults that reinforce the misconception that it is unhealthy for a child to be openly curious and fearful about death" (Reisler, 1977, p. 332), teachers worked against these inhibitions and protective tendencies to ensure students developed the ability to work through and manage their grief. Clara drew upon her own grief to connect with children's grief:

> In my life there's a fair amount of grief, mostly loss, mostly recently . . . . I think I grieved pretty well, and I feel like I can be present to it, but I can also keep moving. It allows me to feel empathetic. I don't know what it's like to be a young child and lose somebody super significant.

Leveraging her own experiences grieving and recognizing the way she carried her own invisible weight of loss day-to-day, Clara reflected on and initiated a conversation with a grieving student in her class:

> I said, "I miss people at Christmas, do you miss anybody?" "Yeah, I miss my Mom." I said, "The nice thing is you love your brother and sisters, and your dad and your grandma. You have all these people coming over and that's like me, too. I miss my mom but I'm also super happy so there's a mix of feelings." I said, "I just want you to know that I remember. I remember that you miss your mom."

Clara recognized—and became a witness to (Dutro, 2008)—her student's grief, as well as her own, as a precursor to creating opportunities for her class to engage with *The Heart and the Bottle* (Jeffers, 2010). Rather than wait for the student to approach her about his grief, she initiated discussion, grounding it in her own mixed emotions of the holiday season. Perhaps most important is Clara's assertion she wanted her student to know she knew he missed his mom, an availability to repeatedly bear witness to grief as a member of a community *across time*. The conversation doesn't end with the first read-aloud. Clara sees a read-aloud like this as an opportunity to begin relevant, supportive, ongoing discussions with children: "We don't have to get mired, to let it drag us down. We acknowledge it and . . . I can follow up one-on-one with them."

Clara's tactic—following up one-on-one with a child experiencing particularly relevant struggles after the read-aloud—is a proactive way to show grieving children that an adult cares and their feelings matter. Creating supportive conversations, and reciprocally supportive relationships, is the real impetus to opening up conversations on death and grief in elementary classrooms. To "witness" (Dutro, 2008) grief in the classroom requires teachers to subvert portions of their identity, to acknowledge their own vulnerability, and to make that known to their students, while also resisting cultural policing of grief by defining which life spaces and times are suitable for grieving.

HOW EDUCATORS READ AND DISCUSSED THESE BOOKS IN THE CLASSROOM

While intentional decisions and some degree of thoughtful preparation for reading books on death and engaging in discussions about grief may help, uncertainty about how to do so lingered for these educators. Allyson, who received pushback during her read-aloud, sees it as important to read books on death, regardless of how prepared one feels. (See Table 4 for additional books about grief suitable for the elementary classroom.) She advises:

> If I were to share with another book, I would have more than one book, so I could back up what I wanted to convey. This is one of several things you should consider having access to, not *if*, but *when*, you will need this.

Reflecting on her colleagues' resistance, Allyson decided an important additional step would be frontloading:

> I didn't do enough activating of prior knowledge. It would have been good for me to mention, upfront, the church shooting in Texas, . . . the little girl who died of cancer in our school district, and different things where they would be set to make mental connections before they were exposed to the book.

Allyson felt sharing risky books with colleagues might be made easier by connecting to current traumatic events at school and frontloading the importance of a book to address such events.

Remembering one's own personal experiences with grief, or imagining how children might experience grief, was also a helpful preparation exercise.

TABLE 4

Additional titles of picturebooks dealing with grief

Alvarez, A. (2016). *Where do they go?* (S. Field, Illus.) New York, NY: Triangle Square.

Cobb, R. (2013). *Missing mommy: A book of bereavement.* New York, NY: Henry Holt and Company.

Golstyn, J. (2017). *Bertolt.* Brooklyn, NY: Enchanted Lion.

James, M. (2018). *The funeral.* Toronto, ON: Groundwood.

Lies, B. (2018). *The rough patch.* New York, NY: Greenwillow.

Parr, T. (2015). *The goodbye book.* New York, NY: Little, Brown & Company.

Seeger, L. V. (2018). *Blue.* New York, NY: Roaring Brook Press.

Clara has experienced the death of significant people in her life, creating an ability to resonate with bereaved students and providing her insight into helpful empathetic responses to the child in her class who surely missed mom at Christmastime. Humanizing grief became important for John, a preservice teacher, as he prepared to engage his fifth graders with *The Scar* (Moundlic, 2011). While John hadn't experienced death as an adult, reading the book several times allowed him to empathize with what that experience might be like:

> The boy talked about like really small details about his mom his dad would never be able to recreate, . . . the squiggle on the toast or maybe it was jelly but it was small things like that the other parent might not even know about. . . . I just thought those were important details in the book . . . it just brought up some emotions for me about their [his parents] potential loss and, well, eventual loss.

For John, preparing himself for sharing the book with his students required him to project himself into a future without his parents; the book's portrayal of a young boy mourning the small, quotidian things his mother did that his father can never replicate made him uncomfortable. John willingly entertained discomfort, considering his own future bereavement, which provided potential insight into grief his students may be presently experiencing.

Typically, preparation for reading any read-aloud entails paging through the book noting talk-about spots, ideas children might connect with, themes to expand, and potentially tricky concepts to clarify. Due to the uncharted territory of teaching about death, Meredith explains how in retrospect her preparation varied and how, subsequently, the reading felt rushed and uncomfortable:

> I kind of regretted the first time I read it through. I literally just read it. . . . I wanted to be done with it and the kids didn't push it then, but they clearly weren't done with it and brought it up later. I wish I had chosen some places to really pause or to just say, "What do you think is happening?" Or just maybe some key questions . . . I don't know what questions. I wish I had been a little bit more thoughtful, but I think I didn't really know how to teach the book. . . .

TEACHING TIPS

Death and grief are natural parts of the human life cycle. Yet, according to the authors, many teachers struggle with talking about death with students. Create a professional learning community with teachers (and administrators) and discuss the four educators' experiences in* Death Didn't Come Up at Center Time. *Which educator resonates most with you? How so? Choose a picturebook about grief. Discuss the book with your colleagues. How might you implement a lesson/unit that includes a trauma-informed and healing-centered conversation about death in literature? Describe what micro- and macro-level supports you may need to implement a lesson/unit with students.

If supplying key questions for children to think through proves difficult, preparing and asking authentic questions you wonder about as a reader is a starting point for discussion. John did just that. He diligently approached preparation for using this text in reading groups with 5th graders as he would with other texts, noting points in the story he wondered about himself:

> Well, I read it a bunch of times. I tried to put myself in the place of the reader and think about when I would need to stop, what questions I would ask as we read, and where we would stop. I anticipated a lot of questions about why [death] happened, and there's not a good answer for kids. Death just happens, and sometimes there's not necessarily a reason. I anticipated having a lot of questions about why the kid was acting the way he was because, as someone who has not experienced that, it seems like his behavior didn't make sense, like him lashing out at his father and his grandmother at times when they were trying to help. . . . We had a lot of discussion about that, and the more we discussed it, the more it made sense to the readers about how he was acting.

John also considered how to integrate the book into existing literacy routines and student groupings, deciding this text would work best in small reading groups, not a whole-class read-aloud with his 5th-grade students:

> I chose to read it in small groups so we could have a closer discussion around the book. . . . Kids might feel more open about discussing it in a small group instead of in front of the whole class. Because I was with fifth graders, they do a little more emotional guarding than other grades would. . . . I don't think anyone wanted to comment first, but the more we read it, the more the students knew the plot already, so they were looking for details to discuss.

John, Meredith, Allyson, and Clara all indicated that however uncertain the first reading felt, increased exposure and invitations to talk more would be key for their students to dig deeper into the ideas in these books on death and subsequent experiences of grieving.

All four educators recommend facilitating meaningful conversations through repeated readings, encouraging readers' authentic connections, preparing texts to pair with the book, and inviting questions of all sorts. A common characteristic of these picturebooks is their sophistication. As Meredith reflected on *Duck, Death, and the Tulip* (Erlbuch, 2011): "It's a great book for critical thinking. It's not one of those books where you read it and you're like, *I really understood that*. I'm actually going to admit for myself that I read the book and I don't think I understand it." In Allyson's words, these books take "more than one read to begin to develop a really strong appreciation for what was happening." These books require readers to return to them repeatedly; for some teachers, like John, this was surprising. He shared:

> Students were pretty uncomfortable with it at first; they were being quiet, and yet toward the end of the time reading, after multiple times reading it, students were more open to discussing it. We talked a lot about behavior and how that made sense to the main character.

For John, grounding this initial reading in the book's basic plot and character development flattens the text's emotional impact, creating a mirage of it being "safe" for discussion. Through repeated readings, John gives the book dimension; through repeated readings, students are able to unpack emotional aspects of the book.

John's specifically designed repeated readings came over the course of a week. Meredith, however, was cautious about rereading; even so, the book worked its way into the intellectual fabric of her classroom:

> We eventually came back to the book as we, weeks later, read another book. I thought I'd never read books about death, but I've become more attuned. . . .we were reading *Tough Boris* (Fox, 1998) about a pirate whose parrot dies and he's crying. The book is about how it's okay for even tough pirates to cry if they're sad. . . .the kids were immediately like "oh yeah, and that's like *Death, Duck, and the Tulip*" (Erlbuch, 2011), and I'm like "where did that come from? We read that book like over a month ago!" The book stayed with them; they were still pondering it.

Clara also read the book to her kindergarteners once. Throughout the reading, Clara paused to have students turn-and-talk to a friend about a connection they made. She didn't hear all conversations around the room, but noted, "A lot of them did talk about a pet that died, maybe a fish, and so if your goldfish died, you loved that goldfish." Other children had more significant experiences of loved ones dying. Clara shared:

> I had one little boy who was like "my great grandfather died" and his eyes got all teary. I said, "Tell me about that." "Well, I miss him." Part of me was like, well, that's okay. You know, if [my student] had cried, would that have been the worst thing? I don't think so.

Conclusion: Be Vulnerable, Be Brave, and Witness

"Because literacies and life experiences are not separable things," Dutro (2017) reminds us, "we have to be concerned with what counts as trauma, for whom, and what it does in classrooms" (p. 335). We have sought to explore, alongside four educators, what conversations about death and acknowledgment of grief do in classrooms, using children's literature as a starting point. These conversations are never easy, as demonstrated by these educators as they sought to make sense of their own and their students' responses to the experience. Despite our own discomfort with the subject matter, as

WE NEED TO BE VULNERABLE, WILLING TO MUCK AROUND IN OUR OWN FEELINGS OF GRIEF. . . . WE MUST MODEL FOR OUR STUDENTS HOW GRIEF IS NEGOTIATED AND MANAGED.

educators, we need to be vulnerable, willing to muck around in our own feelings of grief, accepting that we do not need to be "all knowing." We must model for our students how grief is negotiated and managed, and to respond to students' needs. Through their active engagement in addressing death and grief in their educational spaces, these educators ensured trauma in classrooms was not forced underground, but rather was out in the open, where it could be addressed through everyday classroom activity.

AUTHORS' NOTE

The writing team would like to thank Allyson Henseley, Meredith Labadie, John McDermott, and Clara Thiry for their participation in this project, which required complex, responsive, and considerably brave teaching.

REFERENCES

American Federation of Teachers and New York Life Foundation. (2012, Dec 10). Grief in the classroom: Groundbreaking survey of educators shows overwhelming interest in helping grieving students—and strong demand for training, more support. Retrieved from http://www.aft.org/sites/default/files/release_bereavement121012.pdf

Bargiel, S., Beck, C., Koblitz, D., O'Connor, A., Pierce, K. M., & Wolf, S. (1997). Talking about books: Bringing life's issues into classrooms. *Language Arts*, 74, 482–490.

Boler, M. (1999). *Feeling power: Emotions and education*. New York, NY: Routledge.

Boler, M., & Zembylas, M. (2003). Discomforting truths: The emotional terrain of understanding difference. In P. P. Trifonas (Ed.), *Pedagogies of difference: Rethinking education for social change* (pp. 110–136). New York, NY: Routledge.

Carspecken, P. F. (1996). *Critical ethnography in educational research: A theoretical and practical guide*. New York, NY: Routledge.

Child and Adolescent Health Measurement Initiative. (2013, May 10). Overview of adverse child and family experiences among US children. Retrieved from http://www.childhealthdata.org/docs/drc/aces-data-brief_version-1-0.pdf?sfvrsn=2

Corr, C. A. (2004). Bereavement, grief, and mourning in death-related literature for children. *OMEGA—Journal of Death and Dying*, 48, 337–363.

Doka, K. J. (1989). *Disenfranchised grief: Recognizing hidden sorrow*. Lexington, MA: Lexington Press.

Dutro, E. (2008). "That's why I was crying on that book": Trauma as testimony in responses to literature. *Changing English: Studies in Culture and Education*, 15, 423–434.

Dutro, E. (2009). Children's testimony and the necessity of critical witness in urban classrooms. *Theory Into Practice*, 48, 231–238.

Dutro, E. (2013). Towards a pedagogy of the incomprehensible: Trauma and the imperative of critical witness in literacy classrooms. *Pedagogies: An International Journal*, 8, 301–315.

Dutro, E. (2017). Let's start with heartbreak: The perilous potential of trauma in literacy. *Language Arts*, 94, 326–337.

Dutro, E., & Bien, A. C. (2014). Listening to the speaking wound: A trauma studies perspective on student positioning in schools. *American Educational Research Journal*, 51, 7–35.

Johnson, J. (2004). Historical perspectives and comments on the current status of death-related literature for children. *OMEGA—Journal of Death and Dying*, 48, 293–305.

Kimmel, S. C., & Hartsfield, D. E. (2018). "It was . . . the word 'scrotum' on the first page": Educators' perspectives of controversial literature. *Journal of Teacher Education*. Advance online publication. doi: 10.1177/0022487117751126

Klingman, A. (1980). Death education through literature: A preventive approach. *Death Studies*, 4, 271–279.

Kvale, S. (2007). *Doing interviews*. Thousand Oaks, CA: SAGE.

Lewis, C., & Tierney, J. D. (2013). Mobilizing emotion in an urban classroom: Producing identities and transforming signs in a race-related discussion. *Linguistics and Education*, 24, 289–304.

Lewison, M., Leland, C. H., & Harste, J. C. (2015). *Creating critical classrooms: Reading and writing with an edge*. New York, NY: Routledge.

Mahon, M. M., Goldberg, R. L., & Washington, S. K. (1999). Discussing death in the classroom: Beliefs and experiences of educators and education students. *OMEGA—Journal of Death and Dying*, 39, 99–121.

National Institute of Health. (2015, April). Talking to children about death. Retrieved from https://clinicalcenter.nih.gov/ccc/patient_education/pepubs/childdeath.pdf

Neimeyer, R. A., Klass, D., & Dennis, M. R. (2014). A social constructionist account of grief: Loss and the narration of meaning. *Death Studies*, 38, 485–498.

Poling, D. A., & Evans, E. M. (2004). Are dinosaurs the rule or the exception? *Cognitive Development*, 19, 363–383.

Poling, D. A., & Hupp, J. M. (2008). Death sentences: A content analysis of children's death literature. *The Journal of Genetic Psychology*, 169, 165–176.

Reisler, R. (1977). The issue of death education. *The School Counselor*, 24, 331–337.

Rowling, L. (1995). The disenfranchised grief of teachers. *OMEGA—Journal of Death and Dying*, 31, 317–329.

Thiry, C. (2018). Second reaction: Wrestling with *The heart and the bottle*. *First Opinions, Second Reactions*, 11(1), 27–29.

Wiseman, A. M. (2013). Summer's end and sad goodbyes: Children's picturebooks about death and dying. *Children's Literature in Education*, 44, 1–14.

Wollman-Bonilla, J. E. (1998). Outrageous viewpoints: Teachers' criteria for rejecting works of children's literature. *Language Arts*, 75, 287–295.

CHILDREN'S LITERATURE CITED

Erlbuch, W. (2011). *Duck, death, and the tulip*. Wellington, New Zealand: Gecko Press.

Fox, M. (1998). *Tough Boris* (K. Brown, Illus.). New York, NY: Houghton Mifflin Harcourt.

Jeffers, O. (2010). *The heart and the bottle*. New York, NY: Philomel.

Moundlic, C. (2011). *The scar* (O. Tallec, Illus.). Somerville, MA: Candlewick Press.

Ringtved, G. (2016). *Cry, heart, but never break* (C. Pardi, Illus.). New York, NY: Enchanted Lion.

NICHOLAS E. HUSBYE is an associate professor of elementary literacy education (K-6) at the University of Nebraska–Lincoln. He can be reached at nhusbye2@unl.edu.

BETH A. BUCHHOLZ is an assistant professor of reading education in the Reich College of Education at Appalachian State University. She can be contacted at buchholzba@appstate.edu.

CHRISTY WESSEL POWELL is an assistant professor of literacy and language education in the College of Education at Purdue University. She can be contacted at cwesselp@purdue.edu.

SARAH VANDER ZANDEN is an associate professor of literacy education in the College of Education at the University of Northern Iowa. She can be contacted at sarah.vanderz@uni.edu.

This article originally appeared
in *English Education* 53.2

WHEN TEACHERS HURT: Supporting Preservice Teacher Well-Being

In this essay, the author reflects on the importance of accepting and expressing emotion in teachers' lived experiences. By centering emotion work in preservice teacher praxis, teacher educators can make emotion work visible and assign value to it.

MANDIE B. DUNN

I REMEMBER A MOMENT when I felt something break open in a class I was teaching with preservice English language arts (ELA) teachers. My students had been working in pairs to write and perform short skits addressing an issue of practice that had more than one appropriate teacher response. The last pair to perform had framed their skit with a question: What is the line between the personal and the professional? In their imagined scenario, a student joined a teacher on a bench outside school and shared that she was pregnant and did not know what to do.

I do not remember how the skit resolved. What I remember is that, while the class sat in a circle around the performers, one student announced in dismay that she was overwhelmed by "just how much" responsibility there was in teaching. Another student worried about the legal implications of advising a pregnant student; still another expressed concern about not attending fully to the student's vulnerability in that moment. Preservice teachers began talking with one another and over each other, and my first thought was that I should have let them have this space sooner.

As the preservice teachers talked, my thoughts drifted to my own early years teaching high school ELA, when I often struggled with how distinct the roles of *human* and *professional* seemed to be for me as a teacher. I sometimes hid my thoughts about school policies or events to protect administration or other teachers' reputations. The one time students made me cry, I left the room because I thought I should not cry at work. While my preservice teachers debated the role of a teacher in a student's personal life, I wondered about the role of a teacher's personal life in the lives of students. I shared these thoughts with the class when I eventually joined them in discussion.

I also told them about Ann, a sixth-grade ELA teacher who once shared a story with me about telling her students she was pregnant, only to then tell them that she had lost the baby. Ann said the most difficult moment teaching that year was the week after she miscarried. Two students arrived in class and one asked why there were flowers on their teacher's desk. The other student responded loudly, without thinking, "Duh, because her baby died." Ann expressed sincere guilt over her inability to make that moment "teachable." She said she wished she could have asked: *How might these words affect someone? Who might help this student rephrase their comment?* Instead, she didn't say or do anything. She started class.

I told my preservice teachers that, when I think about this story, my stomach screams. I want to say to Ann: No, *you don't have to make that moment teachable. You don't have to move on.* Why do teachers have to push down what they feel? Why can't we say, *you hurt me*? What is the line between the personal and the professional?

My teaching experiences and my work with grieving ELA teachers, Ann included (Dunn, 2019), inform my interest in teachers' experiences of feeling pulled between what they think their job requires and what they want to do or feel, a dissonance that can be heightened during a period of bereavement. As I write these words, a global pandemic means that loss is everywhere and more teachers are hurting, yet politicians and administrators seemingly remain focused on the logistics of making school happen. I don't see much focus on the grief teachers and students may be carrying. Systemic racism means that this current pandemic exponentially harms Black people, indigenous people, and people of color (BIPOC) in every way: our health care systems, schools, and economic structures are built on stealing health, knowledge, and wealth from BIPOC so that white people benefit. This violence makes loss more painful.

I BELIEVE THAT THE STORIES OF TEACHERS I HAVE WORKED WITH HAVE WORTH. THEY HIGHLIGHT THE REALITY THAT TEACHERS FACE, ESPECIALLY NOW: THEY ARE PEOPLE EXPERIENCING LOSS WHILE THEY CARE FOR THEIR STUDENTS—AND I AM CONCERNED FOR THE WELL-BEING OF OUR TEACHERS.

Because of this context, I am conflicted about whether or not I, as a white woman, should be writing about grief and loss in this moment. As a white researcher, I do not want to extract the grief of Black teachers for career gain: theirs is not my story to tell. I know that the stories of white teachers' grief cannot attend to BIPOC's experiences in ways that account for racial trauma. Still, I believe that the stories of teachers I have worked with have worth. They highlight the reality that teachers face, especially now: They are people experiencing loss while they care for their students—and I am concerned for the well-being of our teachers.

Drawing on what I've learned in my research with grieving teachers, as a pre-service teacher educator I've worked to more directly address teacher well-being in my classroom by making the *emotion work* of teaching both visible and valued. My hope is that by recognizing the expertise required for teachers to manage emotions in the context of their work, I can also validate teachers' emotions as influential experiences they draw on when they teach.

Emotion Work

Emotion work is the work teachers do to suppress or change their emotions in service of preserving pleasant emotions for clients (Hochschild, 1979). English language arts pedagogical traditions do not typically foreground teachers' emotion work, done in the service of students' needs, as part of the teaching of ELA. Most purposes for teaching ELA center students' gains and how to make them happen: students should gain knowledge, skills, or the benefits of personal growth (Bickmore et al., 2005). With these purposes in mind, teachers may perceive their emotions as obstacles in the work they need to do to help students learn. This perception can leave teachers feeling guilty for exhibiting emotions or believing that certain parts of their humanity do not matter (Dunn, 2019).

Emotion work is connected to what Noddings (2005) called the ethics of care in teaching. Caring about students by responding to their needs forms the foundation of the learning relationship. However, teachers often assume that caring is a natural part of the job, and they may not recognize that caring can indeed be work. In particular, when a teacher is hurting, they may perceive their emotions as negatively influencing students and work harder to suppress them. Too much emotion suppression, however, can be harmful for teachers, who may become "estranged or alienated from an aspect of self" (Hochschild, 1983, p. 7). Too much suppression of emotion, then, might contribute to a teacher not feeling well.

For example, Rachel, an eighth-grade ELA teacher, told me about pushing through a thematic analysis of *The Giver* (Lowry, 2002), even though topics such as end-of-life care and euthanasia were upsetting to her because her mother had recently died in hospice. Rachel spoke at length about being worried that sharing her sadness would make students uncomfortable or would make the reading experience about *her* when it should be about her students. Rachel's effort to hide her emotional response was an effort in preserving a particular experience for students, as was addressing the subsequent guilt she also managed. Still, Rachel did not necessarily recognize the effort she was making to suppress her emotions as work; she saw work as her efforts to help students comprehend texts or identify themes. Rachel described this year of teaching during her mother's decline and death as painful, upsetting, and exhausting, but she also blamed herself for not being a better teacher.

Emotion Work in Praxis

I want to make the emotion work that Ann, Rachel, and other teachers do visible and valued in my PST classroom. I tell my students about emotion work and encourage them to include emotions that they might be trying to change or suppress in the course of their teaching in their discussions and writings. I also make conversations about emotions in teaching routine in my classroom.

For example, I have taken the traditional field placement journal and invited preservice teachers to "remix" reflections from these journals as a way of processing emotions over time and considering how emotions affect the relationships they are building with students (Sulzer & Dunn, 2019). When discussing literature instruction with students, I talk with preservice teachers about deciding when to share personal loss as part of engagement with literature, a move that first requires addressing that teachers are people who have experienced losses (Dunn & Garcia, 2020). I also share times when I engaged in emotion work, such as when I recently admitted to preservice teachers my efforts to hide the irritation I felt while fulfilling mandates for "seamless" instruction during the global pandemic.

I TELL MY STUDENTS ABOUT EMOTION WORK AND ENCOURAGE THEM TO INCLUDE EMOTIONS THAT THEY MIGHT BE TRYING TO CHANGE OR SUPPRESS IN THE COURSE OF THEIR TEACHING IN THEIR DISCUSSIONS AND WRITINGS. I ALSO MAKE CONVERSATIONS ABOUT EMOTIONS IN TEACHING ROUTINE IN MY CLASSROOM.

One question that arises when considering emotions in teaching is whether or not I would suggest mitigating the burden of emotion work by encouraging teachers to share their emotions more openly in classrooms. While I do think reciprocal sharing (Dutro, 2019) between students and teachers can be powerful, it is critical to consider that sharing involves different stakes for different people. White teachers do not have to think about if, how, or when to include emotions related to racial trauma when they discuss loss experiences or manage emotions in the context of teaching. The risk and stakes for sharing hurt are not equal, and sometimes doing emotion work can be a protective act.

For example, sharing about a miscarriage may carry additional risk because it is a relatively hidden painful experience, as well as an experience associated with women. Hochschild (1983) argued that women are expected to do a higher amount of emotion work and are already considered more emotional than men. BIPOC also do significantly more emotion work than white people (Evans & Moore, 2015). White norms for professionalism position Black women teachers, in particular, as emotional (Dixson & Dingus, 2008). When BIPOC resist the white ideological norms that permeate our workspaces by sharing their experiences, they risk being positioned as "overly emotional or problematic" (Evans & Moore, 2015, p. 441).

I explain to preservice teachers that, even in times when I have done significant emotion work as a teacher, I benefited from whiteness. I have often shared, for example, that following a terrible car accident that left my spouse in trauma care, my colleagues seemed to expect me to be positive about the situation because my spouse did not die. I *was* grateful that my spouse was alive, but I was also still managing intense worry and stress during his recovery that I felt compelled to hide. Teaching during this time was exhausting as I tried to maintain the quality of my instruction on top of navigating caretaking responsibilities and managing my emotions of helplessness and anger. Still, the risk of showing what might be perceived as negative emotions or even weakness was low because negatively perceived emotions are more heavily regulated for BIPOC as part of maintaining oppressive social hierarchies (Ahmed, 2004).

TEACHING TIPS

Educators experience all human emotions. Dunn describes different types of "emotion work" that educators might experience in different stages of their teaching careers: pre-service, in-service, and as a teacher educator. By doing this, Dunn makes emotion work visible and assigns value to it. Consider the scenarios that Dunn describes: do any of them resonate with you? If so, which ones? How have you navigated the emotion work involved in teaching? In your professional learning community, discuss what micro- and macro-level supports you may need to safely and productively engage in emotion work. This work is especially important now, as stress, grief, depression, and anxiety are elevated during the pandemic.

Furthermore, I benefited from whiteness even during the traumatic experience itself. Right after my spouse's accident, a social worker from the trauma ward sent a police officer to my door as part of a protocol for notifying family. I was asked a series of questions, such as whether or not my spouse had children, without being given any information about my loved one's condition; I only had news that there had been an accident. This experience was upsetting enough without someone asking these questions. Still, I never once thought that the police officer would harm me. When I was having one of the worst moments of my life to date, my whiteness meant that I didn't also have to live through fear and helplessness with the added fear that I would be hurt or killed.

MY GOAL IN CENTERING EMOTION WORK IN MY PRESERVICE TEACHER PRAXIS IS TO MAKE EMOTION WORK VISIBLE AND ASSIGN VALUE TO IT. DOING SO ATTENDS TO TEACHER WELL-BEING BY RECOGNIZING THAT TEACHERS ARE PEOPLE WHO CARE FOR OTHER PEOPLE WHILE ALSO TRYING TO CARE FOR THEMSELVES.

Closing Thoughts

My goal in centering emotion work in my preservice teacher praxis is to make emotion work visible and assign value to it. Doing so attends to teacher well-being by recognizing that teachers are people who care for other people while also trying to care for themselves. When teacher educators acknowledge teachers as human beings who do emotion work, we name the experience, make space for it, and possibly reduce the isolation teachers may feel when they find themselves teaching in the midst of difficult experiences. My hope remains that this perspective also attends to and validates human experience and its accompanying grief, sadness, anger, love, hope, and joy.

REFERENCES

Ahmed, S. (2004). *The cultural politics of emotion*. Routledge.

Bickmore, S., Smagorinsky, P., & O'Donnell-Allen, C. (2005). Tensions between traditions: The role of contexts in learning to teach. *English Education*, 38(1), 23–52.

Dixson, A., & Dingus, J. E. (2008). In search of our mother's gardens: Black women teachers and professional socialization. *Teachers College Record*, 110(4), 805–837.

Dunn, M. B. (2019). *English language arts teachers' experiences teaching while grieving a death* (Publication No. 13896038) [Doctoral Dissertation, Michigan State University]. Proquest Dissertations Publishing.

Dunn, M. B., & Garcia, A. (2020). Grief, loss, and literature: Reading texts as social artifacts. *English Journal*, 109(6), 52–58.

Dutro, E. (2019). *The vulnerable heart of literacy: Centering trauma as powerful pedagogy*. Teachers College Press.

Evans, L., & Moore, W. (2015). Impossible burdens: White institutions, emotional labor, and micro-resistance. *Social Problems*, 62(3), 439–454.

Hochschild, A. R. (1979). Emotion work, feeling rules, and social structure. *American Journal of Sociology*, 85, 555–575.

Hochschild, A. R. (1983). *The managed heart: Commercialization of human feeling*. University of California Press.

Lowry, Lois. (2002). *The Giver*. Laurel Leaf Books.

Noddings, N. (2005). Caring in education. *The Encyclopedia of Pedagogy and Informal Education*. Retrieved from https://infed.org/mobi/caring-in-education/

Sulzer, M., & Dunn, M. B. (2019). Disrupting the neoliberal discourse of teacher reflection through dialogical-phenomenological texts. *Reflective Practice*, 20(5), 604–618.

MANDIE B. DUNN is an assistant professor of English education at the University of South Florida. Her research and teaching focus on the lived experiences of English teachers as professionals who respond to multiple competing stakeholders. She has been a member of NCTE since 2013.

This article originally appeared
in *English Leadership Quarterly* 43.4

CREATING SPACE FOR GRIEF: Cultivating an Intersectional Grief-Informed Systemic Pathway for Teacher Leaders

Teacher leadership that supports the needs of classroom educators who are experiencing and reacting to loss is an area of growing need. What systems and practices might promote wellness?

SAKEENA EVERETT &
MANDIE BEVELS DUNN

Introduction

As teachers and teacher educators, we are intimately aware of the required and expected work of teachers and teacher leaders during a typical public school day. Space for grieving is rarely, if ever, created in the average teacher's day. Yet, grief is a natural and necessary part of the human experience. We are learning from our personal experiences of living with grief and our research about grief—grief can be devastating for any human, but it has a unique impact on teachers who are grieving (Dunn, 2019, 2021; Dunn & Everett, 2020).

More specifically, teacher leaders are expected to be available and present for others, listen with a desire to understand, and build a sense of community within and beyond schools; they focus on people (and relationships) as the core purpose for any innovation among adults and students alike (Killion et al., 2016). In other words, being a teacher leader requires strong interpersonal skills and a deep commitment for leadership. However, when grieving, even the most skilled and committed teachers can lack the capacity to carry out teacher leadership work.

Connecting Intersectionality and Grief in Teacher Leadership

We have been engaging in research about grief among teachers *before* the onset of the COVID-19 global pandemic, as we explain in more detail in our "positionality" below. According to the US National Center for Education Statistics (2020), approximately 84 percent of teachers are white and 76 percent are women. Living through a pandemic as women educators who study grief has elevated our urgency for cultivating an intersectional grief-informed systemic approach to teacher leadership. Our grief-informed stance is foregrounded by "intersectionality," or what Black feminist legal studies scholar, Crenshaw (2016) articulates as the "intersectional impact of racism, sexism, and classism" because it is impossible to ignore that Black people in the US are dying at disproportionately higher rates from COVID-19.

WHEN GRIEVING, EVEN THE MOST SKILLED AND COMMITTED TEACHERS CAN LACK THE CAPACITY TO CARRY OUT TEACHER LEADERSHIP WORK.

In the past decade, there has been a growing body of literature on teacher leadership. This scholarship brings much-needed attention to the role of teacher leaders within schools and districts, especially with regard to licensure requirements, career advancement opportunities, professional learning communities, school improvement plans, student success, and culturally responsive school leadership (Khalifa et al., 2016; Killion et al., 2016; York-Barr & Duke, 2004). We wholeheartedly agree that teachers are well positioned and are also severely underutilized in making some of the most critical decisions concerning school and districts. At the same time, we are deeply concerned with the lack of systemic attention for meeting the grief needs of teachers, especially amid a grief-stricken climate. Furthermore, even among teachers who are grieving, the burden of grief is inequitably distributed. Specifically, *intersectionality* issues amplify grief among Black women teachers.

According to Killion et al. (2016), "a systemic approach to teacher leadership elevates the significance, visibility, and viability of teacher leadership as a means of improving teaching and learning" (p. 20). Furthermore, they argue, there are four main components that make up a system of teacher leadership: (1) a clear definition, (2) conducive conditions, (3) dispositions, and (4) assessment of the impact of teacher leadership. Further, they argue it's necessary to name these four components because "there remains insufficient practical guidance for developing systemic approaches that advance and sustain viable teacher leadership" (p. 4). We agree. In *The Urgency of Intersectionality*, Crenshaw (2016) asserts that "if we can't see the problem, we can't fix the problem." Crenshaw further explains: It is difficult to address an issue we cannot see or name "because there are no frames for us to see [Black women]. No frames for us to remember them. No frame for us to hold [space for] them." With these underpinnings in mind, we build upon the four components of systemic teacher leadership offered by Killion et al. (2016) to frame our vision of *intersectional grief* as a pathway toward a more robust systemic approach to teacher leadership. Our approach makes intersectional grief visible, offers conducive conditions and dispositions, and assesses impact among teacher leaders. As schools and districts are forced to regroup and reallocate resources amid the COVID-19 pandemic, we urge them to create a systemic space for grief.

AS SCHOOLS AND DISTRICTS ARE FORCED TO REGROUP AND REALLOCATE RESOURCES AMID THE COVID-19 PANDEMIC, WE URGE THEM TO CREATE A SYSTEMIC SPACE FOR GRIEF.

Positionality

Our friendship and professional collaboration began when Sakeena, a Black woman, learned from a colleague that Mandie, a white woman, was doing research with English language arts (ELA) teachers about their experiences with teaching while grieving. Having just lost her beloved sister, Sakeena reached out to Mandie to learn from Mandie's research—with hopes that she might gain some insight into her own grieving process. Since then, we have spent numerous hours examining and unpacking the nuances of grieving while teaching.

As we discussed the nuances of grief itself (a natural part of the *human* experience), we quickly recognized that teachers and teacher leaders are particularly vulnerable in their grief journeys. Specifically, teachers must navigate the unpredictable and often exhausting manifestations of grief, while also caring for and educating others (students and colleagues). In our discussions, we kept returning to the intersectional impact of grief for Black women teachers. Because of the double burden of racism and sexism, Black women are often not afforded the same opportunities as their white women teacher colleagues to grieve. Though our initial conversations began with our individual grief experiences, we soon realized our grieving experiences were not unique but fit within a larger, understudied issue within education.

Unpacking the Reality of Grief

The way we deal with grief in the US is incomplete, at best, and dehumanizing, at worst. The gut-wrenching physiological, cognitive, emotional, and physical effects of losing a close loved one can affect a person's appetite, digestion, blood pressure, heart rate, respiration, memory, and sleep. Living with grief can be an all-consuming mind *and* body experience with no preparation or finite timeline.

Grief is a natural response to death. It indicates that one has deeply loved and lost. Grieving, especially after the loss of a close loved one, *never* ceases. However, our relationship with our grief evolves over time. The survivor has grief reminders with each passing birthday, holiday, anniversary, milestone, fond (or triggering) memory, smell, and/or sound associated with their deceased loved one, even though they may choose not to mention these out loud. Over time, a person learns how to live *with* grief, as opposed to "getting over it." In other words, grief becomes integrated into a person's life. Grief is necessary to heal.

David Kessler, a white man, who has written multiple books about his experiences with teaching physicians, nurses, counselors, police, and first

TEACHING TIPS

In "Creating Space for Grief," Everett and Dunn normalize public conversation about grief: a natural part of the human experience that is rarely discussed publicly. Grief itself is disorienting and can impact a person's mental, emotional, and physical well-being. While much of the impact of grief is invisible to the average person, grief can seriously impede on a person's ability to function, even in areas where they may have previously thrived, like being a teacher leader. Supporting others can be especially difficult for the educator who is living with grief. Plus, the weight of grief is inequitably distributed between BIPOC and white educators. Consequently, we introduce a new framework of "intersectional grief" and offer concrete micro- and macro-level supports for attending to grief in schools like investing in grief-informed training, appointing institutional-level grief advocates, providing financial support to teacher leaders who facilitate grief support, and developing flexible grief leave policies, to name a few. In your professional learning community, discuss ways to implement these supports (or lack thereof) in your teaching context. Brainstorm additional grief supports educators might need.

responders about grief still struggles with grief. In a recent NCTE webinar, when referencing the unexpected loss of his son, Kessler (2020) explained, "It's as brutal as anyone could imagine, if not worse. And being a grief expert didn't help me. In a lot of ways, I was a father who had to bury a child."

Many of the common experiences among those who are living with grief are "invisible" to the average colleague. However, they are impossible for the person living with grief to ignore. If we ask (or expect) our colleagues to rush through these common experiences, we risk alienating and/or hurting them. While we recognize that no amount of knowledge can protect us from the pain of loss, we have learned that creating space to acknowledge the realities of grief can reduce isolation and harm.

Inequitable Distribution of Grief

The grief burden of the pandemic is heavy for most people, but the brunt of the weight and impact is inequitably distributed. Systems of anti-Blackness (Dumas, 2018; Love, 2016; Torres & Johnson, 2019) mean that the negative impacts of the pandemic also were and are exponentially felt in Black communities and communities of color. Ladson-Billings (2020) unapologetically asserted,

> Far too many people keep talking about how to "get back" or "return to normal" without understanding there can be no return to normal with the level of devastation this virus has wreaked upon the world and particularly Black people. As a people with less resources and the least able to work remotely we find ourselves deemed "essential" in jobs like public transportation, sanitation, grocery and pharmacy store clerks, and health care workers. We are also a group of people with less access to quality health care and are likely to be treated unfairly by the health care system.

As of April 2021, there were 574,000 confirmed deaths caused by COVID-19 in the US. "The American Federation of Teachers, one of the nation's largest teachers' unions, estimates more than 530 of their members died of the virus last year" (Kaur, 2021). Hollingsworth (2020) explained some 1.5 million teachers have underlying conditions that make them vulnerable to the virus.

In 2020, we had 12 hurricanes in the US, including six record-tying hurricanes that have damaged the vast majority of the gulf and east coasts (Samenow et al., 2020). Plus, there was an estimated 4.2 million acres of land on the west coast burned during the same year (Center for Disaster Philanthropy, 2020). In short, death is all around us. We need viable systems for processing grief.

Promoting Wellness through Intersectional Grief-Informed Teacher Leadership Practices

While much research defines grief, finds meaning in grief, and documents how teachers can support students through grieving, there is less research about how to support teachers who are living with grief. Grieving can be a lonely experience. Love (2020) aptly notes that even prior to COVID-19, "schools were failing not only children of color but all children" and teachers had "high burnout." Therefore, we endorse the "hard re-set analogy" (Ladson-Billings, 2021) and dream of systemic teacher leadership where schools might function as healing spaces, especially as countless people are grieving loved ones in the US.

The work of teacher leaders is often undefined, unsupported, and sometimes unrecognized and undervalued, thus limiting the potential for positive impact (Khalifa et al., 2016; Killion et al., 2016; York-Barr & Duke, 2004). The teaching profession requires that teachers care for students (Noddings, 2005). Because of this expectation of care, teachers may believe their grief-related emotions are obstacles to fulfilling professional responsibilities (Dunn, 2019, 2021). As a result, teachers often feel shame or guilt when they take time to care for themselves, and they may try to hide any grief they experience. Thus, creating space to talk about grieving experiences among teacher leaders can be a starting point for making schools more humanizing spaces. We believe it is particularly important to create space for an intersectional grief-informed frame to advance and sustain a viable teacher leadership agenda.

Advancing an intersectional grief-informed frame requires cultivating a transformational culture that acknowledges grief *and* dedicates efforts to a collective responsibility in supporting teachers who are living with grief. Love (2019) offered a framework for *mattering* that foregrounds a "collective spirit of accountability, love, and purpose" (p. 48). Furthermore, Love (2019) explains, "For schools to do well, educators need to be well. Educators need free therapy, love, compassion, and healing, and to embrace theories that explain why getting well is so hard" (p. 161). As teachers, we can engage in collective spirit work by committing to humanizing responses to colleagues who are living with grief. "Companionship, reflection, and connection" (Devine, 2017, p. 15) create spaces where we can be honest about the realities of grief.

Below we outline some concrete practices schools might consider as they reallocate resources:

- **Invest in grief-informed training and research** for the education staff.
- **Appoint a grief advocate** to be in charge of fielding questions and organizing support, such as meals and condolences, for a colleague who may be grieving.
- **Provide opportunities for teacher leaders to acquire additional compensation** for creating and supporting the school community in navigating grief.
- **Develop flexible leave policies** that are intersectional and grief-informed (align with the realities of grief).
- **Have a grief action plan checklist** to cover recurring teacher duties like orchestrating hall duty, submitting lesson plans, or volunteering for after school events, so a person who is grieving does not have to worry about these tasks. After losing a close loved one, a person living with grief acquires several new responsibilities at home, such as planning a funeral, managing end-of-life paperwork, and/or tending to physical needs.
- **Be critically aware of the current grief local and global climate** (e.g., increases in anti-Asian violence; unevenly distributed pandemic-related grief among communities of color). Without racial justice, schools cannot be humanizing spaces for grieving individuals.
- **Recognize that for Black colleagues, the pain of grieving is magnified** because Black people are continually grieving. White educators, in particular, need to work to understand how white supremacy inflicts continual pain on Black colleagues (Baker-Bell et al., 2017) through police brutality and the unequitable impacts of the coronavirus pandemic discussed earlier.
- **Listen to a person who is grieving.** Resist corrective impulses, such as "fixing" their grief. Even when well-intentioned, this response dismisses the person's experiences with grief.

If we do not move in this direction, unfortunately, good teachers will eventually leave schools where they do not feel supported.

While these proposed practices cannot bring a loved one back, they communicate to teachers that their loss experiences matter. Further, the practices make the school community more aware of how grief manifests and allow for the creation of space for it. An intersectional grief-informed frame as a pathway toward systemic teacher leadership creates opportunities for us to be supportive companions to our colleagues who are living with grief.

REFERENCES

Baker-Bell, A., Butler, T., & Johnson, L. (Eds.). (2017). The pain and the wounds: A call for critical race English education in the wake of racial violence. *English Education*, 49(2), 116–29.

Crenshaw, K. (1991). Mapping the margins: Intersectionality, identity politics and violence against women. *Stanford Law Review*, 43(6), 1241–99.

Crenshaw, K. (2016). *The urgency of intersectionality*. TedXWomen. www.ted.com/talks/kimberle_crenshaw_the_urgency_of_intersectionality

Center for Disaster Philanthropy. (2020). *2020 North American wildfire season*. disasterphilanthropy.org/disaster/2020-california-wildfires/

Devine, M. (2017). *It's ok that you're not ok: Meeting grief and loss in a culture that doesn't understand*. Sounds True, Inc.

Dumas, M. J. (2018). Beginning and ending with Black suffering: A meditation on and against racial justice in education. In E. Tuck & K. W. Yang (Eds.), *Toward what justice? Describing diverse dreams of justice in education* (pp. 29–45). Routledge.

Dunn, M. B. (2019). *English language arts teachers' experiences teaching while grieving a death* (UMI No. 13896038) [Doctoral dissertation]. ProQuest Dissertations and Theses Global Database.

Dunn, M. B. (2021). When teachers hurt: Supporting preservice teacher well-being. *English Education*, 53(2), 145–51.

Dunn, M. B. & Everett, S. (2020). *Living with grief: Equipping teachers in being companions for grieving colleagues*. National Council of Teachers of English. vimeo.com/449022069/70ce096b30

Hollinsworth, H. (2020). *Empty desks: Coronavirus robs US classrooms of teachers*. abcnews.go.com/Health/wireStory/empty-desks-coronavirus-robs-us-classrooms-teachers-74277447

Kaur, H. (2021). Teachers have lost colleagues to COVID-19 and worry about being next. But, they say, no one's listening. www.cnn.com/2021/02/03/us/teachers-dying-covid-trnd/index.html

Kessler, D. (2020). *National Council of Teachers of English: A conversation about grief*. vimeo.com/426314896

Khalifa, M. A., Gooden, M. A., & Davis, J. E. (2016). Culturally responsive school leadership: A synthesis of the literature. *Review of Educational Research*, 86(4), 1272–311.

Killion, J., Harrison, C., Colton, A., Bryan, C., Delehant, A., & Cooke, D. (2016). *A systemic approach to elevating teacher leadership*. Learning Forward.

Ladson-Billings, G. (2020). *Time for a hard reset*. blackandsmart.wordpress.com/2020/05/25/time-for-a-hard-reset/

Ladson-Billings, G. (2021). I'm here for the hard re-set: Post pandemic pedagogy to preserve our culture. *Equity & Excellence in Education*, 54(1), 68–78.

Love, B. L. (2016). Anti-Black state violence, classroom edition: The spirit murdering of Black children. *Journal of Curriculum and Pedagogy*, 1–3.

Love, B. L. (2019). *We want to do more than survive: Abolitionist teaching and the pursuit of freedom*. Beacon Press.

Love, B. L. (2020). *Teachers, we cannot go back to the way things were*. www.edweek.org/leadership/opinion-teachers-we-cannot-go-back-to-the-way-things-were/2020/04

National Center for Education Statistics. (2020). *Characteristics of public schools*. nces.ed.gov/programs/coe/indicator_clr.asp

Noddings, N. (2005). *Caring in education. The encyclopedia of pedagogy and informal education*. infed.org/caring-in-education/

Samenow, J., Freedman, A., & Capucci, M. (2020). *Atlantic hurricane season breaks all-time record while leaving Gulf Coast battered*. www.washingtonpost.com/weather/2020/11/10/record-hurricane-season-atlantic

Torres, A. B., & Johnson, L. L. (2019). The normalization of anti-blackness in teacher education: A call for critical frameworks. In K. T. Han & J. Laughter (Eds.), *Critical race theory in teacher education: Informing classroom culture and practice* (pp. 103–112). Teachers College Press.

York-Barr, J., & Duke, K. (2004). What do we know about teacher leadership? Findings from two decades of scholarship. *Review of Educational Research*, 74(3), 255–316.

SAKEENA EVERETT is an assistant professor of language and literacy education in the College of Education at the University of Georgia. She focuses her research and teaching on the literacy development of Black male students in elementary and secondary schools; literacy teacher preparation; culturally sustaining pedagogies; and transformative educational experiences for students and teachers. Recently, her research agenda has expanded to include grief among educators, with a special emphasis on supporting grieving Black women educators. Dr. Everett has taught elementary and secondary students, prepared prospective teachers, and provided professional development for in-service educators across multiple school districts. NCTE has been her professional home since 2011, and she is a former Cultivating New Voices among Scholars of Color (CNV) Fellow. Her research has been recognized by the American Educational Research Association (AERA); *RTE*'s Alan C. Purves Award; and the Spencer Foundation.

MANDIE BEVELS DUNN is an assistant professor of English education at the University of South Florida. Her research and teaching focus on the lived experiences of English teachers as professionals who respond to multiple competing stakeholders. She has been a member of NCTE since 2013.

CALL FOR MANUSCRIPTS

NCTE SPECIAL ISSUES SERIES VOLUME 2

TRAUMA-INFORMED TEACHING: TOWARD RESPONSIVE, HUMANIZING CLASSROOMS

DEADLINE: JANUARY 10, 2022

EDITOR: ELIZABETH DUTRO

"The material body is center, and central. The body is the ground of thought."

—GLORIA E. ANZALDÚA, *LIGHT IN THE DARK / LUZ EN LO OSCURO: REWRITING IDENTITY, SPIRITUALITY, REALITY*

"Personal experiences—revised and in other ways redrawn—become a lens with which to reread and rewrite the cultural stories into which we are born."

—GLORIA E. ANZALDÚA, "NOW LET US SHIFT . . ." FROM *THIS BRIDGE WE CALL HOME: RADICAL VISIONS FOR TRANSFORMATION*

As Chicana queer theorist and writer Gloria Anzaldúa writes, bodies hold deep knowledge. Given that all forms of knowledge held by bodies matter, some of that knowledge is gleaned through trauma. Experiences of pain, sorrow, loss, fear, disruption, and systemic and institutional oppression are an inevitable presence in ELA classrooms. Difficult knowledge, born of trauma, not only counts as knowledge but also is central to seeing the world for what it is and what it could be. Literacy practices are the means through which life stories are encountered, shared, and witnessed in classrooms, which not only makes ELA classrooms crucial contexts for engaging the complexities of trauma in schools but also positions ELA educators as leaders in that work.

As the idea of trauma-informed education has moved to the center of many conversations and initiatives in K–12 education, the definitions and actions brought to trauma are complex and consequential for both students and teachers. Too often, approaches to trauma in schools can employ and fuel assumptions of damage and deficit in relation to students, but those false narratives can be resisted and transformed. How can ELA teachers ensure that trauma-informed teaching is taken up in responsive, humanizing, anti-oppressive ways?

This collection of articles seeks to expand and deepen what trauma-informed teaching can mean in ELA classrooms. The aim is to harness ELA educators' commitments, creativity, and expertise to ensure that responsiveness to trauma centers students' knowledge and brilliance; fosters critical advocacy; interrupts damage-focused language and practices; and heeds critical, humanizing, anti-oppressive stances as integral to teaching in response to trauma. This book seeks contributions that provide actionable, vibrant practices toward these goals.

This call invites submissions in two areas: (1) theory and (2) pedagogies and practices.

Theory

A small number of selected manuscripts may speak to conceptualizations of trauma that can support ELA educators to bring critical, humanizing, responsive stances and practices to students' and teachers' navigations of multiple dimensions of trauma. Guiding questions for these submissions might include, but are not limited to, the following: What are the potentials and pitfalls of employing the term *trauma* in considering students' and teachers' life experiences in schools and classrooms? How can and should the idea of trauma-informed teaching be animated by critical theories of race, gender, sexuality, and class? What are the multidimensions of trauma that ELA educators must heed to build anti-oppressive, humanizing pedagogies and practices in classrooms?

Pedagogy and Practices

Most accepted contributions will focus on classroom practices that support K–12 ELA educators in visualizing and enacting trauma-informed teaching. Submissions can include descriptions and narrative accounts of how students' and/or teachers' difficult life experiences have impacted ELA teaching and learning and fueled critical questions and responsive practice. Areas of focus and guiding questions may include, but are not limited to, the following:

> ***The trauma that school systems and curriculum and instructional practices inflict on students and families and how ELA educators can intervene in such harm.*** What forms of institutional trauma do ELA teachers see students navigate in their schools and classrooms? How can ELA teachers resist practices that exacerbate long-standing injustices in education? Toward interrupting institutional trauma, what do ELA curriculum and pedagogy offer in order to provide students vibrant, humanizing experiences with school literacies?
>
> ***Specific ELA curricular and instructional practices, illustrated by particular lesson plans, text selections, and/or student perspectives and responses (e.g., talk, writing).*** How can teachers approach critical, humanizing response to students' life experiences, including trauma, through everyday instruction and interactions in their classrooms? What stances and instructional moves can ELA teachers enact to cultivate a caring, engaged, and connected classroom community for all students, including those who experience trauma?
>
> ***Approaches to building relationships with children, youth, and families that demonstrate care and compassion and provide tangible support in the face of trauma.*** What can ELA teachers do to enfold students in compassion, care, and advocacy in the face of traumatic experiences? How do teachers connect to families and collaborate with them to support students?
>
> ***Examples of how ELA educators collaborate and support one another to navigate the multiple and sometimes contradictory messages educators receive about trauma in relation to students' learning.*** What forms of collaboration and support can ELA educators engage in to deepen and sustain relationships and practices that are responsive to the complexities of trauma in schools and classrooms? How can ELA educators work together to intervene in institutional practices that cause harm, including accountability, mandated curriculum and instruction, and damage- and deficit-centered language and practice?

Submission Guidelines

- Manuscripts should be double-spaced throughout (including quotations and works cited pages) with standard margins.
- Theory manuscripts should be no more than 5,000 to 7,000 words long (including citations).
- Praxis and community manuscripts should be no more than 2,500 to 4,000 words long (including citations).
- Use in-text documentation by following the 9th edition of the MLA Handbook. Where applicable, a list of works cited and any other bibliographic information should also follow MLA style.
- Provide a statement guaranteeing that the manuscript has not been published or submitted elsewhere.
- Ensure that the manuscript conforms to the NCTE Statement on Gender and Language.
- Obtain permission for any student work featured in the manuscript.
- Submit images (e.g., photographs, charts, graphs) in separate files per instructions in Editorial Manager. Contributors are responsible for securing rights to copywritten material.

Submit your manuscript to NCTE's Editorial Manager, Books Program, at https://www.editorialmanager.com/nctebp and mark Special Issues—Trauma as the article type.

If you have any questions, please contact the volume editor: Elizabeth Dutro (Elizabeth.dutro@colorado.edu).